THE GOOD
THE BAD
AND
THE RUGBY

The Official Biography of Tony Ward

by

John Scally

BLACKWATER PRESS

Editor
Brenda McNally

Page Layout & Design
Paula Byrne

© **1993 Blackwater Press,**
Broomhill Business Park,
Tallaght,
Dublin 24.

Produced in Ireland by Blackwater Press

Contents

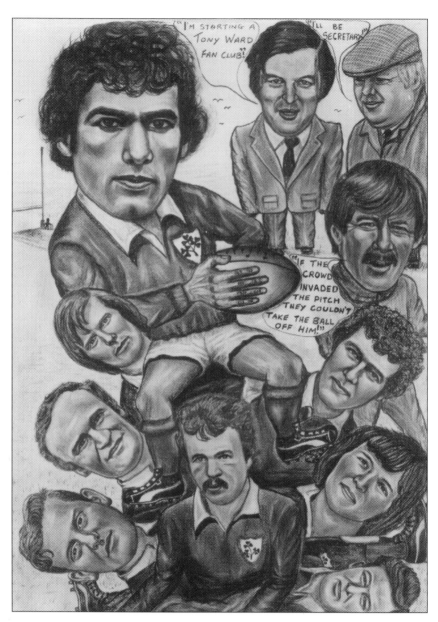

A picture that tells a thousand words.

Foreword

It was in 1983 that the first seed was sown for *The Good the Bad and the Rugby* when Ned Van Esbeck suggested to me the importance of keeping a chronological record of "events" as they were unfolding. While solid advice it most certainly was, I took it on board even though retirement then seemed a million miles away. In March 1989, the season following my retirement, John Redmond all but convinced me as we drowned in a sea of liquid depression in the Pavilion Bar at Jury's following another Irish defeat, that the time was now right to commit my thoughts to print. I remained less than convinced and nothing more became of the idea until the summer of 1992 when P.J. Cunningham arranged a meeting with a well-known publisher.

Suffice it to say, that the angle they sought and my intentions were light years apart. I left that encounter very humbled and if not quite with my tail between my legs, certainly disillusioned and most definitely sure of one thing that *"My Story"* was going to remain just that.

On a balmy evening during that same summer, as Gerry Murphy and I coached a group of Italian youngsters from Amatori Rugby Milano in the wide open expanse of Wesley College, I did a rough and ready taped recording with John Scally on the subject of prayer and how one handles one's innermost thoughts. It was in fact the second time I had worked with him in the context of a sport centred radio interview but this one went much deeper than the norm. What struck me most about my interviewer was his simple ability to listen. It was for me, no run of the mill interview but one with structure, depth and flexibility. That said... interview over... coaching in progress... It was all quickly forgotten... Until that is, the embryonic days of '93 when a phone call from the said same John Scally in his typical inoffensive manner which, was preempted with umpteen apologies, inquiring as to whether I had ever considered "telling my tale".

Happy in the knowledge that I had shortly before made up my mind for once and for all not to go down the memoirs road, this was the last thing I needed. However, a basic inability to say no has long been one of my greatest weaknesses (although I am steadily improving in that regard), so I pawned him off by suggesting he let me chew on it awhile, at least until the Five Nations Championship season was completed. Secretly, I hoped and trusted that he would interpret my reply as a response in the negative. Not so! Within days of Ireland's historic victory over the "auld enemy" in March, on the Monday to be precise, the phone was hopping. It was John. I resorted once again to delaying tactics but alas to no avail. Subsequently, John and I arranged a meeting in the Berkeley Court with John O'Connor of Blackwater Press. The vibes were good. What they both had in mind and what I intended ran pretty much parallel. We were up and running.

Now some six months and many sleepless nights later the fruit of our labour has come to fruition. *The Good the Bad and The Rugby* is – as I had always intended it to be – a rugby book with a human story; my story. Countless journalistic and media people (many unworthy of that name) and many more besides have had their tuppence worth on Tony Ward the rugby player or otherwise. Now it is time, as the title implies, to set the record straight. This is not an exercise in getting even. Who was it that once said: "Don't get angry – get even?" I am neither angry nor do I seek to get even. This is not an exercise in whingeing.

I believe John Scally has got to the centre of my being and captured the essence of my intentions. I presented him with all the primary source material at my disposal and he beavered away relentlessly. His presentation of my story tells of my deepest innermost feelings in times of triumph and despair. I know he has done it justice because he has presented the truth the whole truth and nothing but the truth, warts and all. There is no convenient padding.

It has been a pleasure and a privilege to work with him over the past year. I did not know him from Adam when we did that first radio interview not so long ago. He knew of me from afar. He has no rugby pedigree and was born and bred a very long way from Dublin 4. His total lack of familiarity with me and with the finer points of the rugby psyche appealed from day one. In addition, and even more significant, as I have already pointed out is his ability to listen, ask the pertinent (though not always easy) question and formulate his opinion accordingly. We often differed, but never fell out. I believe the net product does my story both on the field and off, full justice. That, as they say, is the bottom line.

To John O'Connor and John Scally, I owe an immense debt of gratitude for encouraging me to go for it. Their hard work and support has been tremendous.

I think Chapter 12 captures succinctly my feelings for my family. But for this there would be no story. My life has reached a level of contentment I did not think possible. My entire strength today comes from them. Otherwise, I am nothing. Life, as they say, is about living experiences. For better or for worse these are mine.

This book is dedicated to my friend, my hero and my inspiration – a man among men the incomparable Shay Deering.

Tony Ward

Acknowledgements

It takes a great act of faith to entrust someone with the task of writing their biography. I am grateful to Tony for his confidence in selecting me for this task in the first instance and for his generosity with his time, his meticulous attention to detail and his complete candour over the months of research and writing. His penetrating eye was priceless at the proof-reading stage. In particular, I am grateful for his friendship.

I am also deeply grateful to Tony's wife, Louise, for her endless generosity and enthusiasm, in addition to her total honesty in interviews for the purpose of research for this book. Thanks also for her insightful comments at the proofing stage – and she makes a wonderful lasagne! Apologies to Richie, Lynn and Nikki for their father's apparent absence from their lives for lengthy periods throughout the summer.

I am grateful to Dermot Morgan for allowing me to reprint the lyrics of the" timeless classic" *Don't Pick Wardie*. I would also like to thank the sports editor of *The Evening Herald*, P.J. Cunningham, for his interest and encouragement. Very special thanks to Ollie Campbell for his co-operation, kindness and generosity with his time.

My thanks are also due to Blackwater Press for backing this project so enthusiastically from day one and their hard-working staff especially the editor, Brenda McNally, and Anna O'Donovan, for her interest. In particular, I wish to single out the Managing Director, John O'Connor, who appreciated the potential of the story immediately and threw the full might of his energy behind it.

My gratitude to Conail Hamill and Gordon Laing for their help in fine tuning the text, and also to the photographers: Billy Stickland, Austin Finn, Peter Thursfield and Ray McManus.

Introduction

"Can you remember where you were the night John F. Kennedy was shot?"

This was a question I had often heard posed as I was growing up but I never really understood the power of a single event to remain frozen in the memory until Friday, 1 June 1979.

I was in fifth year in school at the time and it was the week of the summer tests. I was not really able to enjoy my breakfast because my mind was a whirlpool of chaotically arranged information about Peig Sayers, Jane Austen and Parnell and the Land Question. As I had finished off my final sausage, my eyes focused firmly on my revision notes which were awkwardly propped up by the milk jug and sugar bowl, when I heard the bombshell. All thoughts of exams were suspended as the shock news was assimilated. Tony Ward had been dropped from the Irish team in Australia. Was it the first of June or the first of April?

The name Tony Ward had exploded onto my brain eighteen months earlier with his meteoric rise to fame in the number ten shirt for Ireland. With his jinking runs and lethal kicking he not only had reviewers furiously scampering for superlatives to describe his performances, he also had the Irish sporting public eating out of his hand. With his ever-present smile off the pitch and outgoing personality he had built the kind of support that, arguably, no Irish national hero had managed since Arkle.

The most vivid quality in sport is fantasy. Wardy was the man who made the impossible possible, conjuring up magic to effortlessly glide past despairing defenders with an icy calm. Often I had nestled comfortably in the armchair and watched him treating a spellbound crowd in Lansdowne Road to another unique display of skills to snatch or set up a score for Ireland. Never had a rugby player made my spine tingle like he did. Each feat of genius was followed by something even more spectacular.

As we streamed into the examination hall on that summer's morning I would never have imagined that 14 years on I would be writing the story of one of Ireland's most charismatic and controversial sporting heroes.

Much has been said and written about Tony Ward already. This book tells the inside story through his own eyes.

John Scally

1. Paradise Lost

Total Disbelief! According to conventional wisdom, nothing is more certain than uncertainty. But when Tony Ward headed off with the Irish rugby team for the summer tour in Australia on 13 May 1979, not even that piece of advice could have prepared him for what lay in store.

Had he been the suspicious type he might have been worried that the date could be an omen for things to come. Yet at that precise moment he was looking at the world through rose-tinted glasses.

The previous evening he had announced his engagement following a whirlwind romance. As he got on board the plane he felt swept away on a tidal wave of emotion and optimism. For just a second it seemed that the world was his oyster.

He forced himself to concentrate. It was time to knuckle down to the real business of the trip. Though best known for his nimbleness of foot and mind, wicked sidestep and searing stride, above all he was consumed by a fierce desire not to let those around him down – believing that if hard work was the difference between defeat and victory, it was unthinkable for him to fall short.

Great Expectations

For this fledgling, international life could hardly be sweeter. While for every impressive debutante who has gone on to be a star there are many more who have fallen flat on their face, Ward, just over a year after his first cap, could hardly have made a more encouraging start.

The background to his explosive entry on the international scene had been Ireland's whitewashing in 1977 and only one win in their previous nine matches. Something magical was called for.

Ward offered new colour to the cloud of gloom which had cast its shadow over Irish rugby, scoring a record 38 points in his first championship season.

In his two seasons as an international player he won almost every rugby award in sight – most notably European Player of the Year. Plaudits had been showered on him with almost wanton abandon. The fans struggled to find still further superlatives to describe him.

The most noteworthy compliment had been recorded the previous February, by no less a person than Cameron Michael Henderson Gibson, one of the greatest players the game of rugby had ever seen:

"He is quite the most important rugby player in Ireland. His legs are far more important to his country than those of Marlene Dietrich ever were to the film industry."

It was a public acknowledgment by one rugby legend of the flair of the new prince on the throne.

But fame has its own price. Ward's performances in the green shirt had placed him on a pedestal as a national hero. This was a heavy burden for such young shoulders.

Ward seemed to have a special aura, almost as much a regular with the social columnists as he was with the rugby correspondents – inhabiting the world of those luminaries who are famous just for being famous. With his filmstar looks and Colgate smile no newspaper seemed complete without him. He possessed the most marketable and recognisable gleaming face for the hoardings and was a constant focus of media speculation and deliberation.

Although the noted commentator, John Arlott, once observed that "No player is bigger than the game", Ward had a popular appeal which was comparable to that of a soccer star like George Best. His style of play was charismatic and his penchant for producing the unexpected endeared him to the masses. Nobody had ever seen such a phenomenon in Irish rugby. Jack Kyle had never won awards for "Best Groomed Man", "Smile of the Year" or "Hunk of the Year".

Ward had been singularly successful yet it had appeared that there might be some who feared the cult of the player and felt that he was getting too big for his boots. His every move on and off the field was watched with interest. Strangely, there were hints that his failure might be gratifying to a few people of influence in the rugby world in Ireland. This remains one of the great mysteries of Irish rugby – how, for all his flair, did he appear to make enemies in high places? Would he have been more acceptable to his detractors had he been less of a success? Some friends with their ears to the ground feared that the knives might be out for him.

Self-confidence is arguably the most important attribute in top class sport. Although Ward was consistently serious about his level of fitness and was assiduous in training, carefully adhering to the basic physical routines as much as skill-work, his most potent weapon was his dashing confidence. Australia was to change all that.

My Heart Is Low

There are two schools of thought as to how the pre-season weeks are best spent. One champions trips abroad, the other vehemently opposes them. Overseas trips are beneficial in the sense that they expose players to a different playing culture, a "hands on" education and an occasion to see other ideas in action. Rugby players are often at their most positive at the start of such tours. With the previous season's trials and tribulations a fast fading memory, the tour bristled with challenges and targets. The downside is the cost, the time away, extending an already lengthy season by another eight weeks – and the unfamiliar playing conditions.

The second match of the tour did nothing to dispel the notion that Ward's place in the Test Side was secure. Against the Australian Capital Territory at Canberra's Manuka Oval, Ireland won 35-7. Ward scored 19 points from a try, three conversions and three penalties, and showed great elusiveness in crossing for the first of Ireland's five tries. His performances earned him rave reviews in Australia, though in general, Ireland was seen as offering little threat to the Wallabies in the Test Series. The hype after the match was on "the clash of the kickers", with the potentially nail-biting duel between Ward and the prolific Australian international, Paul McLean in the First Test. The match was billed as rugby's version of *"The Gunfight at the OK Corral"*.

However, nobody in Ireland knew that what was seen at home as a one-horse-race at the start of the tour for the number ten jersey, was heading for a photo-finish. Ward was out on his own. Old Belvedere's Ollie Campbell, a sound player, had not even reached the starting gate but could be depended on to provide good cover for Wardy in the less important matches. Ward was indisputably Ireland's most outstanding international of recent years, while Campbell was a comparative beginner – his one previous outing, coincidentally against Australia three years earlier, had been a game to forget quickly.

Even when Campbell scored all of Ireland's points when he landed six penalty goals from seven attempts against Queensland on the Tuesday before the First Test, few could have foreseen that Ward would be dropped. While Campbell had given a fine goal-kicking performance it seemed to be more than outweighed by Ward's tally of 77 points in his nine internationals for Ireland.

As the team got off the bus in the idyllic Surfer's Paradise where the First Test Side was to be announced, Ward was discreetly told by another squad member to be prepared for very bad news. Shortly after, the team manager, Noel Murphy, informed him that he would not be playing in the First Test. His first thought was to quietly offer his congratulations to the heir to his throne. That evening he recorded his emotions in his diary. Although the words were sparse, the naked emotion is immediately obvious:

May 31
Told by Noel Murphy 'off team' before official announcement. Total Shock. Unexpected

Through a dull fog of confusion and incredulity Ward attempted to piece together the fragments of his shattered dreams. It would be much later before he would discover just how powerful an impact the experience had on him.

News of the sensational development spread like wildfire. Arguably the most compelling saga in Irish sport had begun.

The Great Debate

No argument would run so long or cause such divisions among the sporting public and journalistic community as the relative value of Campbell and Ward to the Irish cause. It was the stuff of a soap opera. If the print media had an equivalent to the TAM ratings for television, the great debate over Campbell versus Ward would have been the undisputed number one. The only equivalent in Irish life was the long-running battle between Charlie and Garret.

It was extraordinary that such a small country could produce two such great talents at exactly the same position at exactly the same time. Both were great players, though very different in style. In full flow both were a feast for the eyes. Off the field too they were strikingly different. Campbell was red-haired, slim and favoured a low profile, whereas Ward was dark, chunky, and more outgoing. Over the next five years it seemed that it was impossible to speak of one without reference to the other.

It was a high risk strategy for the management to pick Campbell but he repaid their confidence with interest. He scored 19 points in the First Test in Ireland's 27-12 victory and his two drop goals and penalty gave Ireland a 9-3 win in the Second Test. The trivia buffs had a new piece of information to play with. Unusually for an Irish rugby player, Campbell's first three caps were awarded against Australia. Campbell played brilliantly but the rugby world was left to wonder what Ward had done wrong to warrant his exile to the bench. It seemed to many that he had received a raw deal.

I Mourn For My Dream

Controversy has a gift for taking the centre stage and relegating all about it. After the Australian tour in 1979, all the attention had been on Ward, the number ten. Acres were written about the strengths and weaknesses of his game but few seemed to realise that the man had been profoundly affected by the trauma of his exclusion. The old self-confidence gave way to self-doubt.

There were many times in the turbulent seasons that followed when he had to stop himself from wondering how different his career could have been. It was very little consolation to know that he was better-known to rugby followers at home and abroad than many who had collected far more medals and caps. He sometimes wondered if this was his real problem.

His diary of that tour makes for fascinating reading. The language is clipped and stark but the depth of feeling is unmistakable. The entry from the day after his fall from grace, reveals much about the mental state of the vanquished hero:

June 1

Worst day so far. Exchanged words with Murphy. Went to room, fell asleep. Woke again. Took sleeping pill and slept right through. There is no way I will make second test. Regardless of whether I want to or not.

2. Where's Your Party Dress?

The direction in which education starts a man will determine his future life.

Plato

The 1950's are not remembered with great affection by many Irish people. It was a decade when emigration reached epidemic proportions and economic life, both agricultural and industrial, was depressed. The one bright note was that the curse of TB was largely curtailed. It was a time when expectations were low and many looked no further than the emigrant ship. The early life of Tony Ward fits into this pattern.

He was born in Dublin on 9 October 1954. His mother, June Donnelly, used to play camogie, but his father, Danny, though not a sportsman, was a great sports fan and took his wife to every soccer, rugby and boxing match around. The family lived a nomadic existence because Danny was a commercial traveller by profession, moving from Terenure to Sandymount, to Leinster Road, Rathmines and when things were slow in the "auld sod" in 1951, he took his family to England. They settled in Leeds, which they found to be a friendly city not unlike Dublin. Tony went to school there for a year and immediately became a fan of Leeds United – a passion which would endure all his life.

Tragedy afflicted the family when Tony was only five-and-a-half-years-old. His father died from a massive heart attack on St Patrick's Day 1960. To this day Ward knows very little about his father's background:

"He was born in London and was a huge Arsenal fan. In view of his birthplace I would have been eligible to play for England had I so wished. I know precious little about my family tree on my father's side except that somewhere along the line his parents had been in Russia and had fled to escape persecution.

"I have to confess that, because I was an only child, my mother spoilt me a bit. Even to this day I still envy people who grew up having brothers and sisters.

"I go over to Leeds each year to see them play and last year I went to check out where we once lived. My mother couldn't remember the exact address but she had a good idea where it was. Although a lot has changed in the city, I was able to track it down and it was amazing the number of memories that came flooding back.

"I was doing my scouting via a taxi and the taxi-driver and I got chatting. He asked me was I over for the match and I said I was. Then he took me by surprise by saying: 'I know who you are.' I just said: 'Oh.' He went on: 'You are Johnny Giles's son.' Down through the years many people have said I looked like Gilesie but I doubt if John would be too flattered if people thought him old enough to be my father!"

As his mother recovered from the trauma of her husband's death she decided to come home for a holiday to her mother's house in Harold's Cross. Intending to stay just for a visit she quickly settled in her home city. She got a job in the Irish Hospitals' Sweepstakes Trust, a position she retained until 1978 when, like a bolt out of the blue, she was made redundant.

Amongst Women

Ward may have missed his father, but in effect he had two mothers. While June was out at work all day, her mother took care of him and doted on his every word.

"My mother devoted her entire life to me. I was brought up in a house of women. My grandfather was in hospital for a long time and I lived with my mother, grandmother and three aunts. Two of them got married subsequently."

Having made his First Communion in St Louis' Rathmines, he moved next door to the Holy Ghost Fathers in St Mary's. Like most parents of the time, June Ward saw her primary duty to be a good provider for her son:

"It was a struggle financially for her. Most of the local children went to the Vocational School in Clogher Road. My mother went to work by day and four nights a week so that I could go to Mary's. She worked by day in the Irish Hospitals' Sweepstakes Trust in Ballsbridge and for Bord na gCon three nights a week at Harold's Cross and Saturday night in Shelbourne Park. Through her I was able to get a job six nights a week with Bord na gCon when I started college and this made a huge difference in helping to pay my way through third level education.

"I can never thank my mother enough for the sacrifices she made for me."

Although home was a formative influence on the young Ward, his subsequent life was also greatly shaped by his school days. Ward has nothing but happy memories of his time in the classroom:

"I can speak nothing but good for the Holy Ghost Fathers. My memories of Mary's are nothing but the best. They were very happy days.

"My interest in sport began at a very early age when we lived in Priory Road in Harold's Cross. Our Wembley was a square with a statue which had been erected in the Marian year, 1954. There was seldom a blade of grass on it because we would be playing soccer there morning, noon and night and come in covered in dust and dirt.

"*Match of the Day* was a big influence on my life though I seldom, if ever, got to see it in our house because the *Late Late Show* was compulsive viewing for the ladies. I started with OLOR Boys, Our Lady of the Rosary in Harold's Cross. We played in the Rosary field on Harold's Cross Road up to under-13 level in the Dublin and

District soccer league. From under-13 to under-18 I played for Rangers AFC in Bushy Park – the premier under-age side on the south side of Dublin, with St Kevin's Whitehall, featuring Liam Brady, Villa United and Home Farm – the big teams on the north side. Five of us from Rangers were on the Irish schoolboy international team. The Rangers side the year behind me included Kevin Moran, Gerry Ryan who went on to play for Derby County and Ireland, and Pat Byrne the former manager of Shelbourne."

From the day he put his foot inside the door of Mary's, sport was to become the mainspring of Ward's life, as his mother, June, recalls:

"He played everything: soccer, cricket, rugby, tennis and he did a bit of running as well. I just can't remember a time when he wasn't fully occupied, going training or playing matches. I never had a minute's trouble with him.

"I must say the happiest, most carefree days for me were when I went along to cheer through those innocent inter-school games. I'll never forget the exciting atmosphere of those matches in Donnybrook. Just listening to the lads singing their songs, chanting their choruses, and then watching them marching back to school in victory was a fantastic experience."

That Takes The Biscuit

Thursday, 23 March 1967 was a significant date in the life of the young Tony Ward. He had his picture in *The Irish Independent.* He was one of 36 boys from St Mary's who were featured in a full-page advertisement for Marietta biscuits. The common link between the boys was that they all had 'butter-wouldn't-melt-in-their-mouth', altar-boy smiles. Under the pictures of the boys was a picture of a packet of Marietta biscuits and the words: "The way to please two football teams and the reserves for less than a shilling. And you'll even have some left for yourself."

Little did his mother June realise that pictures of her only child in the newspapers would one day become commonplace. Courage is a Ward family trait and she was to need it as she often had to watch her only child lying under a pack of heaving bodies haggling over a rugby ball or receiving a savage swipe in a tackle. However, June Ward is not the squeamish type:

"Sure he could have been killed crossing the road and I was happy for Tony because it meant so much to him to play on the Irish international rugby team. It was not that I didn't worry. I remember him playing against France early in his international career – I knew from watching him that he had been concussed within the first ten minutes. It was obvious to me that he had lost his concentration on the game, and I felt like going out there myself and taking him off.

"Tony would never admit, or even discuss injuries. When it came to news from 'inside the camp', he was as tight-lipped as the KGB. As a lad he was always one to make light of his injuries from football. 'It's only a pulled muscle, or twisted ankle' was his usual way of brushing off any query as to why he was a little lame, or limping a bit. His most serious injury when he was young was only a broken finger, which was fortunate because he was not the type to let anyone fuss over him or try to mollycoddle him in any way."

Words Hurt

However, Ward's great sporting romance was not without its pains. His voice drops to a whisper and he looks into the distance as he recalls the memory:

"I was primarily soccer mad when I was young. Rugby was almost compulsory in Mary's and if there ever was a clash between the two, rugby always took precedence. To that extent I was sometimes begrudgingly a rugby player. At one stage I was picked to play for Mary's on the school under-13 team against Willow Park, the preparatory school for Blackrock College. I was really small at that stage and picked on the right wing. Willow Park always appeared to have a few 'overseas players' on their side. My opposite number was Joe Rekab. Joe was huge for his age, mega-fast and he was black. I was petrified, and I mean petrified of him. I got nowhere near him when trying to half-heartedly tackle him. By half-time we were being annihilated and Joe must have run in for four tries.

"Our coach that day was Fr D'Arcy. We nicknamed him affectionately 'Noddy' because he nodded a lot when he got excited or angry. His face was as red as beetroot at the interval and we all knew he was furious. He asked me: 'Where's your party dress Ward?' That comment cut very deep and I will never forget it. Fr D'Arcy and I became very close over the next few years and he had a huge influence on my career choice, so it didn't ruin our relationship but it could have put me off the game of rugby for life.

"I learned a lesson in that moment about the potentially destructive power of negative comments. That is why I never make any negative comment during, or immediately after, a match to the pupils I teach today. If I have no positive remarks to offer I say nothing. The lads know I am disappointed then and we come back to the mistakes or problems the following Tuesday in a training session, when the heat has gone out of the situation."

The Swinging Sixties

Ward could not have picked a more exciting time to grow up:

"The biggest influence I remember was when England won the World Cup in 1966. It coincided with us getting BBC and ITV on our screens for the first time and we all became soccer fanatics. The other big thing was the music. Radio Caroline and Luxembourg 208 were played non-stop.

"When I look back on the time, I'm struck by the innocence of it all. The songs were so meaningful – remember Dylan and Simon and Garfunkel? There was an idealism which just isn't there today.

"I'm delighted to have lived then, to have been young in a time when there wasn't a serious drug or alcohol problem, when the word AIDS had never been heard of.

"I don't think that I will be the kind of 40-year-old that 40-year-olds were in my youth. I feel I would be much more tolerant of young people and youth culture.

"I went to school in St Mary's College from the age of six and, of course, played rugby there from the beginning. I was a fairly average rugby player then, although I played on the junior and senior teams and captained the latter in my final year. Schools rugby is very important, especially in schools like St Mary's and Blackrock. Apart from your studies you have little else to do or think about and training is very intense.

"In my final year we were beaten in the semi-final of the Cup by High School – John Robbie scored the winning try against us and the result shattered me for we were intent on winning the Cup that year – it was our only defeat during that entire season.

"I failed to get on the Leinster schoolboy team that year – Ollie Campbell and Ian Burns were the out-halves preferred to me – I sat on the subs bench with John Robbie for some of the interpros. Soccer though, was much more important to me.

"I owe a lot to my old coaches at St Mary's, Fr 'Wally' Kennedy and Fr D'Arcy in particular. They both saw me from day one as an out-half though occasionally I was switched to the wing. The fly-half position requires a cool head because the out-half is known as 'the General' in rugby jargon – he is the link along with the scrum-half between the backs and the forwards. It can be the glamour position and conversely, if things go wrong, it's the place not to be!

"In those days Mike Gibson was a very high profile player and I remember long lectures from Fr Kennedy on the Friday afternoons before internationals as we were instructed to watch how Gibson would deal with various problem situations.

"Much later when I played for Ireland myself I couldn't believe that I was actually playing with the self same Mike. Gibson had the most extraordinary recall. After a match he could remember the smallest of moments and he could tell you exactly how you reacted in a particular situation. He occasionally took me aside and analysed my game for me. I found that type of help invaluable when I first arrived on the international rugby scene."

Even at schoolboy level Ward was involved in controversy. In a first round Leinster Senior Cup match against Clongowes, he was preparing to add the points to a try scored next to the posts late in the second half but was adjudged by the referee to have moved forward to replace the ball after it had fallen from the 'mark' without first seeking permission from the official. The Clongowes' players charged the kick and a golden opportunity was lost. The match ended in a draw and Mary's were hammered in the replay.

Chippy

Although Ward made a significant impact in schools rugby, his talents on the soccer field were attracting even more attention:

"I was playing soccer with a very good Rangers' side which included Donal Murphy, who went on to Coventry City, Tommy Maguire who went to Liverpool and Sean Byrne who played with Dundalk.

"I owe a lot to my manager at Rangers, Tony Guy. He was a real footballing manager and I got my philosophy of soccer from him – put the emphasis on skill, not on booting the ball into the 'position of maximum opportunity'. Tony once spent an entire evening with my mother trying to convince her to let me go for a trial to Arsenal when I was fifteen.

"Our great rivals were St Kevins, who had Liam Brady on their side, and we split the trophies 50-50 although they won the important one – the Evans Cup.

"Along with Donal and Liam, I was on the Irish schoolboy side in 1970 and was offered trials with Arsenal and Manchester United but my mother wouldn't let me go. I think I actually hated her for it at the time but she was so right in retrospect because my education came first.

"At 15 I had set myself a real target of playing for the Irish schoolboys and to do that I had to make the trial teams in December. It sounds very silly now but at the time one of the main reasons I wanted to make the trials so badly was to see my name in the paper with my club in brackets after it. I used to read all about the star players in the papers and what always struck me about those reports was that they always had the name of their clubs in brackets after their names. To my mind, that was the sign that you had really made it! I remember rushing out to the newsagents to get the first edition of the evening paper at noon to see was my name there and brackets after it. Sure enough there it was: 'Tony Ward (Rangers)'. It meant so much at the time.

"My first match for Ireland schoolboys was against Northern Ireland in Portadown. Liam Brady was playing and we drew 2-2. On the way back down our manager, Tony O'Connell, probably just for a bit of fun, did a ratings for each player like the *Sunday People* used to do. He gave Liam a 4 (6 is fair, 5 is poor but 4 means a stinker) and he was dropped for the next game which was against England in Sheffield United's ground, Bramall Lane.

"The travel arrangements were very primitive for that game. We travelled over during the night on the mail boat from Dun Laoghaire. It was a very tough crossing and we got a train to Sheffield but there was a snow storm and we got stuck in the middle of nowhere. Eventually we got to Sheffield at 3.30 p.m. with kick-off four hours later having had no sleep the night before. We were told to have a snooze for an hour and after that we went straight to the game and lost 11-0! England didn't have many players that night who made it to the big time apart from Steve Powell who played for Derby and Brian Hornsby who played for Arsenal. Not surprisingly Ireland didn't play England at schoolboy level for many years after that.

"My last cap that year was against Wales in Cork. We had a new manager, Amby Fogarty, but we lost 3-1. Once again Liam was not selected. The star of the Welsh team was Bryan Flynn, still in the news in 1993 for football and other reasons, and what I remember about him most was that he was so tiny.

"In 1989 I met up with Liam Brady for the first time in a number of years when I was over in the UK for an exhibition match in Durham. It was the Sunday before Liam's last international against West Germany when Jack Charlton pulled him off. We met in the airport lounge at Leeds-Bradford. We had a great old natter for hours on end because the plane was delayed. Neither of us could remember details of many of the major games which we had played when we became full internationals, apart from the really big ones, but we could both remember in minute detail the schoolboy teams we played against, the names of all the players we played with and wondered where they were now. It was a real trip down memory lane for both of us, reminiscing about old times. Liam never forgot nor forgave Tony O'Connell for that 4 rating on the journey back home from Portadown."

Liam's humiliating treatment was uncomfortably close to Ward's 'Where's your party dress?' experience. Two great careers of very talented but sensitive teenagers could have perished at infancy because of an adult's thoughtlessness.

Like most youngsters, Ward had meticulously kept all the press reports of his schoolboy career as both a soccer and rugby player. Every time his name was mentioned it was underlined. As his career took off, when he started playing for Ireland, he became much more blasé about keeping such records.

Having realised his first great sporting dream, playing for the Irish schoolboys' side, Ward went on to fulfil his second major fantasy and signed for Shamrock Rovers:

"I had followed Shamrock Rovers since I was a kid. When I was growing up, every second Sunday, at least, was spent in Milltown. I went to all the home games and the away games in Dublin and as far away as Dundalk or Drogheda. When Liam Tuohy, the then manager, came along for my signature after I left school there was no decision to be made. It was a great thrill to wear the green and white shirt having followed them for so long. I was shoved straight into the first team although I was far from ready for it.

"One of the things I have never forgotten from my time in Rovers was a remark made by the great Billy Lord, 'Mr Milltown' himself, to me, one of many because Billy was a very learned man, about the importance of diet: 'Remember Tony, we eat to live not live to eat'."

Summer Holiday

During the long summer holidays in St Mary's in fifth and sixth year Ward took a job with PMPA. One of his colleagues there would also go on to become one of Ireland's sporting greats – Eamonn Coghlan. Neither found it a very stimulating environment:

"We worked together in filing. A phone call came down from on high and you had to go through thousands of files to retrieve the required one. At the end of the day all the files were returned and you spent the following day putting them back. It was misery. The only reason I did it the second summer was that I wanted to be able to buy a Yahama 50 motorbike so I grinned and bore it. I considered it well worth the endurance test when I bought that bike. My mother thought otherwise.

"The PMPA used to have a sports day every year. The first year it was held in the Phoenix Park and we had a cross-country race. Eamonn was not allowed to compete in the race for obvious reasons but he came for a jog to accompany me. I was very fit and won the race but I remember struggling around the course while Eamonn was jogging along beside me. The PMPA experience was my first introduction to the world of work. It didn't really entice me to study hard so I could get a 'good' job.

"In school I was 'academically okay'. I was in the 'A' class but in the bottom half and struggling to keep my head above water. I never really bothered too much about it but pressure at home from my mum, and Fr D'Arcy in school, meant I did enough to get by.

"While I was doing my Leaving Cert all I was really thinking of in terms of career was soccer. When I completed my exams and started to look at the appointment section in the newspapers, it struck me for the first time that I was qualified for only a very limited amount of the jobs which were being advertised. I joined an insurance company, the National Employers' Mutual or NEM in South William Street, and worked there for a year as an insurance clerk. Most people would have thought it a great job but for me it was a dead end. From nine to five I was miserable but when I left work I started living again. I remember each lunch-time looking out the window at the students in College Park, apparently having a great time. I suddenly thought to myself: 'I don't want this'.

"In my final two years in St Mary's, Fr D'Arcy had suggested to me many times that I should pursue a career as a PE teacher. During those days in insurance I began to think about Fr D'Arcy's suggestion very seriously and eventually applied to, and secured a place in, the National College of Physical Education in Limerick."

Ward could never have imagined then all the ramifications that this decision would have for the shape of his future life.

3. What Lovely Legs He Has

All Rising to Great Places is by a Winding Stair

Francis Bacon

The great Irish out-half, Barry McGann, was quoted in *The Irish Weekly Examiner* of 25 November, 1976 as saying to the match referee, Bill Dowling during the Munster rugby trial in Musgrave Park: "What lovely legs he has." The admiring comment was prompted by 21-year-old Tony Ward, a little fellow with black hairy legs, who had just left McGann for dead with a dazzling inside break, and a surging downfield run. The best McGann could do was stand back and watch helplessly. The comment was significant because it was one of the earliest signs that one established great had recognised the emergence of another. Tony Ward had arrived.

Yet his rugby career was an accident. Although he had played at out-half for St Mary's College he seemed set for a career in soccer when he became a League of Ireland footballer after joining Shamrock Rovers on leaving school.

When Ward trotted out for the first time to play rugby for Garryowen Seconds no one had any idea just how good he was and still less had a hint of how great he was to become. People who have known him all his life claim that he has remained unchanged over the years. However, if Ward didn't change, the attitude of people towards him did in a very big way. He was one of the very few people to achieve instant fame – the transformation was incredible.

Throughout his career Ward would build two reputations, one for his skill on the field and the other for the controversies which, arguably, restricted his appearance in the green jersey.

As early as his first match the potential was there but he was hardly in the superstar class at that stage. The attitude was right. It sounds like a cliché but rugby would become Ward's life. Everything else was an intrusion that tended to be pushed to one side as much as was practicable, as he immersed himself in what really mattered – rugby. It was the be all and end all of his life.

Accidental Hero

Ward's introduction to first team rugby came via an injury to the Dooradoyle side's key man, John Moroney, who broke his leg in the 1975 League final against Cork Constitution. It was necessary to find someone who could plug the gap in both the playing and place-kicking departments. Ward was fortunate enough to be in the right place at the right time. Lady Luck would not always be so kind.

Some fans shook their heads and said it would be too high a jump for him to move into the cauldron of a big Cup match. It was an extraordinary burden for such an inexperienced player to carry but, driven by a fierce determination, and that most magical of qualities, a big match temperament, Ward would not buckle under the strain. He would delight in proving the doubters wrong in the same way he had confounded cynics in his early Shamrock Rovers days:

"Ironically, the turning point in my career came just after I 'arrived', you might say, as a soccer player with Shamrock Rovers. I had started my degree course and soon enough I got fed up travelling from Limerick. Then, out of the blue, Garryowen asked me to play for them and four matches later I had won a Munster Cup medal."

Despite Ward's affection for Garryowen he never lost his soft spot for Shamrock Rovers and is bitterly disappointed that Milltown has been lost to the soccer public for development reasons only:

"Milltown was Shamrock Rovers and Shamrock Rovers was Milltown."

Later, in July 1975, he would receive a letter from Rovers informing him that he had been placed on the transfer list. The fee being sought was £500!

"When I signed originally for Shamrock Rovers from Rangers I went with the Rangers' manager, Tony Guy, to meet Louis Kilcoyne in the Burlington Hotel. I felt a real king, discussing professional terms with the managing director of the most famous club in Ireland. The importance of it was that my signing-on fee virtually paid for my first year in college. It made a huge difference to me financially because although my mother was a great support to me in every way, she was in no position to pay for me through college."

Ward did return for a brief liaison with Sean Thomas and Shamrock Rovers on St Stephen's Day 1976 against Sligo in Milltown and played a handful of games with them that season. He turned down a chance to begin again in August 1977, when John Giles tried to sign him after taking the job as manager of the Hoops. Just meeting his childhood idol was an incredible thrill for Ward, though Giles quickly intervened to stop him from saying "Mr Giles" all the time.

An Englishman In Limerick

There were four personalities involved in luring Ward to what was to be a long-running romance with Garryowen:

"I was a student at the time at the National College of Physical Education in Limerick. One of my lecturers there was Tony Lanaway. He was an Englishman with a very strong British accent who played with Garryowen, where he was affectionately nicknamed 'Paddy Lanahoe'. Every one in first year knew him as 'Mr Lanaway' because he ruled with an iron fist. He took us for rugby practicals in college and obviously felt that this first year soccer player might have something to offer rugby. He tipped off Garryowen and spoke to Shay Deering about me. Shay knew me from St Mary's because I had been in the same class as his twin brothers Kevin and David. The Garryowen team trained at the college two nights a week and one night I was approached by Shay, Mr Lanaway and Garryowen's captain that season, Des Quaid. They asked me to play the following weekend with Garryowen's second side against Birr. It was just before then that Johnny Moroney, the regular Garryowen out-half, had broken his leg and the club was in a quandary coming into the Cup campaign.

"We had a typical students' party on the Saturday night so I was still in bed the next morning when the team manager that year, who later became president of the club, Tommy O'Brien, came to collect me for the game. Suffice to say on this occasion I was not particularly well prepared.

"My one vivid memory of the game is of Paddy Lanahoe, who was in the second row that day, getting the ball in his hand and making a run. I ran along side him looking for a pass and instinctively shouted at him, 'Mr Lanaway, Mr Lanaway' because it was the natural, respectful way we addressed our lecturers. He was mortified with embarrassment and stopped his run. Later he told me in the most emphatic way that I was to call him either Tony or Paddy on the rugby pitch but certainly not Mr Lanaway.

"He went back to England to lecture in physical education in Birmingham a couple of years after. I remember one of the first notes I got when I won my first cap in 1978 was from him. It said simply: 'Remember girls love international out-halves' hips.' His thoughtful gesture meant a lot because he had been such an influential figure in my beginning with Garryowen.

"He trained Garryowen when I was in first year. He said it would be good experience for me as a first year student to take some of their training sessions. I would get pocket money for training them which, of course, was Lanaway's real motive in involving me in the sessions.

"That game against Birr was my only appearance in club rugby below first team level until I played my very last game when I played for Greystones seconds against Bective in the Metropolitan Cup in 1991 on the back pitch in Donnybrook. This is possibly unique as I missed out on the normal apprenticeship most players serve before making it on to the first team because of my involvement in soccer. "

After clocking up about half of Garryowen's points during their 58-4 win against Birr in his first match for their seconds, Ward was selected on the senior side for a match against Wanderers in Lansdowne Road the following week. He was still playing soccer for Shamrock Rovers at the time and played for the Hoops against Home Farm on the Friday evening. The next day was to mark his senior club debut but the circumstances were less than auspicious as he recalls with a broad smile:

"The match was on at the same time as the Wales and Ireland game in Cardiff and we had only a scattering of spectators watching our endeavours. I remember the game well, especially Frank Hogan getting the winning try when he was lifted over the line by Shay Deering and Micky Martin.

"Soccer had been my game up to that match but I was immediately struck by the camaraderie of rugby. In the club house afterwards I remember our scrum-half, Liam Hall, getting up on the table and leading a sing-song. It was all so enjoyable and I remember that feeling of kinship and, at that moment, thinking this is the game for me. That weekend was the start of my demise in soccer and my rise in rugby. I never lost my love for soccer, even though I decided rugby was my number one. Throughout my career I always regretted that the rugby and soccer seasons coincided. Had they run at different times I would have combined both."

Ward feels a particular debt to Frank Hogan who nursed him along in the early days:

"He was in so many ways the father I never had."

The following week Ward was selected for his first Senior Cup game for the 'Light Blues' against Sunday's Well in Cork. Ironically Garryowen were coached by a Cork man, Pat O'Riordan, that season:

"I had never heard of the 'Well'. I didn't know which teams were from Cork and which were from Limerick apart from the fact that Garryowen was obviously from Limerick and Cork Con was from Cork. Mind you, I wasn't long in learning I can assure you and the history and traditions attached to each.

"That Cup game was a totally new experience for me as I had only been used to Leinster schools rugby. The passion and commitment of the players in my first taste of Munster competitive rugby will always remain in my mind. It was unbelievable. There were boots and fists flying everywhere. I was taken aback at the time but I learned subsequently that that was a typical Munster Cup match. The only redeeming feature was that the referee was a 'Dub', Martin Walsh, with a real Dub accent, and I like to think he took care of me on that day."

In the semi-final Garryowen accounted for Old Crescent. It was the first time that Thomond Park would see a sight that often thrilled them – those mesmerising runs and side-steps that constituted the Ward jink. Now it was the big one – the Munster final. The opposition would be provided by Cork Con.

Garryowen had a number of great players at the time but the jewel in their crown was unquestionably Shay Deering. Deering had the knack of leading a good team with a mixture of humour, charm and lordly aggression. Leadership by example and his special presence were matched by the loyalty and respect he inspired in others. A fiercely competitive, though well-controlled, streak burned inside him.

There was no doubt that Garryowen could win, but whether they would or not depended largely on how their rookie out-half could handle the pressure.

The match lived up to expectations – a tough, bruising encounter with little between the teams. On the half hour Con took the lead, a typical Barry McGann kick ahead led to a try for Dave Meagher. On the stroke of half-time Ward kicked a penalty from the left-hand touchline and closed the scoring ten minutes after the restart with another penalty. Ward's two penalties brought his total for his three Cup ties to 23 points.

In defeating their old rivals Cork Con, Garryowen set a number of records. Not since 1940 had a Limerick team won the Cup on the banks of the Lee. It was also the first time they had defeated Con in the final since 1932. Moreover, it was the first time since the 1920s that they had won the Cup in successive seasons. Despite their low score in the final, the six points brought their total for the season to 601 points, the first time the 600 mark had been surpassed in Munster.

The Friday after the match Ward won his first "Sportstar of the Week" award from *The Irish Independent*. Ward remembers that award because of an incident in the college canteen:

"A couple of days after the award was announced I was in the queue for coffee when I heard a voice asking me: 'What have you been up to in my absence?' The question was posed by Brian Mullins, the Dublin player. I was only in first year at the time and Brian was in third year. He was a cult figure in the college because he had helped Dublin to win the All-Ireland Football Final the previous year. He had been returning from America with the Dublin team after the All-Stars' tour and noticed my picture as the Sportstar of the Week on the plane home but was at a loss to understand how I could possibly have got there. I hadn't even started playing for Garryowen before he left. Apart from being a great footballer, Brian had a big interest in rugby and went on to play for Clontarf. He also won a McCorry Cup medal with Blackrock.

"One of the most striking things about my time in college was the top class Gaelic footballers we had around the place. Apart from Brian, there were Pat and Mick Spillane, Ogie Moran and Jimmy Deenihan of Kerry, John Tobin, Declan Smyth and Brian Talty of Galway, Dublin's Fran Ryder, Richie Bell of Mayo and many more. It was practically a who's who of Gaelic football. It's no wonder the college won the All-Ireland club football championship a few years later under the guidance of Dave Weldrick."

For all his achievements since, Ward remains obviously very proud of that first Munster Cup performance:

"I really didn't appreciate the significance of the occasion at the time. In later years I came to appreciate that winning the Munster Cup was the ambition of every player in Munster and when you think of the great players like Tom Clifford, Phil O'Callaghan, etc., who never won a Senior Cup medal you begin to appreciate its significance. It was all new to me and even today Leinster players cannot appreciate the passion that Limerick rugby arouses.

"I remember after the Old Crescent game walking down by the flats in Watergate, off Williams' Street, and a couple of corporation workers, literally surveying the roads, shouted over to me 'All the best in the Cup final Wardy'. This would never happen in a million years in Dublin as I was then a complete unknown. I found the experience very strange and very moving.

"I also recall O'Shaugnessy's florists alongside the Franciscan Church with a full window display of white and blue flowers for Garryowen. Dublin rugby fans think I'm exaggerating when I mention these happenings but they are part and parcel of everyday life in that rugby daft city.

"Similarly, there was a big extension being built at the time in the college and I was amazed at the fact that so many of the construction workers knew so much about rugby. This to me was so alien to what I was used to in Dublin, where your parents' choice of education decides what game you should play. To me Gaelic football is a fabulous game and I would love to have played it. But I went to a rugby college and never got a chance. I think that one of the greatest shots in the arm the GAA got was when the Dubs made the breakthrough in 1974. It did so much to heighten appreciation for the game in the capital.

"In fact Garryowen were only beaten twice that 74-75 season, by Constitution in the League final and in a friendly against Terenure. We were the side to beat."

Ward's star rose still further the following month in the Centenary Club Championship in Thomond Park. He scored 19 points in Garryowen's 35-14 win over Galwegians - two tries, four conversions and a drop goal. He kicked all the side's tally in their 9-9 match against Leinster Champions, St Mary's. Mary's were awarded the game because the rules decreed that the side with the greater number of tries would be the winners in the event of a tie – their nine points included a try from Tom Grace.

The jury was still out on Tony Ward as a possible future international player. Prodding a sleeping giant into life is one thing – keeping it awake another. Less than a year after making his club debut Ward would win his first cap for Munster.

Behind Every Great Player Is A Great . . .

Having been reared in an all-female household it was quite a culture shock for Ward to have to fend for himself in college. The old adage 'We learn in the university of life' was never more apposite than in his case, particularly in relation to cooking. He concedes that a significant factor in his development as a rugby player was the facilities and personnel in Thomond College:

"It provided an unequalled environment for a sportsperson, the best advice on training and coaching, video-tape facilities and sports facilities of all kinds were available to me. Also there were some outstanding lecturers at college who were an invaluable help to me. Chief among those was P.J. Smyth who was perhaps the greatest influence on my game. On my very first day in college I was in the queue for books and P.J. was in the queue also, because it was his first day as a lecturer. We got talking and it says a lot about the common bond a funny oval ball can generate that we became friends from day one. It turned out that he was a former captain of Bective. He has a great passion for the game and was a fitness fanatic. His own knowledge of rugby is immense and his analysis of a game or a performance was very sharp.

"I benefited a lot from his physical education expertise – how your body functions, what you can expect of it and demand of it – how to develop special skills and how to train for particular sports and particular occasions. He placed a great emphasis on specificity – by this is meant that we trained in a specific way for a specific occasion. For instance, running around the muck on a well torn-up field would be of little advantage when it came to playing on a smooth surface like Lansdowne Road. So to prepare for those games I trained on a smooth surface in college.

"Also, I did a lot of my running with a ball in my hands. It's not enough to develop speed and stamina without a ball – you've got to get used to carrying a ball. This consideration applies of course to say, hurlers. They shouldn't train without hurleys in their hands, even when they are just doing sprints. This idea was not just confined to Limerick. I remember that when Tony O'Neill was in charge of training us in my Rovers' days he insisted that we do all our training with the ball.

"I also learned how to plan my training properly before a big game. In the early days of the first week before a big match I would do a lot of hard physical training but for the second week I would concentrate on sharpness by doing a lot of sprints, and practise my kicking a lot.

"After a match P.J. would discuss my performance with me. This was very useful, especially as the kind of comment I usually got was simply congratulatory, which was very nice but not really very helpful. Normally I knew instinctively what I had done wrong but it was important to have someone else confirm it.

"P.J. used to take me for a series of 300 metre runs with a short break, that never seemed long enough, where he counted to ten. I was lucky in the sense that I trained two nights with the Limerick soccer team, Monday and Wednesday, two nights with Garryowen, Tuesday and Thursday, Friday I worked on kicking, Saturday I played a match and often on a Sunday I had a squad session which meant that in the season I togged out virtually every day.

"P.J. also worked on the attitudinal side of my game which was a great help to me when I became an international. We went through a process of mental rehearsal before a match, which for me meant that I tended to go over in my mind, in the days before an international, everything that could go wrong. I got in such a state thinking about it beforehand, that I was mentally attuned to coping with failure as the match was in process. Thus if I made a mistake early on, it rarely affected me.

"One sign of a great player is one who does not allow his game to be affected by making a bad mistake. A recent example of this was the way Gavin Hastings immediately put his bad mistake behind him in the Lions' Second Test against the All-Blacks in 1993. However, some players can be visibly upset after a bad mistake. To take an obvious, though over-quoted, example, Dick Spring's infamous incident in 1979 when he dropped the ball against Wales which led to the first try.

"Dick is a good example to illustrate my point because he was normally one of the most reliable catchers in the game. He played so many outstanding games down through the years and it was quite out of character for him to miss a catch. But on this occasion, he allowed it to interfere with the rest of his game.

"It is easy for me to make this point. I know the isolation of a full-back in a place like Cardiff Arms Park must be very intense. Having said that, it's a crying shame the way Dick has never been forgiven for that incident down through the years and all his outstanding performances have been forgotten."

Although Ward's own magic moments lingered long in the memory the incident which is best remembered from that game is

Dick Spring's missed catch. Although his political career has flourished he has never been let forget that incident. Throughout the enormously popular series on RTE Radio One, *Scrap Saturday,* Spring was consistently referred to as 'Butterfingers'.

Ward has no doubts that his involvement with soccer also helped his rugby career:

"Soccer helped my footwork considerably. I always had a natural jink and I think playing soccer improved that. It also made me a two-footed player, which was a great help in rugby. All players favour one leg and I favour my right but I do claim to kick well with my left also.

"Soccer also helped with my goalkicking. I was an around the corner goalkicker and this ability was developed at soccer. Incidentally, I always hated the tag of 'goal-scoring machine'. It was as though I was incapable of doing anything else. Goalkicking can greatly influence the other aspects of your game. If you're successful, it naturally gives the rest of your game confidence. But conversely, if it's unsuccessful it could damage the rest of your game."

Ward admits that many of the most memorable moments of his career were when he played with Garryowen and when he pulled on the red jersey of Munster.

"Many top players would only view the interpros as a stepping stone to the national team but the vast majority of Munster players feel very proud to play for their province. You had great support from your own fans but you were the sworn enemy of the opposition. I always found it very gratifying that when I played for Munster the fans who scorned me when I played for Garryowen would sing my praises when I wore the famous red jersey. I will always cherish those moments.

"I remember a game in 1975 against Young Munster in Greenfields. The game was only 15 minutes old when I heard a shout from the side line: 'Get the film star.' In fact the match, which we won, was not a dirty one but the comment typified the fiery passion of the supporters."

A Man For All Seasons

Ward is deeply grateful to his club teammates for his rise to the top:

"The players in Garryowen were an enormous help to me. When I started playing with them first I was following in the footsteps of John Moroney who had been a dominant personality and highly popular figure in the club before a tragic injury cut him down. Playing alongside Larry Moloney, Seamus Dennison, Liam Hall, Des Quaid, Frank Hogan and so on, inspires great confidence in a player.

"It was probably the greatest Garryowen side ever. I came into a side in which there were players of outstanding ability and it was impossible not to learn quickly from them. For instance, to have Liam Hall as your scrum-half was a wonderful bonus. Many in Garryowen then rated him the best scrum-half in the country – he was peerless at relieving the pressure on his out-half, he had a precise pass and he himself was very fast on the break. Then there was Seamus Dennison who had enormous experience. He gave me a lot of self-confidence in insisting that as out-half it was my duty to call the shots. Initially I tended to turn to him to decide what to do when in doubt but he always insisted in my making up my own mind.

"There was also a great back-up for a relatively inexperienced player like myself in a club like Garryowen. The traditions of the club have a lot to do with it as well as the presence of fantastic players, past and present, who offer valuable advice."

However, one player in particular will always have a special place in his heart – the late Shay Deering. A new range of emotions come into Ward's voice and facial expression as he talks about the man who was, and is, his inspiration. He speaks with even more intensity than normal:

"I first got to know the Deero as a starry-eyed schoolboy in St Mary's in 1966. Shay was in sixth year and captain of the school cup-winning senior side. He became my hero instantly and he has remained so to this day.

"With the arrival of his twin brothers – Kevin and David – in my class I was to get to know Seamus much better and many times, as the years progressed, not alone were our paths to cross but they became very much one and the same. We played together for club (St Mary's and Garryowen), for province (Munster) and for country and I will be forever grateful that it was much more often with, rather than against him I played.

"One particularly fond memory I have of him goes back to when I was in fifth year in Mary's when I went to a party organised by Kevin and David. Their parents were away and we made hay while the sun shone. Shay came in late that night. He was in university at the time and we got him to sing, 'My brother Sylvest'. My admiration for him was total.

"He won eight caps for Ireland between 1974 and 1978, captaining his country in his final appearance. He won Munster and Leinster Cup medals, a Leinster League medal and was capped for both provinces. He had a most distinguished career but long after the cups and caps have been counted, it is the friendships he made along the way that mattered the most. That he was brave on the field is beyond dispute but in his final years his bravery was stretched to the limits because of his battle against a terminal illness. He displayed courageous fighting qualities that one would expect only of him. His passing has left the game he loved much poorer. Shay was quite simply the player's player.

"In recent years I think of him regularly, particularly whenever I hear the Bette Midler song 'Wind Beneath My Wings', from the film *Beaches,* because of the line: 'Did you ever know you were my hero?' Every time I hear that song Shay Deering flashes into my mind."

Wobbling Wallabies

Although Ward's main memory of his second year in college is of the time the rigours of academic life really hit the class as they were bombarded with assignments from their lecturers, his rugby memories are much happier. January 13, 1976 proved lucky for Ward. He was called onto the Munster side to play against the touring Australian team after Barry McGann failed a fitness test following a thigh injury.

There were two noteworthy connections between the 1976 Munster side and the historic Munster side of 1967 – the first Irish provincial team to beat a touring side from one of the major rugby playing nations. Tight head prop, Phil O'Callaghan was the sole survivor on the playing side. Tom Kiernan, who had scored eight points in Munster's 11-8 win in 1967, was the coach of the Munster team.

Down through the years Munster had turned in some remarkable performances against touring sides – the All-Blacks, the Springboks and the Wallabies, only to be narrowly defeated. The more senior Munster supporters could still remember the feeling of being robbed at the Mardyke in 1947 when Australia scored a last minute try to defeat Munster 6-5 despite the suspicion that the winning try came from a forward pass.

History was to repeat itself at Musgrave Park when another dubious pass, which looked well forward, played a decisive role in a 15-13 points win for the Wallabies. The match began promisingly for Ward and Munster. The Aussies were penalised from the very first line-out and Ward floated over a lovely kick from the right-hand touchline after only 90 seconds. He added a second penalty in the 19th minute and before the interval added a drop goal from 40 yards following a swashbuckling, 60 yards run by Larry Moloney on the right wing. However, his good work was balanced by a hat-trick of penalties from the acclaimed Australian fullback, Paul McLean – who was more than a little profligate with his kicking.

The crucial score came 34 minutes into the second half when a forward pass seemed to pave the way for John Weatherstone to score a try under the posts, which McLean converted. Then, when all seemed lost, five minutes into injury time, Shay Deering scored a try. The score set off a temporary pitch invasion and the roar which followed must have threatened the sound barrier.

The conversion, which could have won the game, was a big moment for Ward. It was not the most difficult kick he had faced that day but the circumstances were difficult for a novice with little or no experience of such tense moments. A hush descended on the entire stadium as he faced up to the kick. If tension could be generated into electricity Musgrave Park could have supplied more power than Windscale. His kick from the right was hooked and tailed wide. Munster lost by a point. It was a cruel end to what had been a dream debut:

"I have two special memories from that game. Before the game, the 'non-Cork' players were staying in the Silver Springs Hotel, and I remember, because I was in college at the time, that the food in the hotel seemed bliss when compared with the standards of our canteen. The players were well-treated by the Munster branch.

"I also remember the size of the crowd, seeming huge at the time. When I dropped the goal there was an almighty roar, and I can still hear the applause ringing in my ears. Of course I have played in front of much bigger crowds since but because it was such a novel experience then, it was really magic."

In his first full season Ward shattered all Munster scoring records and wound up with 227 points to his credit. In his second season he threw the Munster trivia buffs into frenzy when he scored 27 points, including three tries, in a 46-9 victory over Munster Cup holders U.C.C. It seemed to be a new record for Irish rugby, surpassing Barry

McGann's 25 points for Munster against Cheshire in 1971. However, it was recognised as being a long way short of the world record – 41 points scored by Joe Karam in 1974, including 15 conversions, when New Zealand beat South Australia.

Ironically the omens for Ward's personal achievement that day were not favourable:

"The match was played on the Monday of the October bank holiday weekend. I had spent the weekend with my friends in Dublin and had been 'a little loose' in my preparation for a match. I had a glass or two more than I should have had to drink the night before and was not feeling too sharp. In the very first minute they got an extraordinary try when Danny Buckley ran the length of the field to cross the line and I remember thinking to myself, 'Oh no, this is going to be a nightmare'. Then for some unknown reason I had an inspired match. I could do no wrong and scored three tries. Anybody who had seen me the night before would not have believed it."

Ward's form was the crucial factor which allowed him to depose Barry McGann from the Munster side in the second match of the interprovincials the following season. Following a poor performance by McGann in the opening game against Leinster, Ward was one of seven changes, two of them positional, for the second match against Connacht. Ironically, Ward's elevation to the Munster team was achieved at the expense of a man who had a significant role in his development as a rugby player, Barry McGann:

"Irrespective of whether we met at a Munster training session or on the occasion of our games against Cork Constitution, Barry always sought to give me good advice. I suppose it could be said that his comradeship rebounded on him in the sense that I took his place on the Munster side but I will always be grateful for his remarkable philosophy of sport.

"Another man I remember with great affection from the same period is Des Barry who coached Munster in my second season with the province. A tough coach but a thorough gentleman. Now sadly no longer with us. I always remember his rallying cry before matches: 'Slash Donkey. Slash Cart.' In other words, get stuck in!"

Munster won the match against Connacht 13-6 with Ward proving to be a real box of tricks, kicking one magnificent penalty, and varying his play like an old head. He opened the scoring with a penalty from 50 yards and closed it by converting a Greg Barret try. In between, Conor Sparks kicked two penalties for Connacht and Colm Tucker scored a try for Munster. The significance of the match for Ward was that it appeared to put him at the head of the queue for the out-half position on the Irish B side's forthcoming match against France in Dijon.

Ward was duly chosen to play for the Irish B side on Saturday, 4 December 1976. He had always associated telegrams with bad news but a message from the IRFU was to change all that.

It was not the fairytale he had dreamed of, as Ireland were comprehensively beaten 16-3. He got Ireland's only score, a penalty from 25 yards after 15 minutes. Apart from winning his first cap, the other significant memory Ward has of his B selection is that he received a letter of congratulations from St Mary's club. Such a piece of correspondence was noteworthy because it was the only time he received such a message from his former club.

"Whereas in Garryowen or Greystones no matter how high you went there was always a message of congratulation. It's the age old story, little things really do mean a lot. I think, certainly in my time, Mary's fell down badly in that regard. While I will always retain a deep love for the school, my admiration for the club is nowhere near as strong.

"When I look back now it is astonishing the number of letters, telegrams and good luck calls I got from Garryowen and Greystones while I wore their colours, congratulating me not just on playing for Ireland or the Lions but for playing in interprovincial matches or representative games of any description. When I won my first cap I got letters from all the priests and teachers in the school in Mary's which meant a lot to me at the time but there was never anything like that from the club.

"I learned a big lesson that day in Dijon about how to prepare as regards the warm-up for a big match. Roly Meates was the coach and Robbie McGrath was the captain and naturally they were psyching us up for the honour of playing for Ireland. Forwards in particular need to be psyched up before a match because they are involved in physical confrontation from the kick off whereas backs' skills are much finer and they get tetchy if they are too wound up and over tense. We went through a really tough warm-up before going out for the team photo and then came back in from the freezing cold and got worked up again so that when we went out on the pitch a second time we had experienced too many extremes of hot and cold. It was very uncomfortable. From then on I always participated in the warm-up but not in the frenzied way I did in Dijon."

The following week he also finished on the losing side in the climax of the interprovincial series in one of the most memorable inter-provincial matches. The match was billed as the clash of the two out-halves. On the one side, the maestro and old fox, Mike Gibson for Ulster and on the other, Ward, the jinking young pretender with a flair for the unpredictable. The match featured some tough forward exchanges which boiled over more than once. The game ended in controversy when 27 minutes into the second half with both sides locked at 24 points each, the Munster hooker and Irish international, Pat Whelan, was sent off after an off-the-ball incident.

It seemed a very harsh decision to send Whelan off. There was considerable speculation among the Munster contingent that the reason for the dismissal dated back to the previous Saturday when the referee who sent Whelan off had been a touchjudge and had spotted Whelan being involved in an off-the-ball incident. At the time touchjudges were not permitted to intervene in the case of dirty play which was out of sight of the referee. The feeling was that Whelan paid a price for the sins of his past.

The game featured vintage performances from both fly-halves with both setting up sparkling back movements and being in superb kicking form. Ward kicked six penalty goals and a conversion of a try by Donal Canniffe. Gibson too kicked 20 points as Ulster ran out victorious, 27-24. Curiously the winning points were scored by Frank Wilson, in his only penalty attempt. However, Ward's performance was not enough to win him a place on either side for the final trial.

If that was a surprise it was as nothing compared to the shock news that he was dropped for Munster's next match in April against Cardiff by a selection committee which included Noel Murphy. Few could remember when a player who scored 20 points in one match could be dropped in the next. Ward gave way to Moss Finn of U.C.C. Munster were beaten by over 50 points.:

"Nobody told me that I was dropped. I just read about it in the papers. A portent of things to come. As the match grew closer they had a lot of injuries and asked me to travel. The travel arrangements were very primitive – the team travelled over by boat and played the game without sufficient chance to recuperate. My exams were coming up at the time and that provided me with a legitimate excuse not to travel."

It seemed just a blind impulse but in the most controversial incident of Ward's career, when he was dropped in Australia in 1979, he would recall that incident with a different perspective.

The 1977-78 season began on a high note for Ward when, in September, he joined Garryowen on a fortnight's tour of Trinidad, Tobago and Barbados. It was a trip which would have a lasting effect on a young, impressionable player:

"Garryowen were very good to me and paid all my expenses. We went via New York and travelled from there to Trinidad. At the time the Americans were pumping millions into soccer. The glamour side of the time was the 'New York Cosmos' because Pele, Franz Beckenbauer and Carlos Alberto played for them and to our surprise, they were also on the same plane as us to Trinidad.

"Pele was unbelievable. The graciousness of the man was extraordinary. He had his photo taken with each of us individually and signed autographs for one and all. At one stage he went to the toilet and I remember Shay Deering saying jokingly, 'Jaysus, Pele goes to the jacks'. Mind you, the biggest shock I ever got was when I discovered in school that priests actually go to the toilet as well!

"I learned a big lesson that day with Pele about humility. I remember Shay saying, this time in all seriousness: 'Isn't that incredible? Pele – the greatest soccer player who ever lived and look at how much time he has for everyone'. That taught me a lot about how to treat fans and always to sign autographs when requested and respond to letters as best I could."

Not surprisingly, Ward regained his place on the Munster side for the interprovincial championship. The opening match against Leinster in Musgrave Park was an ideal showcase for him. Leinster went into the game as hot favourites following a fine performance against Llanelli. Munster upset the odds to win 15-10.

Munster began with the advantage of a stiff breeze but it was Leinster who first drew blood with a try from John Moloney after 20 minutes. At that stage Leinster were completely on top with their pack dominant and backs setting up neat movements. Then Ward stamped his class on proceedings with some typical jinks and huge punts.

Against the run of play, Munster, with a team that featured nine Limerick men, took the lead when a spectacular series of sidestepping movements from Ward paved the way for a Gerry McLoughlin try. Ward kicked the conversion. As if to show that his Nureyev act was no fluke, Ward repeated the feat a few minutes later setting up a move which led to a try for Donal Spring which the out-half converted. At half-time Munster led 12-4. By now the southerners were in the ascendancy. Ward added a penalty goal in the second half while a drop goal and penalty from Mick Quinn gave a veneer of respectability to the score from a Leinster point of view. Ward had surely done enough to earn his place in the final trial already.

In their next match Munster beat Connacht 10-6. Ward converted Olan Kelleher's try though he failed with the conversion of Billy Cronin's try. Lashing rain and a gale force wind ruined the game as a spectacle and as a productive exercise for the Irish selectors.

Ward's form earned him another B cap. This time the match was against Scotland in Murrayfield and he was to finish on the winning side. The game was played on a bitterly cold afternoon with the Irish side surprising everybody by their determination and aggression in loose play. The much-hyped Scottish half-backs, Roy Laidlaw and John Rutherford were something of a disappointment. Instead, they were outshone by the Irish half-back pairing of Ward and Colin Patterson. Patterson scored the only try of the game and Ward kicked a penalty with Colin Mair replying with a penalty to give Ireland a 7-3 win. The match itself was forgettable but for Ward it was a stepping stone to his big ambition to play for Ireland in a full international:

"The match was originally supposed to be played in Ayr but the weather was dreadful that day in both Ireland and Britain. The game had to be transferred to Murrayfield because they had an underground heating system. All the other fixtures, race meetings and so on were cancelled, with the result that RTE had little option but to show the match live. Consequently we got much greater exposure than we would normally have expected and that, I believe, was a significant factor in many of that team winning caps afterwards.

"Another memory was that Moss Finn was playing outside me on the left wing that day. From the kick-off the ball went behind our goal-line and Frank Ennis who was playing full-back, instead of touching it down passed it on to Mossy who had gone back to cover. He was taken completely by surprise and kicked the ball immediately but sliced his kick infield where some of the Irish players were in an offside position. We were penalised and conceded a penalty. They converted it and we were 3-0 down within minutes. It was not the start we were hoping for! One of the things that helped us greatly was that our captain that day, Ciaran Fitzgerald, really got us going in his own inimitable way."

Ward was duly selected to play in his first final trial a few weeks later. However, the trial clashed with his college class field trip to Newgrange in county Meath and the Young Scientist's exhibition.

One of his lecturers informed him that if he refused to go on the field trip he would ensure that whatever Ward's achievements on the rugby field might be, he would never graduate from the college. This threat was repeated by the same lecturer a number of times during the academic year. Ward never completed the field trip but did graduate the following summer.

It came as no surprise to anyone when shortly after the B international, Ward was chosen to make his debut for Ireland. His hour of glory had come. On reflection, he appreciates his achievements more now than he did at the time:

"It was quite a meteoric rise and in retrospect, even more so than I realised at the time. Looking back I think of it in terms of my progression through college and what I remember is that each year coincided with a step on the ladder. In my first year I played club rugby. In my second year I played for Munster. In my third year I became an Ireland B cap and in my fourth year I was playing for Ireland."

Ward retains a cluster of congratulatory telegrams which were sent to him at the time. Among them was one from a man destined to play a big role in his rugby story – Ollie Campbell.

4. From The Sublime To The Conspicuous

Every Beginning is a Promise

Brendan Kennelly

The selection of the Irish team for the opening match of the 1978 season against Scotland provided a number of talking points. Ireland had a new captain, 28-year-old St Mary's College scrum-half, Johnny Moloney. He had won the last of his 19 caps against Scotland at Lansdowne Road in 1976 and had inherited the leadership of Leinster from clubmate and former Irish captain, Tom Grace.

There were four new caps on the team – centre, Paul McNaughton, out-half, Ward, wing forward, John O'Driscoll and second row, Donal Spring. Of this quartet two were former League of Ireland footballers. McNaughton had played for Shelbourne and Ward for Shamrock Rovers. McNaughton had been an Irish amateur soccer international and Ward an Irish schoolboy international. O'Driscoll was a brother of Barry O'Driscoll who had won four caps at full-back in 1971. Astonishingly, there was only one Ulster player on the team – centre, Alistair McKibbin. Tony Ensor had retained the full-back position despite being demoted to the 'Possibles' for the Final Trial. A fifth new cap, Mick Fitzpatrick, was added to the front row. He got a late call-up when original choice, Ned Byrne, had to cry off with a badly damaged knee.

Before the game, Ward was, not surprisingly, a bundle of nerves. Gareth Edwards, speaking before his 50th international against England as he performed his normal ritual – buying shirts and relentlessly patrolling the hotel – was asked how he was affected by big match nerves. He responded with typical candour: "It's always the same, always the same gripping of the stomach, the same catching of the breath."

Ward is like a child in a sweet shop as he recalls his first international:

"I never thought I could match that feeling I had when we beat Cork Con to win the Munster Cup in my first season in front of their own people. Then I ran out in a green jersey.

"That day was like something out of one of those Boys' annuals. That morning I had walked in Stephen's Green with Johnny Moloney trying to talk about everything but football. We had a great relationship both on and off the field which is essential between a scrum-half and his out-half. We trained together because I was doing my teaching practice in Ballyfermot at the time and we talked about every aspect of the game. But in the hours before the Scottish match both of us were too nervous to mention football. It was Johnny's first game as captain and my first cap. There was a lot at stake.

"I was always very nervous the 48 hours before an international. I found it difficult to sleep. In the Shelbourne Hotel where the team traditionally stayed, there was a lot of tension and it was not made any easier meeting rugby followers, ex-internationals and, worst of all, members of the opposition, unexpectedly on the corridors.

"It didn't feel any different from an ordinary game until we left the coach and walked towards the dressing-room. I saw Nigel Starmer-Smith and the BBC cameras first, then all the top brass from the Rugby Unions. Then I realised that this was something completely different.

"I was sharing a dressing-room with players who were heroes a few years ago. Green jerseys were passed around and outside a brass band was warming up. You could hear the crowd outside as Johnny and Noel Murphy exhorted us to go out and win."

Ward experienced mixed emotions just before the match began – a combination of apprehension and excitement:

"To represent your country, be it at soccer, rugby or tiddlywinks, is an extraordinary honour. I was sick before the game. Mike Gibson told me, 'Don't worry, you will never feel any different no matter how often you play at this level.' I felt most unassured.

"But that moment when I ran out the first time in an international match can never be forgotten. It's still clear in my mind. I can remember running on to the pitch and hearing the incredible noise from the terraces. I knew then that I had to live up to the things people expected of me. Barry McGann sent me a note telling me how lucky I was to be winning my first cap for a home game, just as he had won his, because the difference in playing in front of a Lansdowne Road crowd is enormous. I thought I understood what he meant but it was not until I heard the crescendo of noise when I came onto the pitch that I fully appreciated what was meant in that note.

"I was lucky insofar as I had a temperament which was ideally suited to the big occasion."

He did not find the transition from playing in a B international to a full international as dramatic as he had expected:

"As soon as I got on to the pitch, I got an enormous confidence from nowhere. The nerves were gone. Once I got in a nice garryowen early in the game I felt fine. The pace was a little bit sharper, but really I was surprised to make the transition so easily."

Sweet Dreams Are Made Of This

21 January 1978 was the day when Ward made his debut in the Irish senior side. After two seasons in the wilderness it was time to put a halt to Ireland's losing sequence. It was not a game for the purists, but what the home side lacked in skill and technical proficiency the fighting Irish more than compensated for with their guts and determination.

On a chilly day Ireland played with the advantage of the wind in the opening half. However, they seemed to have profited poorly from it when they trailed 6-3 after 40 minutes. The Scottish captain, Douglas Morgan had kicked two penalties from 25 yards on the left after 12 minutes and the second from 40 yards after 26 minutes. Sandwiched in between, Ward had scored his first penalty from 30 yards in the 22nd minute. Two long-range efforts from penalties had failed when he faced up to his fourth kick from the right touchline in the 40th minute. He hit the ball so sweetly that the partisan crowd were cheering long before the touchjudges raised their flags to register the score.

The timing was perfect – as important psychologically as it was on the scoreboard. At least Ireland would face the interval on equal terms – or so it seemed. Ireland's impressive new flanker, John O'Driscoll, had taken a severe knock earlier and had to be replaced by the ever-reliable Stewart McKinney. His impact on the match was immediate and dramatic. Two minutes later he scored Ireland's first try at Lansdowne Road since the game against Australia in 1976.

The Scots were menacingly on the offensive in the heart of the Irish defence when Phil Orr made one of his typical storming runs breaking through the Scottish cover before being grounded. Five Irish forwards were following through and each brought the ball closer to the line before a scrum was awarded to Scotland. Although the Scots won it, the Irish scrum-half, Johnny Moloney, grounded his opposite number, Dougie Morgan, and the ball was taken up by Fergus Slattery who made some ground before feeding McKinney for a try. Ward calmly slotted over the conversion to give Ireland a 12-6 lead at the interval.

In the second half Ireland were forced to surrender the territorial advantage but defended superbly. The Irish grit was typified in the 11th minute of the second half. Willie Duggan was helped from the field holding his left shoulder. Ireland having already deployed their back row replacement, McKinney, the prop, Gerry McLoughlin, prepared to enter the fray but Duggan shook off his assistants and ran once more unto the heat of battle. Despite his obvious handicap, Duggan turned in his customary towering performance. Fifteen minutes later Tony Ensor was carried off the field after a collision with one of his own players to be replaced at full-back by Larry Moloney. In the 75th minute Morgan kicked his third goal to reduce the deficit to just three points and set the stage for a heart-stopping finale. The tension was compounded when the referee played ten minutes of injury time.

Then, in the dying minutes, Scotland, was awarded a penalty just 10 yards from the Irish line and 15 yards to the left of the posts. As the fans braced themselves for the inevitable equaliser, thousands of jaws dropped as Scotland decided to run the ball. The old adage 'Fortune favours the brave' was put under a severe test but happily, from an Irish point of view, it was found to be untrue in this case and the assault was halted yet again by the brave Irish defence. Scottish skipper, Dougie Morgan, explained his decision to run the penalty after the match:

"Given the same situation again, I would do the same. A draw ruled out our chances of the Triple Crown and I wanted to win."

An interested spectator at the match was the peerless Jack Kyle. His comments afterwards were:

"It was a great result for Ireland, especially as the win was needed so badly. They played with wonderful spirit. I think Ireland's out-half, Tony Ward, had a splendid match. It was a great debut for him. I would not be despondent about Irish rugby after that performance."

The Irish side that day was: Tony Ensor; Tom Grace; Paul McNaughton; Alistair McKibbin; Freddie McLennan; Tony Ward; John Moloney (captain); Phil Orr; Pat Whelan; Mick Fitzpatrick; Moss Keane; Donal Spring; John O'Driscoll; Willie Duggan; Fergus Slattery.

Ward quickly appreciated that his life was now going to be different:

"The impact of playing for Ireland did not really strike me at first. I was back into college on the Monday morning. There was some interest before the first lecture from my classmates but no big fuss. Our first lecture was sociology with Roderick Harrison, who was a superb lecturer, a brilliant performer, like Jimmy Davidson in many respects. He alluded to the wonderful occasion we had witnessed on Saturday. The remark was made in the context of the lecture and was not a direct reference to me but it really brought home to me how widely the game is seen and discussed. As my mother would say, it warmed the cockles of my heart."

The Greatest Show On Ice

Four weeks later it was off to France. On their previous visit Ireland had not so much been defeated as routed. The match was to be played on a bone hard pitch in conditions more suited to skating than rugby, and the Irish were very reluctant to play at all because the risk of serious injury was so great. The Welsh referee, Cefydd Thomas, also considered the ground to be dangerous but the French Federation had the final say and they insisted the game should go ahead.

It was one of the greatest, most stirring Irish performances even though they were to lose by the narrowest of margins. Although France were well worth their win, past form considered, their performance was not half as impressive as Ireland's.

The Irish were handicapped by the presence of just one specialist second row when Emmet O'Rafferty, due to make his international debut, was forced by a cruel twist of fate to withdraw four hours before the kick-off having sustained a calf muscle injury in training the previous day. Harry Steele was called into the second row and John O'Driscoll was contacted in London to act as a cover player. This put an added burden on Willie Duggan in the lineout because he had to compete with the legendary Jean Pierre Bastiat at the back. Not for the first time Duggan rose magnificently to the challenge.

Although Duggan was the inspiration up front there were heroes in the backs also. Tony Ensor had perhaps his finest game ever for Ireland – heroic under high kicks, masterful in his positional play and defensive kicking. Honours in the defence were shared by captain, Moloney, who made an enormous defensive contribution with his tackling and safety kicking, and by Ward who lifted siege after siege with relieving clearances. Dancing on the ice in a way that Torvill and Dean would have envied he was a constant thorn in the side for the French with his jinks, delicate chips, and floated kicks giving a great deal of headaches to the French full-back, Jean Michel Aguirre.

Ireland trailed 10-6 at half time. Jerome Gallion scored a try and Aguirre kicked two penalties to Ward's two penalties. Ward kicked the only score of the second half, 10 minutes after the restart – his third penalty. However, the French were camped in the Irish 25 for the final 20 minutes but time after time the Irish fought them off the line and survived a succession of five-yard scrums. The referee was looking at his watch when Ireland, to everybody's astonishment and the anguish of the French hordes, found themselves inside the French 25. The screaming was so frenetic that nobody off the pitch heard the final whistle. Although they lost, their remarkably resilient and brave performance won them many friends and promised much for the match against Wales two weeks later. Ward remembers one incident after the match as vividly as any moment during it:

"We all had a lovely warm communal bath after the game. We were still soaking in it when Johnny Moloney came in, his official duties, like the press conference, completed. He was such a whole-hearted player. He had out of necessity dive-passed all through the game despite the ice and his knees were red raw. I will always remember the agony he was in when he got into the water, especially the way it aggravated his discomfort."

Although Ward was coping well with his apprenticeship in international rugby he was also having to contend with his academic duties, principally, at that time, his final teaching practice:

"I was doing my teaching practice in Ballyfermot Vocational School. I had originally been scheduled to go to St Andrew's College, ironically the school in which I now teach, but it was considered too similar to St Mary's where I had done my teaching practice the previous year. I remember the Monday morning after an international going to school on the 18 bus. I had to bring a group to the swimming pool nearby and there was a supervisor, Carmel Vekins, waiting for me. I was still struggling with the aches and pains of the previous Saturday and the last thing I needed was that kind of pressure."

The Ballyfermot experience was as much an education for Ward as for the pupils he taught. Having attended St Mary's he was insulated in many ways from the day-to-day problems of children from the large section of Irish families that constitute the "have-nots". It was a real eye-opener for him to be in daily contact with kids who came to school without any breakfast – a symptom of a much deeper malady, the poverty of many Irish families. It was one thing to read about it in the papers but very different to see its human face and confront it head on. One incident encapsulated the harsh lesson Ward had to learn about the inequalities which bedevil Irish life:

"Every Friday afternoon I had a geography class in one of the prefabs. Out of the corner of my eye I noticed a paper bag at the back of the class and it was moving. Suddenly it started clucking. I naturally asked what a hen was doing in my class, only to be told that the principal had given permission for it to be there. I discovered that the daily egg from this hen played a crucial part in the family's diet and on Fridays there was no one in the family home to mind the hen so one of the children brought her into school in case she would be stolen.

"The idea of a hen in the class may have seemed funny at first but it was very, very sad, to hear that people have to eke out an existence in this way. It was a great lesson to learn so early on what life is really like for so many people."

Stevie Wonderful

Wales had ambitions of their own as they sought a third consecutive Triple Crown. The evening before the match is as well remembered by Ward as the game itself:

"We were staying in the Shelbourne, the same hotel as the Welsh. This practice has changed since because the last thing you want is to be bumping into the opposition or indeed fans on the eve of a big game. I was trying to keep out of their way, and at one stage, to avoid running into any of the players I went around to the back lift. To my horror, when the elevator door opened Gareth Edwards, Phil Bennett, J.P.R. Williams, Ray Gravell and J.J. Williams were in the lift. I wasn't sure if they knew who I was or not because I was still a novice at international rugby but there was no way I could turn back. I walked into the lift but kept my head down and didn't look any of them in the eye. There was total silence until I pushed the button to get off and Gareth Edwards said, and I can still hear his voice ringing in my ears: 'See you tomorrow Tone'.

"The door was closed before I could say anything. I can still remember the two thoughts that came into my head: 'Gareth Edwards knows my name!' and, 'If only if I had my autograph book'. Mind you I made up for it the following day and got everybody's autograph after the game at the post-match dinner which is standard practice for all players involved."

The game itself was marked by a typically gutsy Irish performance which ended in gallant failure. By the 23rd minute Ireland tailed by 13-3. All Wales' scores came from Steve Fenwick – three penalties and a try; Ireland could only manage a Ward penalty. With Quinnell and Martin in control in the lineouts, Ireland seemed set for a hammering. Ward cut the deficit to seven points with a penalty in the 33rd minute which was the cue for the Irish side to roar to life. Moss Keane and Willie Duggan began to dominate the lineouts, and in the mauls and rucks, Ireland started to gain parity.

A controversial incident arose in the dying moments of the first half when Mike Gibson, winning a record 64th cap, was felled by J.P.R. Williams as he kicked up to the 25 from the halfway line. To the astonishment of the crowd the referee did not award a penalty. Subsequently, every time J.P.R. touched the ball he was booed vociferously.

Early in the second half Ward dropped a goal. The Irish crowd now had the scent of victory in their nostrils and went into a frenzied state for the next 30 minutes. Their joy was intensified when Ireland scored a try in the 56th minute. A high kick from Ward put J.P.R. under pressure and in the chaos, John Moloney crossed for the equaliser. Ward failed to convert from a difficult angle.

For the next 20 minutes a magnificent rearguard action kept the Welsh scoreless until J.J. Williams scored a try in the corner. A minute later Fenwick kicked a penalty. It was the match which firmly established Fenwick's reputation – no longer seen as support player to the genius of Edwards or Bennett but as a class player in his own right. The stage was set for a grand finale when Ward reduced the arrears to 20-16 in the 79th minute. But it was too little too late. It was a victory of experience and guile over grit and effort.

Into The Record Books

Ireland's final match of the season resulted in a 15-9 defeat against England. It was a significant game for Ward as he kicked all Ireland's points – two penalties and a drop goal – and thereby equalled the championship record of 38 points held by the former English full-back, Roger Hosen and Phil Bennett. Yet it was a very disappointing team performance and belied the suggestions of improvement in the previous games. One of the few eye-catching moments came early in the second half when a streaker ran on to the field. The statistics for the season told their own story. All Ward's points came from the boot and he scored all of Ireland's points except for two tries. Later that year though, Ward would be involved in one of the great Irish sporting moments.

Rugby's Miracle Of The Loaves And The Fishes

As dawn broke on Tuesday, 31 October, 1978 the Irish sporting public had no idea of the momentous events that lay in store for them that day. The build-up to the match between Munster and the All-Blacks had been overshadowed with forecasts of doom and gloom. The reasons for these dire predictions were twofold. The tourists had gone through the best of the Welsh and the English sides, like a knife through butter. The rugby cognoscenti on both sides of the Channel confidently proclaimed: "They will go through the tour unbeaten." For their part the Munster side had flopped dismally on their preseason tour of London. It would be like sending lambs to the slaughter. This was certainly the impression many of the St Mary's players had:

"The Thursday night before the game there was a lot of slagging about Munster's chances against the All-Blacks but Shay Deering, now back playing for Leinster, was giving as good as he was getting. One of the most vociferous people in the dressing-room was coach and former winger, Noel Kenny. Shay said, 'Okay, Noel, put your money where your mouth is'. A £20 bet was agreed between the pair of them. I'm sure it was not the most confident bet that Deero ever made. It was more pride in Munster than anything else, but he was very happy to collect his money after the game. Noel was not too bothered about paying up because it was such a great occasion."

One man who had not read the journalistic script was Munster's coach, Tom Kiernan. His infectious iron-willed determination had been transmitted to the players to the point where they would have died for their jersey.

The day before the game was a bank holiday Monday and while a thousand people or more had watched the final All-Blacks preparation, only a handful had bothered to watch Munster train at St Munchin's College. Throughout the rugby world the general belief was that Munster would do well to hold the tourists to a ten point winning margin. Ward attributes great significance to the day before the match:

"On the afternoon before we played the All-Blacks we went to Lough Derg. No, not that Lough Derg! The one near Killaloe. It must have been a strange sight but three boatloads of Munster rugby players descended on one of Ireland's quietest lakes and we were anything but quiet. Buckets of water and duckings were the order of the afternoon and, as they say, the craic was mighty. When we arrived back in the Limerick Inn Hotel nobody was wetter from head to toe than T.J. Kiernan. I can still see Tommy with a bucket of water in one hand and an oar in the other, enjoying the larking as much as the youngest member of the side.

"Something happened that afternoon that transformed a group of interprovincial players into a group of blood brothers almost with one common aim – the destruction of the mighty All-Blacks.

"TJ had insisted all along that we could win. The night before the game we rewatched videos of the New Zealanders' previous matches. We watched a video of the All-Blacks annihilating the London Division. The London Division were even a stronger side than Middlesex who had destroyed us a few weeks earlier. For the life of me at the time I could not understand this because it's not the sort of thing that gives you confidence. While playing for Ireland, I never enjoyed watching videos of the opposition before games. I preferred to concentrate on our game rather than worrying about the opposition.

"Again Kiernan stressed that he wanted to see how good the All-Blacks were going backwards. My job was to put them under pressure by putting the ball behind them, so in the opening few minutes I launched a massive garryowen – the pack were charging like roaring lions and Seamus Dennision was breaking the opposition in half with his first tackle and the rest is history."

The Clare hills provided a scenic background for the New Zealanders as they performed their traditional "haka" before the game. Somewhat against the run of play Munster took the lead in the 11th minute – a delicate chip from Ward was followed through and won by Jimmy Bowen, who made an incisive run and as he was caught from behind, he fed Christy Cantillon, who crossed the line beside the posts. The great surging roar from the crowd could be heard for miles around. Ward kicked the conversion with ease.

In the 17th minute the tourists were penalised for indiscriminate use of the boot. Ward's penalty attempt fell five metres short but was knocked on by Brian McKechie. From the ensuing scrum Donal Canniffe fed Ward and he dropped a goal.

The home side hung on to their 9-0 lead until half time but realised that a modern day siege of Limerick awaited them in the second half when the men from down under would do all in their formidable power to protect their unbeaten record. Their fears were justified as the All-Blacks exerted enormous pressure. Metaphorically, and literally, the tourists did not know what hit them as they were stopped in their tracks with a series of crunching tackles by such players as Seamus Dennison, Greg Barrett and most notably Colm Tucker. Jack Gleeson, the All-Blacks' manager, subsequently described them as "Kamikaze tacklers".

As the seconds ticked by agonisingly slowly in the second half the crowd became more and more frenzied, sensing that here lay history in the making. "M-U-N-S-T-E-R! M-U-N-S-T-E-R!" rang out at deafening sound levels. Ward got the only score in the second half – a drop goal – and Munster held on to become the first touring side to beat the All-Blacks. Russ Thomas, the tourists' coach, generously saluted 'fifteen great players'. It was an extraordinary team performance.

The Munster team that day was: L. Moloney (Garryowen); M. Finn (U.C.C.); S. Dennison (Garryowen); G. Barrett (Cork Constitution); J. Bowen (Cork Con); T. Ward (Garryowen/St Mary's); D. Canniffe (Landsdowne); captain; G. McLoughlin (Shannon); P. Whelan (Garryowen); L. White (London-Irish); M. Keane (Lansdowne); B. Foley (Shannon); C. Cantillon (Cork Con); D. Spring (Dublin University); C. Tucker (Shannon).

The victory was overshadowed by the news that while Donal Canniffe was leading the Munster team to an historic win his father, Mr Dan Canniffe, collapsed and died in Cork listening to the match. At the banquet in honour of the team's victory a minute's silence was observed and Pat Whelan, vice captain, stood in for Donal.

One of Limerick's best-known sons, film star Richard Harris, swept away by the euphoria of victory wired the following message from a movie set in Johannesburg:

"Your historic victory over New Zealand made roaring headlines in every South African paper. I've been on the dry for 10 months, but I can't think of a better occasion or excuse to re-acquaint my liver with the drowning sensation of a drop. I wish I was there. I rang Richard Burton and although he extends his congratulations, I detected a tinge of jealousy".

Although Ward could not have foreseen at the time the moments of deep despair that would cloud his career, the memory of that feeling of exhilaration will linger forever:

"There is something special about putting on the red Munster jersey, and beating the All-Blacks was an historic achievement. Nobody who played that day will ever forget the feeling.

"The All-Blacks were god-like figures, with a reputation for invincibility. The atmosphere that day in Thomond Park was incredible.

"We had won convincingly and left the pitch in a state of bliss. However, the crowd demanded that we come out again. It was the only time that I've witnessed a sporting occasion when all around people were crying. To be able to say you were there was great, but to have been at the centre of the action was just fantastic.

"I remember earlier that season going over to London for the 'Golden Boot' awards, and doing an interview with Nigel Starmer-Smith after the lunch for *Rugby Special*. He asked me what I was looking forward to that season and I said the All-Blacks tour, particularly the game against Munster in Limerick. And we had just been annihilated at the time by Middlesex. Nigel was recording at the time so he didn't really comment. But afterwards he said: 'You weren't really serious were you?' Yes I had no doubt that we could beat the All-Blacks. That was definitely the highlight of the year for me. In fact I will go further and say it was the highlight of my career. I have talked about this with Moss Keane many times. Unlike me he was lucky enough to be on the Triple Crown winning side in 1982. He was also on a Lions' tour but he too says that the famous Munster victory was the high point of his career."

The only biblical story which appears in all four gospels is that of the loaves and the fishes. Munster's victory over the All-Blacks has spawned a similar miracle. Although the official attendance at the match was only 12,000 – since then hundreds of thousands of people have said, often with the benefit of generous liquid refreshment: "I was there the day Munster beat the All-Blacks."

Ger Cusack wrote a song to mark Munster's most famous victory called "The Mighty Men of Munster". It concluded with the lines:

About half-four on that historic day
We shouted with delight
The mighty men of Munster had given the Kiwis a fright
The scenes after the match that day will live in memory still
As we walked from Thomond Park Hurray,
Know Munster had won twelve nil
Hurray Hurray Hurray for the boys in red
Hurray Hurray Hurray for the boys in red.

Trying To Pot The Blacks

The tourists extracted retribution for their slip-up the following Saturday to beat Ireland 10-6 courtesy of a try in injury time by Andy Dalton. It was a clash between New Zealand steel and Irish fire with the steel winning by a short head.

Ireland's scores came from two Ward penalties which were cancelled out by two drop goals by his opposite number, Doug Bruce. The closeness of the score made for an exciting contest but the standard of rugby was disappointing with the tourists winning the overwhelming majority of possession but then needlessly kicking much of it away.

From an Irish point of view the pluses from the game were the fine showing of their two new caps – Colin Patterson and Terry Kennedy. Over a week later Ward was to receive the following letter from the IRFU – who were unhappy with his extravagance in relation to expenses.

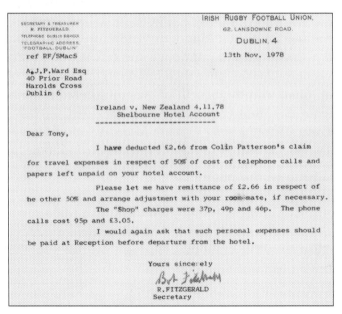

Ward is quick to point out that he was not the only player to receive such correspondence:

"Only recently I heard the story about a home match when Michael Kiernan and Moss Finn were rooming together in the Shelbourne Hotel. One of them went down for a haircut and charged it to their room. Some time later the two lads were billed for a half a haircut each!"

In his book on the All-Blacks' tour, *Mourie's men: The All-Blacks' Tour 1978,* Wallace Reyburn attributes the tourists' defeat to Munster's fearless tackling and Ward's kicking. The book makes for interesting reading particularly the chapter on likes and dislikes. Ireland features prominently in the positive categories:

Best Country:
Ireland ("We felt at home there – they're more like us than the others.")

Best Town: (*???* - author's italics) Limerick.
("Despite the result of the match there – just like being home in a one-street town like Hamilton or Timaru or Invercargill.")

Best Crowd: All the Irish crowds.

Most popular Sightseeing: Bunratty Castle.
("We all went to one of the banquets they have there. Medieval food, serving wenches with cleavage and you're allowed to pinch their bottoms – and Barry Ashworth got locked in the Dungeon!")

Ward was the only Irish player mentioned in the best opponent category along with Andy Irvine, Mike Slemen, Graham Price, Peter Wheeler, Alan Martin and Tony Neary.

A feature of the book was the explosion of the myth that the New Zealanders and the Welsh are beloved enemies: "It's just so much heifer dust. The Welsh hate our guts. . . You never really beat the Welsh, you merely scored more points than they did."

Munster rounded off a magnificent season by beating Leinster 12-3 in Lansdowne Road in December, to win their first grand slam since 1968, their first championship outright since 1973 and to record their first win at Lansdowne Road since 1972. Ward scored all of Munster's points – a try, a conversion and two penalties:

"That game was played on a Sunday. The previous day the All-Blacks were playing against the Barbarians and the Munster team watched the match in the hotel together. The All-Blacks only won with a late drop goal and I still remember the roar that went up when they got that score because it meant that the All-Blacks had won 17 out of 18 highlighting the uniqueness of Munster's achievement. It set us up for the performance the next day, without question Munster's finest season."

A Try In Business

Shortly after the victory over the All-Blacks, Ward made an important career decision. He decided to forsake his teaching position to go into the business world. He teamed up with international colleague, Pat Whelan and Garryowen F.C. administrator, Frank Hogan, to open a sports store at Thomas Street, Limerick. The shop was opened on 2 December 1978 by Johnny Giles.

Having such a public workplace presented its own joys and problems:

"If I hadn't taken the opportunity, I might well have regretted it. It was great to be able to go back to live in Limerick and play my club rugby for Garryowen.

"However, everyone knew where I worked. Without wishing to sound conceited I never felt pressure at the time when it came to playing rugby. The only place I felt pressure was outside the game. In the shop, it got to the stage where I never answered the phone and rarely took calls. The amount of pressure I was put under from various people for this, that and the other – and a lot of them were 'mickey mouse' things - that was where I felt the pressure.

"I always had one other problem with the shop. My mother came down for the opening with John Saunders. It was a miserable night weather-wise. She was staying in Jury's that night, about a half a mile from the shop, as the crow flies, and on the other side of the Shannon. She looked out the window and all she could see was a gigantic sign with my name on it. She got an awful shock, though mind you not half as big a fright as I did when I saw it. This was a sign that Frank Hogan and Pat Whelan had ordered and organised because they wanted to make sure it was clearly visible from O'Connell Street. Talk about putting your name in lights! It was horrendous."

A Tony Award

Ward's achievements in his first international season were recognised when he was chosen as the recipient of the Texaco rugby sportstar award. Other winners that season included John Joe O'Neill, John Treacy, Derek Daly, Pat Spillane, Pat Horgan, Pat Jennings and Barry McGuigan. Ward also won a number of awards from rugby magazines in Britain and France. The IRFU were very anxious to know the nature of these awards and pointed out that he needed their approval to receive such awards.

Throughout his career Ward received a huge amount of correspondence from his fans. Most related to the highs and lows of his rugby career. However, a feature of his first two years in international rugby was the number of letters he received from girls about his looks – most of them from lovesick teenagers. Many of them are not just letters, but weighty tomes full of such romantic sentiment as to put the average 'Mills and Boon' writer to shame. Typical of this was a letter from a young teenager in Meath who wrote that even her horse had fallen under the spell of Ward's charms:

SECRETARY & TREASURER
R. FITZGERALD
TELEPHONE DUBLIN 684601
TELEGRAPHIC ADDRESS,
"FOOTBALL, DUBLIN"
Ref: RF/AH

IRISH RUGBY FOOTBALL UNION
62, LANSDOWNE ROAD,
DUBLIN, 4.

RECEIVED
22 APR 1983
KEVANS

A.J.P. Ward Esq.,
40 Priory Road,
Harolds Cross,
DUBLIN 6.

29th September, 1978

AWARD

Dear Tony,

      It has come to the notice of the IRFU Committee that you have been in London as recipient of an award as an Irish International Rugby player.

      I have to ascertain from you, for the information of my Committee, details as to what organisation was responsible for the award in question and also the nature of the award.

      I look forward to hearing from you.

Yours sincerely,

R. FITZGERALD.
Secretary

SECRETARY & TREASURER
R. FITZGERALD.
TELEPHONE DUBLIN 684601
TELEGRAPHIC ADDRESS
FOOTBALL, DUBLIN
Ref: RF/AH

IRISH RUGBY FOOTBALL UNION.
62, LANSDOWNE ROAD.
DUBLIN. 4

A.J.P. Ward Esq.,
40, Priory Road,
Harolds Cross,
Dublin 6.

16th November, 1978

Awards

Dear Tony,

      The Union Committee has considered your letter of the 3rd ult., and has accepted your very full explanation of the position regarding the "Golden Boot" award.

      In future, if you should receive offers of similar awards, the Union Committee would like you to kindly seek its approval before your acceptance.

Yours sincerely,

R. FITZGERALD.
Secretary

*"I have finally decided to register my horse under the name 'Outside half'.
She is at present known to her friends as Trotskie but something tells me she's
got a crush on you! Thrills I hear you say. That's all you need isn't it, a horse
with a crush on you! We were grooming her yesterday when she was in a bad
mood. Then I said 'Tony Ward' and ever so slowly she pricked up her ears and
went all floppy . . . Meeting you had such an effect on me I went back to school
today and it doesn't start until tomorrow."*

He also received a letter from a girl informing him that she had
called her dog after him 'Ward of Cooley'. In 1979 a mother from
Wales wrote:

*"I am writing on behalf of my daughter Alison, she really is one of your
greatest fans. We thought she would go through the television on Saturday
when you got your head hurt. She kept saying, 'Leave him alone, come on Tony
they cannot keep you down' . . . Tony, the purpose of this letter is that she
would really love to have your autographed photo. We shall have no peace
Tony if you do not send her one, so please do."*

There were also letters from more mature ladies. Typical of this
kind was a flattering letter from a lady which ended on a surprise
note: "Wife need have no fears of a rival. I am a granny."

Ward cringes with embarrassment when reminded of these letters.
However, he never allowed himself to be overly impressed by this
flood of fanmail - part of which bordered on idolatry:

"While I suppose it was very nice to have a horse called after me,
for example, I never let it go to my head. On the Lions' tour in 1983
Ollie Campbell had a horse called after him. The difference was that
whereas I had an auld plough horse named after me, Ollie had a
thoroughbred racehorse in New Zealand called after him. The
contrast speaks for itself!"

I Can't See Clearly Now

Ireland's opening match of the 1979 season was a home game against
France. It was a match of which Ward can remember little. Midway

through the second half he considered withdrawing because he could see little or nothing as a result of concussion sustained in a 10th-minute tackle. Only in the second half did he recover his senses. He went on to kick three penalties to tie the score at 9-9 each, though his best moment was a break midway through the second half where he stopped twice in his tracks like a toreador in the bullrings of Spain, beating two tackles before being brought down in a move which yielded Ireland's final score. France's scores came from a try by fly-half, Alain Caussade, and a conversion and penalty from full-back Aguirre.

The game finished on a controversial note when Ireland were awarded an indirect free kick 20 yards from the French posts. Ward asked the English referee, Roger Quittenton, if he could take back the ball a few yards but his question went unanswered. The ref explained his silence afterwards:

"The laws state that the referee cannot consult with the players, and I thought it might offer an advantage if I answered the question. Tony was pretty badly concussed. He even joined the wrong team when he came back after treatment at half time, and I had to lead him back to his colleagues. I think he was confused about the position, but I felt he had to make his own decision, so I deliberately ignored his question."

In the event, as was clearly demonstrated by the evidence of the TV replay, the French failed to retreat the requisite 10 yards and Ward's kick was blocked down. A match winning chance had been lost.

Ireland's four debutants had reason to be proud of themselves. Gerry McLoughlin, the carrot-haired Shannon prop, came through his baptism of fire against the hallowed French front row very much with an enhanced reputation. Flanker, Colm Tucker and full-back, Dick Spring, acquitted themselves well, with Tucker bringing much of the fire that he played with in Munster's win over the All-Blacks.

However, a new star was born with a famous name in the tall, lean Mike Gibson. He dominated the lineout as he ranged along the line to deny France the platform to launch penetrating attacks. He enabled Ward to use the touchline to set up attacking positions or to ease the pressure when the visitors attacked.

The Tragedy Of Errors

After that it was off to Wales. Cardiff Arms Park was Ward's version of the promised land. He really looked forward to getting onto the pitch to display the full range of his talents but as the big day approached he became increasingly nervous:

"I always worried about my game. I am a natural pessimist. And to be honest the pressure at international level is fierce. I was always on edge until I was actually out there on the pitch, then I just got on with it.

"The first night in Portcrawl before the Welsh game I hardly slept a wink. Then the Friday night was better. Fergus Slattery brought us all to *Adventures of a Window Cleaner* and *Adventures of a Taxi Driver*. Those films certainly took our mind off the game!

"That afternoon while the rest of the team played golf I went for a long walk on the beach alone. I found that more physically relaxing."

In normal circumstances, for an Irish side to score 21 points in Cardiff Arms Park (and thus establish a new scoring record for an Irish side against Wales on any ground), on that most sacred soil, would have been considered a great achievement. The 1979 fixture was an exception. The problem was that Ireland gifted the home side with 15 points to lose on a scoreline of 24-21. The game was a catalogue of errors on both sides but the difference was that Ireland's were punished more severely. In fairness Ireland had shown commendable spirit in coming from 21-9 down, when all seemed lost, to haul themselves back to 24-21 with four minutes to go.

After 22 minutes Ireland led 6-0 courtesy of two penalties from Ward – from 50 and 35 yards respectively. The 12-year-old dream of a win in Cardiff was starting to look as if it might be fulfilled. In the 25th minute the picture changed dramatically. Davies, the Welsh fly-half, lofted the kick towards the Irish posts but Dick Spring was under it and there seemed to be no danger. Somehow the ball slipped through his hands and bounced over the Irish line for Alan Martin to rush on and score a try which Steve Fenwick converted. A minute later Spring failed to find touch with an important clearance attempt. From the fall-out Ireland were penalised and Fenwick kicked the points. Before half-time Fenwick and Ward exchanged penalties to leave Wales leading 12-9 at the interval.

Eight minutes into the second half Ireland were feeling generous again. Slack, untidy play as they defended a scrum close to their line allowed Paul Ringer to score a try which Fenwick converted with ease. A late challenge from Fergus Slattery presented Fenwick with another gift-wrapped penalty score. Ireland rallied and their best moment of the match came when Ward kicked through for Freddie McLennan to score his first try for Ireland which Ward duly converted. However, the good work was partially undone when a careless lineout infringement provided Fenwick with his fourth penalty goal. Colin Patterson redeemed himself somewhat after a poor performance to score a try which Ward converted again. It had been Ward's best performance to date in an Irish jersey, preventing Ireland from being lost without trace and making loaves from crumbs.

Ward has one distasteful memory of that game:

"One of the Welsh forwards, Paul Ringer, declared himself out to get me from the moment we got on to the pitch. He kept shouting at me throughout the match and eventually he did give me a belt off the ball. I mentioned this to him after the game and he shrugged it off with the comment that it was all part of rugby.

"Another thing that started to distress me at the time was the cruelty of much press comment. At the time I was getting nothing but adulation but some players, particularly Paul McNaughton, were getting a dreadful time. What bugged me most about it was that much of it was hopelessly misinformed. Paul was a great player in my view. He gave me great confidence and he had a marvellous ability to adapt quickly to situations. For example, on quite a few occasions that season we called a move around the backs that was not on. Paul was always remarkably swift in adjusting. That is something that would not be readily recognised from the sidelines, but it's an invaluable asset on the pitch."

Get Your Retaliation In First

An unfortunate postscript to the match came in a subsequent article written by the Welsh flanker, Paul Ringer, for a tabloid newspaper after his defection to Rugby League. Commenting on the dual standards over dirty play in rugby union he cited the example of an instruction five minutes before the kick off in that match to "sort out" Ward:

"The meaning was clear and I set to it. Trouble was he was so good I couldn't lay a finger on him until late in the game but I eventually flattened him off the ball and we went on to win. I got such a booting from the Irish forwards afterwards that I couldn't get out of bed for two days. After I'd laid out Ward that time he turned up late at the after-match reception with a massively swollen eye."

Ward winces ever so slightly as he reminded of that incident:

"Ringer had the reputation of being a fly-half's nightmare. As we were coming out onto the field for the match he stood on my ankle and then winked at me as he ran away.

"Rugby is a physical contact sport but it is no more dangerous than any other similar sport like Gaelic football or soccer. If the referee gets on top of the game then everything flows smoothly but, if not, you can run into problems. I was livid when Ringer flattened me but it's important not to retaliate when you do get hit. You have just got to hold the head because, if you are caught retaliating, you will rightly be sent off. The best way to get back at them is to put some points on the board. That's what really hurts".

Brain Over Brawn

Two weeks later Ireland had a welcome opportunity to redeem themselves with a home game against England. Willie Duggan had been recalled to the side in the unfamiliar wing-forward position in place of Colm Tucker, even though Tucker had turned in fine performances in his previous two matches. His tremendous physical presence proved invaluable. After their performances against Wales, Dick Spring and Colin Patterson could have considered themselves lucky to retain their places.

Ward recorded the build up to the game in diary form:

Wednesday, Feb. 14.

I escaped for an hour's kicking practice at the college and travelled up to Dublin in the evening. The roads were grand in Limerick but not so good further up and I got a bit of a skid at Monasterevin which aggravated a wrist injury I have been suffering from for some time.

Thursday, Feb. 15.

In the morning, I did a T.V. interview for Thames television talking about Liam Brady and he did a similar piece talking about me.

The build-up for the English match began with the assembly at the Shelbourne Hotel for lunch at 12.30. And from this point on the players are put under intolerable pressure from people seeking tickets. We receive two free tickets and an option on two more and when you have looked after your family and close friends, you don't have much left (the situation has changed, now the players receive four stand tickets, an option of buying six more stand tickets and 20 ground tickets). *But so many people don't appreciate this. After lunch and a brief team meeting, we go by coach to Anglesea Road ... if there's a new cap he must sing a song, but Moss Finn escaped because he had obliged at the Welsh game, when he was a sub for the first time. It was a hard session of two hours ... after this, Gerry McLoughlin and I went to St Vincent's Hospital for treatment and after a meal at 6 o'clock, we watched videos of both our match with Wales and the England/Scotland game as well. Noel Murphy and the other selectors do what they can for you. I shared a room with Colin Patterson and found getting to sleep no great problem, although I couldn't sleep a wink before my first cap.*

Friday, Feb. 16.

After breakfast in bed, we went to Anglesea Road for another much quieter session, and there I was one of a few who taped a T.V. piece for RTE News. After lunch at the Shelbourne came the bit I love – bowling at Stillorgan. I'm absolutely useless at it and the best I could manage was 37 pins out of 200. Imagine the slagging when Moss Keane cleared everything out of sight and came out tops. All the team went – except Pat Whelan, who spends the afternoon before every international in bed. When you get back to the hotel around 6.30, you sense the atmosphere. Suddenly the place is crammed. After a meal, we all went to 'The First Great Train Robbery', but I fell asleep as soon as the film started. This time, it's bed at 11 and again thankfully I slept well.

Saturday: Match Day

"Now you really feel it, the lump in your throat, the butterflies in the tummy. At 11.15, Colin and I went for a walk in St Stephen's Green and though I am not superstitious, I always take the same route and follow the same routine. Colin is superstitious ... he insists on following me from behind, everywhere. I go for lunch, I have my usual meal – just a few pieces of plaice and orange squash. The worst part is between 12.20 and 1.40; firstly you're just hanging around and then the team talk. Here we had a

psychological boost when we saw Eamonn Coghlan running his great race in the States . . . that set us in good humour. I love the journey from the hotel to the ground when the people on the sidewalks and coming out of the pubs give you the thumbs up. The motor-bike escort makes you feel a real VIP for the day.

The first thing you hear on arriving at the ground is the wail of the bagpipes. You go out and test the pitch. At 2.05, you tog off; at 2.20 it's team pic time. Warm-up begins at 2.30 and from 2.45 it's just the 15 players with Fergus Slattery and Pat Whelan doing their motivation bit. Superb the pair of them are. The ref checks the studs and suddenly out you go for the most fabulous moment of all, once you are out there you forget all your nerves.

After the match, I did TV interviews with BBC Grandstand (live), BBC Rugby Special, RTE and a radio piece with the BBC. When that was all done, I joined the others in the tea room and from there we went back to the hotel before diving into the dress suit and heading straight for O'Donoghue's pub just around the corner. It was there that I heard 'the Late Late Show' wanted to put Colin and me out that night, so we had to watch the jar! The dinner began around 8 o'clock, and we duly left that at 10 to go by taxi to RTE for 'the Late, Late Show'. I enjoyed it all very much; Gay Byrne really puts you at your ease, and Colin and Harry Booker of the IRFU also got a great kick out of it.

The clash with the "auld enemy" was a bruising battle that had the Lansdowne Road crowd at fever pitch. From the kick-off the English forwards made their intentions clear, but their strategy boomeranged because it was the Irish pack that finished in the ascendancy. Ward was the subject of thinly disguised intimidatory tactics. As early as the fifth minute, Tony Neary crashed into him with a late tackle which left him nursing a bruised right cheek. Scottish referee, Alan Hosie, officially warned Tony Bond when he clattered Ward into the ground with a late charge. Yet Ward had the last laugh scoring eight points in Ireland's 12-7 win.

For all their possession the English backs failed to capitalise and had only a try and a penalty goal from fly-half, Neil Bennett, to show for their efforts. Ireland made a dream start with a try in the sixth minute. Ward kicked ahead and Freddie McLennan took advantage of a bungled pass to Peter Squires to score an easy try which Ward converted. However, Ireland spent much of the rest of the half penned into their own 25. Ward's defensive kicking and stout tackling kept the English at bay. In the 38th minute Ireland's new cap at wing threequarter, Moss Finn, went off injured and Terry Kennedy the man he had replaced, came on. Despite their inferior possession Ireland led 6-3 at the interval.

In the second half, Ward turned the screw on the opposition with a succession of long kicks which kept them away from the danger area. After 57 minutes he dropped a magnificent goal. The score prompted a chant from the Irish crowd: "Nice one, Tony, nice one, son, nice one Tony, let's have another one!" In the 70th minute he added a penalty to complete Ireland's scoring.

Ward rubs his chin ruefully at the memory of that drop goal:

"The drop goal came from a tap down in the lineout from Mike Gibson but just before that the English forward, Nigel Horton, had deliberately short-arm tackled me. I very stupidly never wore a gum-shield. I remember that incident because of something the great, former English number eight, Andy Ripley, said to me afterwards.

"Andy is one hell of a nice blocke. He's a lovely man and you won't find anybody who's got a bad word to say against him. He used to go to his work on a motor-bike with his pin-stripe suit, long hair, bowler hat and leather jacket. He works in high finance and is a very intelligent man who enjoys the simple things in life. He was subbing and watching the game in the stand and although he was an Englishman he was cheering for me for the rest of the game. He told me that the best answer I could have given Horton was that drop goal."

The English press reports were totally monopolised with talk of Ward – highlighting that his armoury was not solely stocked with kicking boots. Particular emphasis was attached to his clever runs, his positional sense, his poise under pressure and his remarkable handling.

An Error Of Judgement

Ireland's last match of the season was against Scotland in Murrayfield. The evening before brought an unexpected surprise for Ward:

"In a profile piece for *In Dublin* magazine I had been asked who I would most like to meet. I had said Tony O'Reilly. We were staying in the North British Hotel in Edinburgh for the Scottish game. Paddy Madigan came to me and said, 'There's someone waiting outside to see you'. I went out and there was Tony O'Reilly. I was dumbfounded."

In the build-up to the next game Ward was in the public eye though not in the manner he would have wished when, the morning of the game *The Daily Mirror* published a page three style pin-up of him in his swimming trunks much to Ward's embarrassment:

"It was totally my own fault. A photographer contacted me with a view to doing a photo with a difference. In my foolish innocence, I did not know it was to be a pin-up or page three. His exact words were that he wanted a 'beefcake photograph'. Of course that should have put me on red alert but in my blind foolishness, I agreed to it. It was done in the pool at Newpark, when RTE were filming for *Superstars.*

"The minute I saw the picture in the paper it had a devastating effect on me because I am a particularly sensitive person by nature. What made it worse was to find out later that Liam Nolan had shown the picture on RTE in the build-up to the game which meant that although only a minority of Irish people would have seen that photo in the paper a lot of them saw me on the television.

"Colin Patterson had pinned it up in my room and that did nothing for my troubled mind. I was dreading getting on the team bus because I expected a ribbing from the lads about it. The chances of someone like Paul McNaughton letting you away with something like that were zero. There was a very strange atmosphere on the bus but nobody said anything about it. I found out later that Noel Murphy had gone around to the lads individually and told them to say nothing about it. The whole episode really cast a big shadow over my game that day.

"In the early days I was not in the least selective as to whom I gave interviews to. Page 3 would not happen if I had the chance to do it all again. That's being honest. I was very naïve then, really naïve, when that happened. They really caught me out on that one. You live and learn but at the time it was very embarrassing for me, my family and those close to me. I can fully understand the ire of the IRFU and Noel Murphy about that particular one. Noel was fuming about it and gave me a right ticking off and he was fully entitled to.

"I learned something from the incident. I was determined not to allow myself to be at everyone's beck and call where interviews and other types of publicity were concerned. It has always been hard for me to say no to people from the media and unfortunately some people took advantage of that."

The fact that it was Ward who was pursued in this way says a lot not just about his star status but about the changing face of rugby at the time. Rugby in Ireland and Britain was changing dramatically. With ever-increasing media exposure, and the subsequent search for personalities like Ward, it was developing a popular feel similar to that of soccer, even pop music. No Irish rugby player in history had been so eagerly hounded.

The Year Of The Two Mike Gibsons

Two changes were made in the Irish defence before the game. Dick Spring was dropped to make way for Bangor's Ronnie Elliott, and Mike Gibson was a surprise late replacement for Terry Kennedy. Kennedy was less than happy about the circumstances which led him to cry off:

"Terry was very unhappy about the sort of fitness test he was asked to do on the morning of the game, where Freddie McLennan, John Moloney and Mike Gibson were each asked to do two sprints against him. He had to do his six sprints consecutively but the three others had a break between their two sprints. He felt that was very unfair and was, not surprisingly, out of breath afterwards. He spoke to Johnny Moloney who was always a good bet for giving sound advice and John's advice was to the effect that there was a seed of doubt in the selectors mind about him and if he played badly they would hold it against him. On foot of this advice he withdrew but it was a reluctant withdrawal."

The match was dominated by the swirling wind – causing a proliferation of dropped passes, wayward kicks, crooked lineout throws and a feast of interceptions. In an error-ridden match it was appropriate that both sides finished on level terms – only the fourth draw between the two teams in 89 matches. Two tries by Colin Patterson and a Ward penalty were matched by tries by Andy Irvine and Keith Robertson and an Irvine penalty.

The performance was Ireland's worst of the season. The set scrum was poor and the feed through the channel was especially disappointing. Despite the presence of four big men, Mike Gibson, Willie Duggan, Moss Keane and Donal Spring, Ireland won almost a negligible proportion of quality ball in the lineout. Willie Duggan, one of three number eights in the back five, looked distinctly uncomfortable on the flank. For once Ward was off form with his place-kicking though the treacherous wind made a lottery of scoring chances.

Ireland's hero was Colin Patterson who gave a typical display – liked the fabled curate's egg he mixed the diabolical with the brilliant and, not allowing himself to be affected by his mistakes, he scored two fine tries. Ward had, and retains, a particularly close friendship with Patterson and helped to broaden the scrum-half's education:

"Colin liked to be involved in everything. He wanted to be able to sing the national anthem in Irish like the rest of us on match day. That is the great thing about rugby, it unifies different religious and political creeds. The pride Ulster Unionists took in wearing the green jersey was every bit as strong as their southern, 'nationalist' team-mates.

"I can only once recall politics raising its head in a build-up to a match. Colin and Donal Spring got involved in a heavy discussion of the politics of the north. Their views were diametrically opposed in this instance. Those of us who were sitting around feared it might get a bit out of hand but it didn't and eventually, it petered out to nothing."

Ward himself was faced with something of a dilemma when he was introduced to Queen Elizabeth before a match against Scotland. He did not know what to call her so he settled on saying a simple, 'Hello':

"The other thing I remember from the shaking hands with dignitaries was that our former President, Paddy Hillery, always had a little chat with me before matches. As a Clare man himself I think he must have felt a sense of neighbourliness with me, a Limerick player."

Clocks And Controversy

Ward's performances during the season earned him many plaudits and awards. This latter tendency was to draw the ire of the IRFU:

"In three of the four international matches in the '79 season, I won the 'Man of the Match' award, given to the player voted the outstanding performer in each national team (Colin Patterson got the other). The IRFU let me accept the first – an inscribed clock –

and the presentation was made by the late Paul McWeeney, then rugby correspondent par excellence, but they stopped me receiving the other two.

"The award itself was not of any great significance but what I cannot comprehend is the inconsistency of attitude by the IRFU towards awards.

"Apart from organising the 'Man of the Match' awards, *Rugby World* also awarded a Golden Boot to the 'Player of the Year' in each country in the Five-Nations Championship. I won the award in '78 and '79. I was allowed accept the Golden Boot by the IRFU as Irish Player of The Year and subsequently I made use of the honour to help the David Egan Fund (since returned very kindly by David I might add). Then, in '79 I was named European Player of the Year and again they allowed me to have my name inscribed on the perpetual silver salver and to accept a small piece of glass.

"However, when it came to my acceptance in London of the Player of the Season award in a rugby writers' poll, the IRFU stepped in. The dinner was fixed for Lingfield racecourse and it was graced by some of the most famous players of that era, including Terry Holmes (Wales), Andy Irvine (Scotland) and Jean-Pierre Rives (France). Before I departed for London, I received an instruction from the IRFU that I wasn't to accept the award, though I could attend the dinner itself. We then had the ludicrous situation where I walked up to the applause of fellow internationals, shook hands with the person making the presentation but couldn't even touch the actual trophy. It eventually went to Sunshine Homes and I had the satisfaction that, indirectly, I was helping the cause of underprivileged children.

"I have come to the conclusion that the IRFU's attitude can be summed up in the fact that they shun individual awards because they see rugby as a team game. Nobody agrees more than myself with that concept and nobody believes in the team approach more than I do, despite hints down through the years to the contrary in the media.

But in all team sports you cannot get away from the fact that individual players can dominate a game and it will continue to happen that a player will be named 'Man of the Match' or 'Player of the Year'.

"That in no way affects the team approach and neither should it. And it could be argued also that if an Irish player was elected in a vote of rugby followers as the outstanding player of the season in the Five Nations then, through him, the team as a whole was being honoured. To argue otherwise would be to contend that the fifteen members of a team should become faceless individuals, that there should never be any individual expression and that we should be like fifteen Chinese cyclists cycling in line down a street teeming with humanity.

"There is a further consideration in all this. No player that I know looks for, or expects to get, money for playing. The Irish game is unique in that respect. Players will gladly pay reasonably substantial membership fees to join a club. They don't object in the least. That's what makes rugby so special and such a great amateur game. Does accepting an occasional trophy damage the ethos of the sport? I feel that a significant factor at the time was that that the administrators refused to accept that the game was evolving and they had a very begrudging attitude. Today my generation of players are becoming administrators and thankfully they bring a more 'player-friendly' approach."

A highlight in any rugby player's career is to be selected to play for the Barbarians. In March, 1979 Ward received a letter from the IRFU "requesting" him to decline a forthcoming invitation to play for the Barbarians that season.

```
SECRETARY & TREASURER                    IRISH RUGBY FOOTBALL UNION.
   R. FITZGERALD.
TELEPHONE DUBLIN 684603.                     62, LANSDOWNE ROAD.
TELEGRAPHIC ADDRESS.
FOOTBALL DUBLIN                                 DUBLIN, 4
                                             27th March 1979
```

Barbarian FC.

Dear ~Jimmy~,

      It is understood that you may receive an invitation
from the Barbarian FC to play in matches during the Club's Easter Tour.

      While the Union Committee decided to place no restriction
on members of the Team for the Australian Tour from playing in Club
matches to the end of this season, I have been asked to let you know
that the Hon. Tour Manager, Mr. J.F.Coffey would prefer that you did
not accept an invitation from the Barbarian FC on this occasion.

      Yours sincerely

R.FITZGERALD
Secretary

P.A.Orr Esq
M.I.Keane Esq
C.S.Patterson Esq
A.J.P.Ward Esq
M.E.Gibson Esq

The season finished on a high note for Ward as he steered Garryowen to their 32nd Munster Cup when they beat Young Munster 3-0 in Thomond Park. Ward got the game's only score in a disappointing match when he kicked a penalty.

The next item on the rugby agenda was Ireland's tour to Australia. Nobody, least of all Ward himself, was prepared for the shocks that lay in store.

5. Catch A Falling Star

Every possession and every happiness is but lent by chance for an
uncertain time, and may therefore be demanded back the next hour.

Schopenhauer

Rugby tours are notorious for their unpredictability. The Irish tour to
Australia in 1979 was no exception. More accurately, unpredictability
was the order of the day.

Consider the case of John Moloney who went on the tour as a
cover scrum-half for the incumbent, Colin Patterson, and won a
shock call-up as wing threequarter for the Tests. Then there was the
case of Willie Duggan – yesterday's man, or so it seemed, when he was
discarded by the Irish selectors before the championship that season.
Duggan, like fellow forward, Moss Keane, was an Irish national
institution. A man with little enthusiasm for training, his most
celebrated comment was: "Training takes the edge off my game." He
was also very partial to cigarettes. Asked once in a radio interview if
this was a major problem for him fitness-wise, Duggan took the
interviewer by surprise by saying that it was a positive advantage: "Sure
if it was not for the fags I would be offside all day long."

However, in the match situation it was a different reality, he played
with the same joi-de-vivre that Brendan Behan had exhibited when he
played at Borstal: "I became a dab hand at this rugby and a bull-
shoving bastard at getting the ball back." He had got onto the tour by
the back door when Donal Spring was injured and forced to cry off
but he grabbed his chance with both hands and played like one of the
greatest forwards in world rugby.

At the other end of the spectrum was the case of 22-year-old St Mary's full-back, Rodney O'Donnell, who went out as an uncapped unknown and returned a hero.

But nothing could compare to the fairytale of Old Belvedere's Ollie Campbell. Enid Blyton could not have emulated his story. The 25-year-old's international career had been launched and almost abandoned courtesy of one shattering appearance at Lansdowne Road against Australia three years earlier. He missed six penalties and was immediately written off by many who purported to be judges of international players. Despite injury problems (he had been out of rugby the previous season from September to February with ligament trouble), he had shown good club form and justified his recall to the Irish squad as cover for the out-half position. In the greatest selection shock in living memory he displaced the biggest superstar in Irish rugby since the emergence of Mike Gibson. Campbell's subsequent text-book performances were a revelation and he kicked Ireland to victory in both tests.

For Ollie Campbell all his Christmasses had come at once but his dream was Tony Ward's nightmare. It had all promised to be so different. In the previous two seasons at the top, Ward was heralded the most exciting find in the British Isles since Gareth Edwards. He became an instant pin-up in a sport that historically preferred to play down its heroes. He was regularly spoken of in the same breath and awed tones as Barry John and Phil Bennet and was hailed internationally as the best out-half in the world at that time.

Parting Is Such Sweet Sorrow

At the airport, as the team departed, all the players had emotional farewells with their wives, children and loved ones. One of the biggest challenges facing a touring side is to quickly adapt to the new conditions – training grounds, accommodation, and food. Stories, real and apocryphal, abound about the poor quality of food available on rugby tours. Some of the most famous such anecdotes to enter rugby folklore concern the great Welsh hooker, Bobby Windsor, in particular his comments during the Lions' tour of South Africa in 1974.

One morning he made a very precise order at breakfast:

"I want one egg boiled for exactly 26 seconds and I want another one boiled for 25 minutes 14 seconds. And I want three slices of toast which are pale gold on one side and burned pure black on the other."

The baffled waiter could but splutter out a despairing protest:

"But sir. That's simply not possible. We can't go to all the trouble to fill an order like that.

"Oh yes you can, sonny boy. That's exactly what you dished up to me yesterday."

What It Says In The Papers

The Irish touring party was weakened by the late withdrawals of four key players – full-back, Larry Moloney, centre, Alistar McKibbin and both number eights, Donal Spring and Mike Gibson, the younger. Press attention in Australia centred on Ward and the elder statesman of Irish rugby, Mike Gibson, the most capped international of all time. Gibson was then 36-years-old but still feared, because although his flesh was not as willing as in the golden days of his prime, when he was one of the most outstanding players in rugby union, his keen brain and polished skills still functioned unimpaired. It was widely expected that the tour would mark his swansong and the press looked forward to one last hurrah in which he would weave his magic just one more time.

There were not high expectations from any other of the backs apart from Ward. The prevailing wisdom was that Australia could not afford to give away any penalty within a range of 40 metres of the posts because it would almost certainly yield a score.

Other aspects of Ward's play which were singled out for special attention were his calmness and tactical kicking, particularly his ability to kick with both feet, his acceleration and side-step and the fact that his huge thighs made him a difficult opponent to bring down. What seemed most worrying to the Aussies was his "admirably complete repertoire" and the fact that he was in "a class of his own in Europe".

The general feeling was that Ireland would not be a pretty side to watch but had the talent and work-rate to make life difficult for the home side, particularly in the pack. The Irish forwards had a reputation of being marauders and spoilers, quick to the break-down in play and maintaining a persistent harassment of opposing half-backs. The hard core of experienced Lions' players spread through the pack, flanker, Fergus Slattery, prop, Phil Orr, the great Moss Keane in the second row and Willie Duggan in the backrow were seen as a major threat.

The weakness of the pack was considered to be the lineout. During the previous season the giant Mike Gibson had given Ireland a mountain of possession at the back of the lineout. His enforced defection was a huge loss. With Gibson the younger in the side, Ireland would have hoped to dominate this phase of play in Australia, but without Gibson, the feeling was that they would be hard pressed to do so.

After their crushing defeats of Wales the previous year logic dictated that Australia must be warm favourites for the series but logic seldom comes into sport and no match is ever won by the intellect alone. The touring party received an early setback when 31-year-old prop, Ned Byrne, was knocked down by a hit-and-run motorist in Perth. His left leg was broken in several places, necessitating a plaster from the stomach down – an injury which would effectively end his career. A few eyebrows were raised when Ward was omitted from the opening match of the tour against Western Australia. Ward's diary entry for the day is surprisingly short of details:

Sunday 20 May
Woke at 11.30. Had lunch. Left for match at 2.00 p.m. Won easily 39-3.
They were very poor.

His replacement at out-half, Ollie Campbell, had kicked 14 points in Ireland's facile win. It was a very gentle introduction and offered very little of a clue as to Ireland's real worth.

A Capital Start

Ward shook off the disappointment of not playing in the first game of the tour in the most effective way possible with a sterling performance in the second game, against Australian Capital Territory. The scoreline was 35-7 in Ireland's favour but the press reports damned the tourists with faint praise.

Ward seemed anxious to make up for lost time and to show the Australians that all the hype about him was more than hyperbole. Within five minutes he had scored his first try for Ireland – a magnificent effort following a pass from Paul McNaughton which saw him taking a run close to the touchline, beat one opponent off his right foot and two more off his left to cross over the line. Six minutes later he kicked a penalty from 40 yards and in the 20th minute he set up Terry Kennedy for a try in the corner – a try which Ward converted.

He went on to score 19 points in the game – a try, three penalties and three conversions, beating the previous Irish record in a tour match of 17 points set by Tom Kiernan against Queensland in 1967. The only blot on his copybook was a missed tackle. The other Irish scores were tries from Phil Orr, Paul McNaughton and Harry Steele. A feature of the game was an excellent performance at full-back from Rodney O'Donnell culminating in a magnificent try-saving tackle late in the game. If success at international level is measured by performance and commitment then Ward was one of the few players on the field who could have been happy with his game that day.

The Irish backline that day had no less than five players who had attended St Mary's College – an unprecedented achievement – John Moloney, Paul Andreucetti, Terry Kennedy, Rodney O'Donnell and Ward. It was an extraordinary testimony to the school's tradition for producing great backs – particularly in the light of its relatively small numbers.

Years later Ward can see that perhaps many of his problems may have sprung from the aftermath of that game:

"My scoring achievement made headlines in the Australian papers. I found myself being singled out for interviews; rugby writers seemed to follow my every step. It was never my way to reject media representatives in such circumstances as I feel they have a job to do and it is only right that one should co-operate with them. To simply run away or meet their queries with a bland, tight-lipped 'no comment' was never my way. The only thing that interfered with that was when my trust was abused. Then I closed the curtains as it were.

"I hadn't thought that publicity about me in Europe – winning the European Player of the Year Award and so on – would have been so well-known down under. I was rather naïve in that. But they knew everything about me.

"In retrospect I now realise – older and wiser – that in order to make sure of my place on the Irish team for the First Test, perhaps I should have gone to ground at that point and ignored the media. It would certainly have spared me a moment that left an indelible imprint on my mind. I have pondered it again and again when reflecting on what developed into a most traumatic experience that affected my confidence thereafter.

"We were in the dressing-room preparing to go out for a training session for the match against New South Wales when Jack Coffey, the team manager, came over to me and said: 'This is absolutely ridiculous. It's crazy what's going on – all this media stuff. I suggest that you stay away from these fellows altogether.'

"I looked at him aghast. I didn't know what he was driving at. It was only at the end of the tour that the true relevance of his remarks that day fully registered.

"I knew before I left Ireland that I was under pressure and consequently made certain that I played well in the preliminary games on that tour. I suspected certain undertones. I knew Noel Murphy was no fan of mine; when I started with Garryowen he would call me 'the soccer player' from the sideline.

"To this day I still feel that it was totally unjustified and unjust. It hit me like a thunderbolt – no warning, no explanation, nobody seemed to care. It was extremely traumatic. The immature side of me wanted to come home immediately.

"Inwardly I reacted like a spoilt brat. I felt as if I wanted to get on a plane and get out of there. How dare anyone drop me! Of course I didn't and I would like to think I learned a lot from that experience. I suppose that is what life is about – learning from our experiences because if we could all live with the benefit of hindsight wouldn't it be just wonderful?"

The following day it was off to Sydney for a match against NSW a few days later, the first real test for the tourists, though they emerged victorious 16-12. The game, which featured a vintage performance by Willie Duggan, provided a dramatic ending. Ireland led 16-0 with only eight minutes to go but conceded two goals. Mike Gibson was playing on the right-wing and his opposite number, Phil Crowe, ran in for two late, soft tries. Gibson was at pains to attribute the two tries to the weaknesses of the inside backs. A change on the right wing was inevitable for the next match. Ireland's scores came from a try by Harry Steele, a conversion and two penalties from Ward. Again the real stars of the Irish team were the pack.

After the Queensland game the Australian coach, David Brockhoff looked ahead to the Test and was quoted widely saying:

"We have to accept that we have one hell of a fight on our hands. . They are not the sort of team that will score a lot of tries. But they don't give anything away either, and with Ward in there directing things they will be a lot better than they were against Queensland. He'll give striking power to their backs. He'll rest the forwards when they need it and generally make a tremendous difference."

The Irish Joke That Wasn't

WARD OUT – IT'S THE LATEST OF IRISH JOKES
IRISH DROP 'SOLO' STAR WARD
WHY TONY WARD WAS DROPPED – THE ASTONISHING
PRICE OF STARDOM
WHAT'S WRONG WITH WARD?
NO IRISH JOKE – WARD **IS** OUT

These headlines taken from Australian papers reflect the fact that Ward's omission from the Test side was as big a sensation with the rugby cognoscenti down under as it was at home. A flavour of the coverage was provided in the opening sentence to the seasoned Australian rugby correspondent, Jim Woodward's report:

"The Australian team rated it the Irish joke of the year when Ireland yesterday omitted champion five-eighth Tony Ward from the team for Sunday's First Rugby Union Test at Ballymore, Brisbane."

The Aussies were thrilled. Their coach at the time, Dave Brochhoff, commented on Ward's demotion:

"I am absolutely staggered . . . They will be a ten per cent better side with Ward."

Travelling Irish rugby correspondents, conscious of the likely reaction at home, sought to explain the story behind the selection. The then rugby correspondent with *The Irish Press* group, Bob Messenger wrote in *The Sunday Press* on 3 June, 1979:

"As far as I am concerned the Ward controversy was predictable from an early stage of the tour – perhaps long before it even started. Ward must have had some inkling . . . . Individual likes and dislikes become well-known in a tour environment."

The article went on to advocate a new selection system for Irish tours abroad and concluded with the opinion:

"Somehow I very much doubt, however, that an Irish Five at home would have come to the remarkable decision to leave Tony Ward off an Irish international team."

The Irish Independent's Australian report came from Colm Smith. He was in no doubt about the reasons for the startling decision:

"Tony Ward has been sacked as Ireland's out-half. That in itself is sensational but the potential impact on the tour that has already exceeded the hopes of most, defies comprehension . . . . What worries me about the entire issue is that the decision came as no surprise to me personally. I had heard even before the party left Dublin that Ward's test place was in jeopardy and during the last week the vibes were even stronger. It is becoming dangerous to be a star in Irish rugby."

The Evening Echo's Dermot Russell had a similar view and drew a parallel with one of the most infamous Irish selections of all time:

"My interpretation is that at least one selector had definite opinions about which of the two out-halves he would like to see in the test and had them before the party left Ireland. Certainly the decision to leave out Ward ranks as one of the most incredible ever made by an Irish group of selectors. It is even more unbelievable than the incident in 1970 when the selectors picked Tony O'Reilly as a last minute reserve for the match against England despite the fact that he was so long retired he had even written the article for the match programme. The decision is still laughed at throughout the rugby world."

Never one to sit on the fence, John O'Shea writing in Dublin for *The Evening Press* drew the same parallel.

The Irish Times' Edmund Van Esbeck posed the question: "Were there preconceived ideas about Ward even before a ball was kicked on the tour?"

Mitchel Cogley in his "Corner" in *The Irish Independent* wrote:

"I have often felt in the past that something strange seems to happen to the thinking of normally rational people when they become selectors, and this particular decision fits right into a crazy pattern . . . One is left wondering if performances on the field are really the criterion of Irish rugby selectors or if the formation of teams is, instead, based on personality clashes. How else could Ward be passed over? It's like an Irish soccer team dropping Liam Brady or a Dublin football team without Jimmy Keaveney."

The media consensus was that Campbell was a fine player and would be well worthy of selection if the quality of Ward's performances had dropped – but the evidence indicated the exact opposite. Ward himself evidently had realised that his face might not fit. As early as 3 June he accurately predicted his fate:

Definite fight on hands next season.

Paradise Lost

Ward himself clearly remembers the chain of events as if they were yesterday:

"We were on a coach journey to an idyllic spot just outside Brisbane for a training session when I got the first inkling that I was not going to be selected as out-half for the First Test. Pat Whelan, my team-mate from Garryowen, had been tipped off that there was something in the wind. He whispered: 'Prepare yourself'.

"He had been injured and was therefore out of contention for a place on the Test side. That morning a journalist told him that I was to be dropped. Pat was much closer to Noisy than I. He went to Murphy on the bus and asked him if he would prepare me for the shock that was coming. When Murphy declined to do so he took the initiative himself.

"After getting off the bus, I went over to Ollie Campbell and said: 'Ollie, congrats – you're in'. Later when we talked about it, he would concede that he had never expected to be selected before me at that juncture.

"Noel Murphy saw this gesture and had words with me for congratulating Ollie before the official announcement – this was the last thing I needed at the time. My world was falling around my shoulders and when I most needed a bit of sensitive treatment I ended up getting a verbal dressing down. To be dropped would have been bad enough at the best of times but the insensitivity in the way I was treated just rubbed salt into my very deep wound.

"The team for the First Test was picked by a trio comprising Jack Coffey, Noel Murphy and Fergus Slattery. Later the point was made to me one evening in the Lansdowne clubhouse by Ray Carroll, a former Irish international and the chairman of the Irish Selection Committee prior to the tour – that what happened in Australia would not have happened at home with a five man selection committee.

"Fergus Slattery has never been a fan of mine and I have no problem with that. Neither, I think it's fair to say, was Jack Coffey a particular admirer and Noel Murphy was Munster coach on the one and only occasion I was dropped from a provincial side.

"Before departing for Australia, at squad sessions at Lansdowne Road, Noel Murphy kept emphasising that there was going to be no star system and that, in effect, everything was to be subjugated to the needs of the team. He stressed also that no player must think that he was automatically assured of a place and that there could be no superstars on the team. I am very sensitive in such matters. I couldn't escape the feeling that such comments were aimed specifically in my direction.

"I remember talking to Frank Hogan in his garage after one of our final sessions before our departure to Australia and telling him I was worried about my place because of the comments being made in training. He told me: 'Don't be an idiot. Just go out there and play your normal game and everything will be fine.' When I came home he told me that he often thought about that conversation while I was on tour after I had been dropped.

"The night I was dropped Pat Whelan and Moss Keane took me up to their room straight after dinner and we were reflecting on the events of the day when Noel Murphy came in. He said to me: 'Come on Tone we'll go for a walk?' We went outside but there was no explanation nor words of consolation or encouragement. Instead we ended up in a nearby cinema. The one thing I clearly remember was watching an Australian film on the Vietnamese war. I was looking at the screen but taking in nothing. After a short while Noisy turned around to me and said: 'This is rubbish isn't it. Will we go back to the hotel?" I agreed and that was that.

"The last game before the first test against Australia was against Queensland in Brisbane. Ollie was selected at out-half. He scored Ireland's total of 18 points in an 18-15 triumph. It was suggested by some writers that Ollie would be selected in the centre for the first test and that I would be the choice at out-half, that in view of my 19 points against New South Wales and his record against Queensland, the selectors would make room for both of us.

"It is not just the 19 points that I had scored that made me satisfied with my performance against ACT. I always know when I play well and when I play poorly. I don't have to wait to read the papers to come to that conclusion. I knew deep down that I had played extremely well, just as Ollie did against Queensland.

"What rankled and hurt me deeply was that I had no inkling that I was going to be passed over. In later years, there would be times when I hoped to be recalled but I wouldn't be disappointed when I wasn't named. In Australia in 1979 it was different. The whole bottom fell out of my world.

"Noel Murphy admitted to Irish rugby correspondents covering the tour that he had grave reservations about omitting me and that he had a few sleepless nights wondering if he had made the right decision and he was quoted as saying: 'I knew that if we had lost there would be a terrific outcry at the dropping of Tony Ward.'

"There is one point I will never concede – that the selection of Ollie Campbell before me for the First Test was justified. I know that my critics will contend that the end justified the means – that Ollie won both tests for us. However, when they made their decision the evidence they had before them hardly warranted dropping me. There was no guarantee that Ollie would produce the goods. They must have known that they were taking a gamble and a big one at that. I am convinced that factors other than form on the field at the time were used in that selection meeting."

It Always Comes In Threes

Not only did the controversy about the selection and the debate about "Ollie versus Tony" run and run but in the following days it spawned two sequels.

There was a suggestion that some of the senior players in the party were consulted before the team was picked. Captain, Fergus Slattery, was liberally quoted in the newspapers, in a reference to the team at large, saying that this had been done. But team coach, Noel Murphy, offered a different account saying that management did not have such consultation but that Slattery as an individual might have had.

The Australian and touring British and Irish reporters widely reported the fact that Ward had been prohibited from speaking to the media about his reaction to the selection. The previous two seasons Ward had been allowed to speak freely to the press. A number of journalists commented on the U-turn in sealing Ward's lips the moment he was dropped. *The Sunday People*'s headline echoed the question on many tongues: "Why gag Ward now?"

The official line from the management was that Ward had taken the decision well. However, the Irish press corps were far from certain that this was in fact the case. Tour manager, Jack Coffey, was quoted as saying; "It is not the end of a star." Colm Smith's musings in *The Irish Independent* about Coffey's remark painted a radically different picture:

"I wonder. Quite clearly Ward was not happy when I saw him. Nor is he taking it as well as the management think. . . A star has not fallen. He has been dragged down. And despite Coffey's assertion that the rest of the party have taken it well, there is an uneasiness in the camp that is not healthy."

Leading rugby journalist, Vincent Mathers, offered a similar verdict:

"The dropping of record-breaking points scorer Ward has driven a wedge through the touring party, and a rather dazed Irish public is struggling to understand why the world-class player is suddenly out of favour."

In both the August and September issues of *Irish Rugby*, Bob Messenger dealt with the important influence of Mike Gibson on the tour, claiming: "His power far outstripped that of any other consultant. Indeed their influence may have paled by comparison." After the New South Wales debacle, when his immediate opponent had run in virtually unchallenged for two soft tries, Gibson was not dropped but switched to the centre and stayed to play in all eight tour matches and win caps in both Test games. These two appearances added to his 12 Lions' appearances, edged him one ahead of Bill McBride (63 and 17) on the overall international match list with 81 (69 Irish caps). Messenger attributes the decision, at least in part, to play Campbell rather than Ward to Gibson's influence:

"Gibson unquestionably had his say on selection and on general playing policy, and in the end his approach must be seen to have been successful no matter who it hurt in its execution."

There was some surprise that although Gibson was the oldest member of the touring party he was one of only three players with Moss Keane and Fergus Slattery to play in each of the games.

Ward smiles with pleasure as he savours one sweet memory from that tour:

"Our doctor on that trip was a wonderful man, Bob O'Connell, now sadly departed. I was very friendly with Bob and I always remember after I was dropped for the First Test sitting on the bench close to him. Ireland were doing particularly well and Ollie was kicking all the points. No matter what subs say on most representative teams, on the one hand they do want the team to win, but they don't want the man in their position to do too well, because obviously they aspire to getting into that position themselves. If they don't there's something wrong with them and they're being less than honest.

"As he watched the game, Bob was jumping up and down. He was a great Old Belvederian and his feelings for the club, for Ollie and for Ireland were coming very much to the surface and quite rightly so. Then out of the corner of his eye he saw me and got embarrassed. I felt so sorry for him because he thought he might in a sense be 'rubbing my nose in it'. He had the sensitivity to appreciate that what he was doing might have upset me. It didn't, knowing the kind of man he was. On the way home from the game he sat beside me on the bus and apologised unnecessarily. It was such a thoughtful gesture but so typical of Bob."

I Just Called To Say I Love You

Although Ward's despair on the Australian trip is graphically documented in his diary from the period, the one constant thread of joy and vitality in his diary are his comments on his calls home to his mother and fiancée. Correspondence and calls from friends were another source of joy for him. It is like reading the work of two different people. The bulk of his comments are on rugby. The entries detailing his calls from family and friends at home show a totally different man. One can feel him coming to life just at the thoughts of home.

For all the excitement of being away from home there was a price to be paid – for many players, particularly those who were self-employed, this was literally the case:

"One aspect of the tour which the fans normally don't think of is that it costs some players dearly to represent the country. Our allowance was just four pounds a day on that tour!"

All Is Changed, Changed Utterly. A Terrible Nervousness Is Born

After the euphoria of the First Test win the touring party was off to Orange for a match against the home side on the Tuesday. Ward's mental state is indicated by his brief entry in his diary about the game:

June 5
Team meeting at 1.15 p.m. Left for ground at 2.00 p.m.
Game at 3.00 p.m. VERY NERVOUS. Won 28-7. Scored 12.

The key entry is the one which reveals the extent of his nervousness. Like all players Ward had experienced butterflies before big games but not nerves. With his confidence shattered, nerves would become a constant companion in the years ahead. He could not have known it at the time but this nervousness was the first tangible sign of how pivotal the experience of being dropped in Australia would be for his subsequent career.

However, the press attention quickly moved onto the game scheduled for the following Saturday against a powerful Sydney side packed with potential test players. With the Australian selectors in attendance these players had a powerful incentive to show their best form. Ireland's victory in the First Test had been a severe shock to the

Wallabies, and they were frantically searching for new talent to stop the rampant Irish.

Press interest was fuelled when Rodney O'Donnell was forced to withdraw from the Irish side having damaged his hamstring in training. Ollie Campbell was chosen at full-back ahead of the official second choice full-back, Frank Ennis, who had won his first cap in the First Test when he replaced the concussed O'Donnell. Ward was chosen at out-half.

Sydney inflicted the first defeat in seven matches on the Irish side, despite trailing 12-3 at half time. Ireland had taken the lead in the third minute when Ciaran Fitzgerald scored a try, which Ward converted. Nine minutes later he put over a penalty to make it 9-0 and added another before half time. The Sydney side, which included such classy backs as Mark Ella, Tony Melrose and Laurie Monaghan, moved into overdrive in the second half and achieved a deserved win. Despite Ward's fine kicking performance he knew deep down he hadn't done enough to regain his place. His diary's evaluation of the game was short and to the point:

June 10
Beaten 12-16. 8 points. Poor personal second half.

Light Entertainment

Ward has one other vivid memory from that time in Sydney:

"When you are on tour a huge problem, potentially, is boredom. The day before one of our matches the management got a rush of blood to the head and decided we should all go on a boat-trip so they decided we should take the hydrofoil from Sydney to Manly. The only problem was that it was rush hour, which was the equivalent of the city centre in Dublin on a Friday evening, and we were all crammed in the hydrofoil like sardines. The boat dropped off all the passengers to

Manly except us and turned around straight away. The only redeeming feature was that we had the vessel to ourselves on the way back.

"It is important to have light moments on a tour whether it is with province, country or the Lions. One deliberate effort to induce this is 'the court session'. This is good, innocent fun and part of the ethos of tours because it certainly contributes towards improved morale. They take place two or three times on every tour and involve taking in more than a modicum of alcohol. People are fined for different reasons and the more fines they get the more alcohol they enjoy.

"On the Lions' tour, Nick Popplewell was the judge. Brian Moore was the prosecutor. Stuart Barnes was the defending barrister. Players are charged for incidents in training or in matches, e.g., somebody who dropped the ball a few times in training might be charged with being a 'butterfingers'. The fine might be to drink a bottle of beer without using their hands.

"Rugby tours also have their own requirements, like 'duty boy'. Normally there are 26 or 30 players on a touring party. Each player has at least one day as a duty boy when the task is to perform duties like informing the rest of the players when the next team-meeting is. On the days when the side is travelling it is the duty boy who wakes up the players, reminds them what kind of gear they are supposed to be wearing, official or casual, makes sure everyone is on the coach and knows the time of flights, etc."

A Different Perspective

For Ollie Campbell the memories of the Australian tour evoke very different emotions than for Ward:

"I had missed a lot of the previous season because of injury but when I came back I felt really fresh and things went very well for me. I had no thoughts though of making it onto the Australian touring party. I was obviously delighted with the news of my selection. When I saw the itinerary I thought I would probably get two games. I was delighted then to hear I would be playing in the Queensland game which meant that I would then get three matches, or so I thought at the time. For me that was going to be my Test Match. I thought the selectors were just resting Wardy.

"When we got to Surfers' Paradise something had obviously been said on the bus because when we got off Wardy came up to me and said: 'Congrats Ollie. You're in.' Before the tour some of my friends back in Belvedere told me that there was a chance that I might get a cap in one of the Test games as a centre. It never even crossed my mind that I would be selected at out-half.

"Shortly after, the team was called out. I heard no name other than my own. The rest of the team could have all been from Manchester United for all I knew. I do remember though that my name was not called out as quickly as I expected. It was only a half an hour later when we were on the training field that it slowly dawned on me I was playing at out-half. I was probably the last to know that I was playing in that position.

"I voluntarily became a social outcast until the Test match. I attended all the team activities but apart from that I locked myself into my room listening to my Billy Joel tape over and over again as I prepared mentally for the game, making notes about what I should and shouldn't do during the match.

"My first cap had been a weird experience because I had come in at the last minute for Barry McGann and missed out on all the telegrams and letters and so on. The Test match was the first time I had been an original selection so I always think of it as my first cap. I was totally oblivious to the bombshell that my selection had been, not just in Ireland but in the international rugby world, since Tony had been recently crowned European Player of the Year, until, that is, we came home.

"So many things got lost in the furore about the two of us – like the fact that we were the first country from the Northern hemisphere to win all our Test matches in a tour of the Southern hemisphere. At any other time Ciaran Fitzgerald's selection ahead of Pat Whelan would have been big news.

"To use the buzz word of today all I wanted to do was 'focus'. I really had no idea how Tony was feeling at the time. The only thing I was aware of was that he was particularly quiet and kept himself to himself. I don't know how much support he got from the team but I suspect very little. As I think back on what he must have been going through I suppose we let him down in that respect.

"It was an incredibly brave decision for Noel Murphy and the others to select me. It took a lot of guts. I feel it is something that has not been sufficiently acknowledged that they had the courage of their convictions.

"It was a turning point for both Tony and I and the start of a circus. I never thought of it as me against Tony. My reason for playing rugby was not to play for Ireland. The passion with me was to play to the best of my ability. Even in friendly games for Belvedere there never was an easing down on my part.

"I read an interview just recently with the Australian coach, Bob Dwyer. He was saying more or less the same thing though it was the first time I had seen anybody else expressing that kind of thought. As coach of Australia he had no interest in a player who wanted to be the best in his position so that he could play for Australia. Rather he wanted somebody who saw being the best in his position as an end in itself. Then he would be delighted to pick him for Australia.

"However, if I didn't see it as Campbell or Ward, everyone, apart from Tony, appeared to do so. You know the old song. At one stage it could have gone:

Love and marriage,
Horse and carriage,

Wardy and Ollie
You can't have one without the other.

"From then on people often called me 'Tony', and as the 'Ward-Campbell' saga escalated, this trend accelerated. I remember vividly meeting a man one day and he being absolutely convinced that my name was Tony. After countless examples of this I started to get a bit of a complex at the whole thing. I can honestly say that the single greatest moment of relief in my life came a few years after the Australian tour when Tony came up to me after a training session one day and said: 'Can I ask you a funny question? Do people ever call you Tony?' Immediately a load was lifted from my shoulders because I knew I was not suffering alone. Tony was going through the exact same thing in reverse – being called Ollie. From then on being called Tony never bothered me."

Home Thoughts From Abroad

Only a severe personal crisis could determine if friends are real or fair weather, as Ward discovered on the Australian tour. Some, like his mentor in Thomond College, P.J. Smyth, passed the test with flying colours. Immediately he heard the news of his protege's reversal he dispatched a telegram which read:

> *Sorry about setback. Now U have a challenge. Others have had the same – McBride, Meads, B. John, Bennet. Keep cool. Be positive, while doing the basics right.*

Others were deafening by their silence.

A few weeks after the tour Ward received a timely reminder that he was still as highly thought of as ever by the great players when he was presented with the *Rugby World* magazine's prestigious 'Player of the Year Award' by Gareth Edwards. In his address, Edwards offered words of sympathy:

"Unless you know your downs you cannot appreciate success. You must always remember that you have the admiration of players and rivals. What stands out about your game is talent. You appeared as a great hope for Irish rugby and I sympathise with the burden you had to accept."

On Mature Recollection

As always, looking straight into the eye of anyone to whom he is talking, Ward chooses his words with deliberate care. The scars from Australia have never been entirely healed:

"I could never be accused of having an arrogant or cocky personality. But I must confess that I bordered on arrogance where rugby playing was concerned. I know that sounds strange but please let me explain. I used to worry dreadfully before big games and especially before international matches but once I stepped on the field of play I became totally self-confident.

"I loved the atmosphere of big matches. I loved nothing better than coming out at Lansdowne Road and hearing the 'Irish roar'. The bigger the occasion, the more I loved it and the more I seemed to become inspired by it. It seemed as if my game lifted with the tide that the surging atmosphere of great occasions created, both at home and abroad.

"What the Australian experience did for me was to undermine my self-confidence. The Ward versus Campbell saga took off. My game and my approach to rugby was analysed and dissected. I couldn't pick up a paper but the hype was there in cold print.

"At one stage of my career I did not think about my game. I was an intuitive, instinctive player. It had all seemed to come naturally to me. After Australia I began to believe what I was reading. It reached a point where I sat down one evening and asked myself – can I really play rugby at all? My confidence just went. And went almost totally. As I look back now on my diaries from that tour and the Lions' tour the following year, I am struck at how often I use the word 'nervy'. Of course I always had butterflies before a game but not nerves.

"It's all right for people to say that you shouldn't worry about what the papers say, that much of what is written is meaningless anyway. I don't think players who exclaim loudly to the heavens that they 'never read a paper' are telling the truth. The papers reflect public thinking and fashion it. And in the Ward versus Campbell debate everyone seemed to be taking sides. There were no neutrals.

"It took me two years to get over the 'Australian Experience' even though I played in the International Championship in '81.

"I came through it and it taught me a lot about life and human relationships. My values in life changed and rightly took on a different perspective. I became much more philosophical about life in general.

"Sometimes, though, my mind goes back to a dressing-room in Sydney in 1979 and I can hear Jack Coffey saying to me as clearly as if it was only yesterday – 'It's crazy what's going on, all this media stuff . . I suggest you stay away from these fellows altogether.' "

"What Murphy, Slattery and Coffey did on that tour was to tear the heart and soul out of my game. My confidence was shattered and mine was a game based entirely on that confidence. A little of the self-fulfilling prophecy perhaps, but tell me that I am the best and I will be just that. Tell me I am not, and I will react accordingly.

"Now looking back in the context of my career, that decision and the insensitive way in which it was handled was certainly the crossroads and downturn in my career. It is something 14 years on I can forgive but never forget.

"I resent very much the decision that was made before that First Test side was announced. I know certain senior players were consulted and of course, I accept that, subsequently, the end was seen to justify the means but I had done little to deserve the cold and loaded silence which followed my dropping. Indeed, from my first B game for Ireland in Dijon in 1976 to my final game in Auch in 1988, nobody but nobody has ever pointed out any weakness in my game or told me why I was dropped or what I needed to do to get back in again. It's just not rugger's way chaps. Bullshit. It is surely common courtesy if nothing else.

"To this day people ask me why I was dropped in Australia. I have to say in all honesty I don't know, but I have little doubt that my public persona did not help and that some people felt I had to be brought down to size. On the balance of evidence at their disposal I should not have been dropped. The selectors were blessed that their gamble paid off and Ollie played so well. However, I have absolutely no doubt that factors other than rugby entered into their decision.

"Today a peculiar relationship has developed between Murphy and I. Contrary to what many would have expected in these circumstances I have no respect for what he and his fellow 'jurors' did or for how it was subsequently handled, but any bitterness has long since evaporated. Whenever we meet now Murphy's greeting is warm and sincere but it does not alter the fact that the out-half who went with him to Australia on the 12 o'clock flight from London on May 14, 1979 never came back."

6. The Race For Number Ten

Experience is a good teacher, but she sends in terrific bills.

Minna Antrim

Ward returned from Australia with his self-confidence in shambles. Within days he was planning marriage. His great friend and father figure, Frank Hogan, advised him not to rush into anything but Ward turned a deaf ear. He needed a still point, a sanctuary to restore him to an even keel. Marriage would provide that – or so he hoped.

On the rugby front he knew it would take a lot of hard work and patience to win his place back on the Irish side but he was not going to roll over in the face of adversity. There was considerable press speculation at the time that he might defect to Rugby League on foot of some reported attractive offers to him. These articles were treated seriously in certain quarters:

"Shortly after the Australian tour Noel Murphy called to the shop one day and we went outside and talked in his car at length. He told me that I had to put what happened in Australia behind me and that I shouldn't allow myself to be seduced by offers from England. I suspect that he must have had an inkling of how vulnerable I was at this time and the serious possibility that I might do something foolhardy. His gesture was appreciated."

As ever, storm clouds lurked ominously on the horizon. He was chosen to compete in the European Sportstars competition in Tel Aviv which was to be held from the 4-8 November 1979. The event was just a day after Munster's match against Cardiff. Ward had ruled himself out of the fixture because of an injury. He knew that even if he started there was no way he was going to finish the match and his chances of competing in the *Superstars* would be gone. This time Noel Murphy did want him to play against the Welsh side and was much aggrieved to find out that he was prepared to travel to the *Superstars* event when he had declined to play for Munster:

"Noisy 'told' me that if I was not going to play against Cardiff there was no way I was going to compete in Tel Aviv."

Ward ignored Murphy's 'suggestion' and travelled to Israel. The event is noteworthy because it was the one time that Ward made a defiant stand against the wishes of an influential member, or group, of the rugby hierarchy.

New Decade Old Problems

After the dizzy heights of his performances in the Five Nations Championship in '78 and '79, Ward prepared to begin the new decade in the shadow of Ollie Campbell. However, the new decade began for him with an unpleasant surprise when it seemed that he would not even be able to celebrate his past achievements in the green jersey. He received a letter informing him that the IRFU did not want him to accept his awards from 1979 as

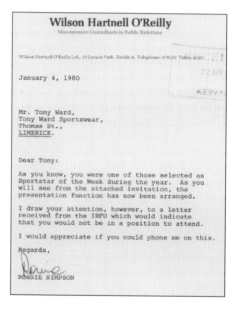

The Irish Independent's 'Sportstar of the Week' at their present-ation ceremony.

Ward did not attend the presentation ceremony: "I meekly gave in to the IRFU's request. It was the fear factor, pure and simple."

A troublesome and long-running knee injury meant that Ward was unable to play in the final trial to try and reclaim his place for the following season. He spent the day before the trial at Anfield. Although it was an interesting experience, especially the opportunity to have a long chat with Tommy Smith, the trip did not yield the desired result because they were unable to diagnose the source of his injury. Eventually he was treated by a doctor in Limerick who gave him a cortisone injection. It was a calculated risk because the side-affect of too many cortisone injections is arthritis, but it did the trick.

The Mighty Quinn

9 February 1980 was an eagerly awaited event in Irish sport – the first clash since the controversial Australian tour between Ward and Campbell on the rugby pitch. The occasion was a friendly match between Old Belvedere and Garryowen on a rain-laden, windswept Saturday afternoon. Ironically the fixture attracted twice the crowd who went along to the Munster League final which was played in Thomond Park on the same day. The thousands who descended into Dooradoyle had no doubt about the importance of the game. It would decide whether the public, particularly in Limerick, or the selectors were right. Such was the magnitude of the event that the chairman of the Irish 'Big Five', Paddy Madigan and fellow selector Brian O'Brien, attended.

In the duel of the kickers Ward kicked three penalties to Campbell's two. On the rugby pitch neither got a chance to shine. Campbell was, as usual, rock solid while only once did Ward get a chance to show his old flair, when, in a carbon copy of a play he had made against France in his debut season, on his own 22, he executed a wonderful dummy kick, showing the ball to the Old Belvedere backs and pulling it back into his body to break and run 10 yards.

On that day one star glowed brightly but he wasn't an out-half. Ward smiles ruefully as he remembers the match:

"Everybody had come to see this great clash between Ollie and myself but neither of us shone on the day. The only winner was Old Belvedere's Frank Quinn who gave an absolutely masterful performance on the wing. I have absolutely no doubt in my mind that his subsequent caps for Ireland can be attributed to that game."

Although Ward spent the 1980 season on the bench, he still managed to bring himself the wrong sort of attention from the IRFU for exceeding the bounds of their generosity during the match against France.

SECRETARY & TREASURER
R. FITZGERALD.
TELEPHONE DUBLIN 68460.
TELEGRAPHIC ADDRESS.
"FOOTBALL, DUBLIN"
REF RF/CN

IRISH RUGBY FOOTBALL UNION.
62, LANSDOWNE ROAD.
DUBLIN, 4.
18th March, 1980.

A.J.P. Ward. Esq.,
15, Pinewood Avenue,
Caherdavin Heights,
Caherdavin,
LIMERICK.

France v. Ireland 1.3.80.

Dear Tony,

Please let me have the sum of £1.92 being 50% of telephone calls charged to the room which you shared with John Robbie in hotel in Paris for the above match.

An early reply would be appreciated so that match accounts may be finalised.

Yours sincerely,

R. FITZGERALD.
Secretary.

The Great Experiment

In autumn 1980 the combination that many people had longed to see in an Irish backline, Ward and Campbell, finally happened when Ireland played Romania in Lansdowne Road. Originally Ward had been chosen in the replacements but was brought onto the side when Paul McNaughton was forced to withdraw with a broken cheekbone. Ward was brought in at out-half with Campbell moving to the centre.

"It has been suggested to me that I must have felt slightly smug about joining the Lions and then playing in the First Test, particularly when I hadn't been in the Irish team. But the truth is that I viewed it simply as a marvellous adventure.

"Although playing for the Lions was great, nothing compares with playing an international game before a home crowd at Lansdowne Road. That is a pinnacle. Everything else fades by comparison. That was one reason why I was nervous about playing against the Romanians. I knew the public were expecting great things from Ollie and I, which in itself created extra pressure. I was very sorry for Paul but it was great to be back on the Irish side. It was a tremendous surprise but wonderful news.

"There was also the fact that I found it difficult to think of Ollie as simply another centre. It was an experiment and I was well aware that we had only 80 minutes to make it work."

It would be their fourth time to play together – for the Irish side in 1979 against Sydney when Campbell was at full-back and Ward was out-half; for Old Belvedere Selected in September 1980 when Campbell was at out-half and Ward in the centre and for Bill Beaumont's Lions XV in Cork two weeks before the Romanian match when Campbell was in the centre and Ward was at full-back.

The game for Old Belvedere Selected was particularly well-timed. It took place at 5.30 p.m. the evening of the All-Ireland hurling final when Galway beat Limerick and Joe Connolly made his famous victory speech. The rugby match drew a huge crowd as Limerick supporters flocked from Croke Park to Anglesea Road to see the rugby match.

Ward was Old Belvedere's only guest player. The original plan was to rotate the out-half position between himself and Campbell but Ward was enjoying himself so much in the centre he asked to be left there for the whole game. It was a shrewd ploy on the part of the organisers to bring Ward and Campbell on to the same team because it guaranteed a full house given the Ward-Campbell hype at the time.

The Romanian match ended in a 13 all draw – a try and three penalty goals each. The Romanians were ecstatic but Ireland were disappointed and in some respects disappointing. The Ward-Campbell combination worked one moment of magic to set up Frank Quinn for his first try for Ireland. Campbell kicked three penalty goals and contributed some good passing and kicking in an Irish threequarter line that never really came to terms with the fierce tackling of their opponents. Ward's return was a triumphant one – kicking well, tackling enthusiastically and foraging energetically. His reward – he was dropped for the next game at home to France in the Five Nations Championship.

By The Rivers Of The Taff We Sat And Wept

1980 ended with a timely opportunity for Ward to remind everyone of his capabilities on the international stage, adding further fuel to the controversy about the number ten shirt on the Irish team. The 29th November saw an England-Wales selection play an Ireland-Scotland selection to mark the centenary of the Welsh Rugby Union.

One of the big buzz phrases of the day was 'forward supremacy is the key'. Indeed the superior power of the pack paved the way for England-Wales to take a seven point lead at the interval. When that lead was extended to 13 points, two minutes into the second half it looked a one-sided affair. But in a memorable 40 minutes, the setting, once described by the inimitable Con Houlihan as 'rugby's La Scala', Cardiff Arms Park seemed to lift Ward and he engineered a magnificent revival. In a free-flowing game of no less than 12 tries,

Ward scored a super goal to give his side a 33-31 lead and they held on to the lead until the second minute of injury time when Gareth Davies got a goal. Like anglers who had hooked a "big one" only for him to break free at the point of landing, Ireland-Scotland had victory snatched away from them. The real winners were the fans who saw an exhibition of running rugby at its best.

Ward scored 15 points – a try, four conversions and a dropped goal. The headlines the following day on both sides of the Irish Sea made great use of the phrase, "Ward's wizardy". Particular emphasis was placed on his eye for the opening of a try-scoring opportunity that did not appear to be there. Those who criticised Ward for being 'only a place kicker', 'not able to involve his threequarters', and 'not a team player' could thank their lucky stars that humble pie is only a metaphorical item on the menu.

Opportunity Knocks

Ireland's opening match of the Five Nations Championship in the 1981 season was a home game against France. It was a match which revived an old Irish failing – an uncanny ability to concede defeat from the jaws of victory. It was a match which recalled for many a comment from Mike Gibson in 1965 when Ireland had somehow contrived to lose the match in Cardiff to present the home side with the Triple Crown, when it should have been crossing the Irish Sea: "We couldn't make a move unless we got permission in triplicate."

On a positive note, the one good thing about the game was the impressive debut of Hugo MacNeill – he played with assurance and panache and capped it all with a fine try. Ireland lost 13-19. Despite kicking three penalties, by his own incredible standards Ollie Campbell had a poor game, which seemed a contradiction in terms. His place-kicking was below par, but it was his normally impeccable tactical kicking which really let him down. Moreover, he failed to bring his threequarters into play. A number of other big name players did not play up to scratch.

However, only two changes were made after the game: Paul McNaughton and Brendan Foley were dropped. Both players could have considered themselves extremely unfortunate to have been excluded. Equally, some of the more illustrious names on the side must have deemed themselves very lucky to escape the ignominy of being dropped. Campbell replaced McNaughton in the centre, a position he confesses he was never really comfortable in, with Ward recalled to the out-half position and a fit again Donal Spring recalled into the second row.

Gareth Edwards, commenting on Ward's selection at the time, stated: "We in Wales believe him to be a better tactical kicker than Ollie Campbell and, regrettably, if you like, kicking plays a big part in modern day internationals. Also the fact that you have both Ward and Campbell in the side gives you a big advantage in the place kicking area and Wales, this season, have been very generous with penalties."

Meanwhile, in his sports shop in Limerick, Ward received a telegram from Ollie Campbell which read:

Congratulations on your selection Stop Looking forward to playing with you in Cardiff.

Ward cringes in embarrassment as he looks at the telegram:

"After, and even before '79, Ollie sent me a flood of telegrams and cards whenever I had something to celebrate but to my shame I never sent him one."

Renaissance Man

Irony is no stranger to sport in Ireland. There is no finer example of this than the phenomenon of Jack Charlton – arguably Ireland's most loved sports personality, even though he is very much an English man. The Ireland-Wales game of 1981 abounded in ironies. Ireland went into the game with two of the all-time great place-kickers, rugby's versions of William Tell, but neither of them could land a kick on goal in the whole match.

Wales strangely went into the game with no recognised place-kicker. Their designated kicker was Gwyn Evans and he had reportedly spent much of the week practising his place-kicks – like a wayward student frantically trying to cram for an exam at the last minute, not having opened a book all year. In true fairytale tradition, the debutant Evans kicked a penalty goal in the opening minutes with his first kick in international rugby despite the swirling wind.

As Campbell settled down to master his new position with his customary aplomb – with his bravery in defence, his ability to batten onto possession in midfield, and make some excellent tackles; Ward quickly showed his touch with a beautifully placed kick for Wanderers' winger, Freddie McLennan, to run on to – strong Welsh rearguard action prevented a try.

Then in the 24th minute, like a forgotten actor turning in an Oscar winning performance, Ward announced his return in bold print. Following a deep kick from Ward Ireland won possession with Campbell feeding Ward and the out-half cut diagonally right. He beat two tackles and then threw out a long pass for Fergus Slattery to take with his outstretched right hand to dive over for a try. It was a try conjured out of nothing, a worthy tribute to Ward's innovation, but also significant because it suggested that Campbell and Ward seemed to thrive on each others' play. Disappointingly Ward shaved the post with the conversion – having earlier missed penalties from 50 and 53 yards. The try was the cue for the Irish side to show their best form but it was not until the stroke of half time that Ireland turned their possession into scores. Again it was Ward who made things happen. He cut loose and gained possession on the left, ran in-field, wrong-footed several defenders to make a clear opening on the right which yielded a try to Hugo MacNeill, his second in consecutive games, via David Irwin and Freddie McLennan. This time it was Campbell who was narrowly wide with the difficult conversion attempt.

Although Ireland led 8-3 at the interval the second half was a different story with the Irish backs living on a starvation diet because the Welsh pack took over completely. Jeff Squire and Allan Martin owned the lineouts for the home side – though it was the scrums which glaringly exposed the Irish weakness. Ireland only got one chance of scoring in the second half with Ward missing a 30 yard penalty. His main contribution subsequently was a succession of relieving clearances as Wales camped in the Irish half. Their only reward was a second penalty from Evans and a fine drop goal from the new out-half, Gary Pearce, enough to give them a 9-8 victory.

The match is vividly remembered by Ollie Campbell for two specific incidents:

"I will always have two very vivid memories of Tony's career. The first was his little chip over the heads of the All-Blacks' backline on that memorable day, 31 October, 1978 in Thomond Park. It set up Jimmy Bowen for a long run and he in turn set up Christy Cantillon for the only try of the match which in turn set up the rugby folklore that the game has become.

"The second was his mesmerising little runs which set up both tries in Cardiff in 1981. This was one of the few games in which we played together and, ironically, it was a game that not only did we lose by two penalties and a drop goal to two tries, but we couldn't kick a point between us! Both these memories were classic examples of Tony's brilliant individualistic play."

If nothing else, the match produced a vintage report of purple prose from Con Houlihan in the following Monday's *Evening Press*. Like St John's Gospel he began with a dramatic flourish – comparing Ward's reappearance to that of Captain Dreyfus' return to Paris after his long and unjust exile. But that was just a warm-up for his next analogy, claiming that Ward's return: ". . . made the return of Jesse James seem about as dramatic as the coming home of a man who has taken the dog for a stroll."

His next analogy was a biblical one: "Alas, although he twice parted the Red Sea in a manner which Moses would thoroughly approve, he failed to lead his people out of the desert." When he got down to analysing the game as distinct from simply Ward's return, he claimed that: "Ward began kicking up-and-unders that had the Welsh backs hypnotised by a swooping hawk." Moreover, his use of the ball was like "a ventriloquist's dummy" and his running was constantly "changing course with the bewildering eye of a politician" leaving the Welsh "like puppies trying to corral a jack-rabbit" because of his ability to "transmute base metal into gold".

His final remark was on the various observations of the Welsh supporters on the way home: "Their comments varied – but on one thing they were unanimous, they made Tony Ward a freeman of the valleys."

With the benefit of hindsight Ward feels the experiment in 1981 did not bring the one advantage everybody expected:

"The idea of having two place-kickers in the team did not work out too well in reality. It inevitably led to the attitude that if one player missed a few kicks then the other would have to take over. It is far better if someone takes total responsibility for the job beforehand. When you go out on the pitch and know you have total responsibility for the kicking you are totally focused on the task. But when there are two kickers both have the attitude at the back of their minds that if one doesn't do it the other guy will. You are not mentally right to accept full responsibility. That experiment worked to the team's detriment. Neither of us mentally could take full responsibility or was completely focused on the job."

The Exorcism

The visit of a touring Australia side in the autumn of '81 presented Ward with the possibility to exorcise some of the ghosts of his '79 nightmare. In Munster's match against the Wallabies on 17 November in Musgrave Park he set about this task with a vengeance. Although Munster emerged victorious, 15-6, such was the ineptitude of the Australian team that the victory did not compare with the victory against the All-Blacks in 1978.

Although Munster played with their customary fire and determination it was not simply a victory of spirit as the home side dominated in all phases of play. Their pack was in near total control in the line-out and in the loose exchanges. Behind the forwards Ward called the shots. Apart from scoring 11 points (two penalties, a 30 yard drop goal and a conversion of Paul Derham's try) his contribution was immense – his strategic kicking pinning the Australians down and, whenever the tourists threatened, his long clearances sent them back on their heels. In the final quarter, Peter Grigg scored a try for Australia which Michael O'Connor converted but it was too little too late.

A crowd of ten thousand people came to watch the final trial a few weeks later. It was an extraordinary attendance and testimony to the drawing power of a Campbell-Ward confrontation. The game yielded no conclusive outcome. Campbell clashed heads with Fergus Slattery, and Ward replaced him as out-half on the Probables and Paul Dean switched to out-half on the Possibles. Ward and Dean subsequently clashed heads, with Dean sustaining a suspected fracture of the cheek bone. The only significant long-term consequence of the game was that Dean retains a small scar from the incident to this day.

Campbell's Kingdom

The Ward/Campbell experiment was deemed a failure by the Irish selectors and for the 1982 season Ward was not even a sub, as the Irish team, superbly marshalled by the all round brilliance of Ollie Campbell, went on to win the Triple Crown.

His total omission came as a big shock to Ward himself because he had played in the final trial and in Munster and Ireland's matches against Australia. After Ireland's team for the opening match of the season against Wales was announced, Ward went AWOL for the next squad training session. There was considerable media comment about this the following day. The official explanation for Ward's absence was that a misunderstanding arose. Ward played along with that illusion to prevent any embarrassment, particularly to Tom Kiernan. However, his decision to stay away was deliberate. He was hurt, not at losing his place to Ollie Campbell, but at being dropped totally from the squad without even a hint as to the reason. It was a perennial problem which galls him to this day. Being dropped is one thing but to lose your place and not know the reason is another. Ward glows visibly as he recalls one little incident which is his enduring memory of that season:

"I was on the steps of the Shelbourne Hotel after the team was announced and feeling despondent about the whole situation when Ollie Campbell came and apologised to me for the way I had been treated. It was a lovely gesture and so typical of Ollie."

On the eve of Ireland's match with Scotland to decide the Triple Crown, Ward was asked his thoughts on his great rival Campbell, in an interview in *The Evening Herald*. His frustration at the hype about the controversy is clearly evident:

"It has all been so stupid and unnecessary. I personally am sick to death of the so-called Ward versus Campbell issue. It is the result of total sensationalism and it's the sort of thing which takes all the enjoyment out of the game. Of course it has put pressure on Ollie in the championship – people may claim they don't read the newspapers but it's only human to take notice of what has been said. The media has gone totally overboard. Ollie and I get on well together and we also do business.

"Ollie has been playing superbly since his return from a three month break. Against England, he had the best game I have ever seen him play, especially since he was under far more pressure than against Wales. His covering and support play was phenomenal. He had the type of game I would love to play myself. Campbell will once again be the key man for Ireland against Scotland.

"Last season we lost four championship matches we could and possibly should have won. I am delighted to see things click into place. Munster's win against the All-Blacks wasn't a flash in the pan – Tommy Kiernan is a superb coach and tactician. I know from my days at St Mary's what a fabulous organiser Fitzy is. He has also taken pressure off Fergus Slattery who has been playing extremely well since giving up the captaincy. Donal Lenihan has made a big contribution to the side – we now have four men in the lineout while, of course, Ollie Campbell has had a remarkable season so far."

That season Ward and Campbell had come close to being clubmates when Ward returned to Dublin for personal and business rather than rugby reasons:

"Paddy Madigan had been a big help to me when I moved back to Dublin in arranging a new business premises for me and so on. Paddy was a great Old Belvedere man and naturally wanted what was best for the club and asked me to join. I was tempted at the time but looking back it would have been a disaster. Whatever about Ollie and I being rivals for a place on the Irish side competing for the out-half berth at club level would have been folly."

Owenly Magnificent

Although Ward was forced to miss out on Ireland's Triple Crown glory the season was by no means a barren one for him as he helped Garryowen to a Munster League title, their first since 1954. His team went into the final against U.C.C. at Musgrave Park as outsiders because they were missing a number of key players through injury. Their win was the fruit of a gallant team effort in the face of seemingly insurmountable adversity.

The college side had the benefit of a towering performance from up-and-coming Irish international star, Donal Lenihan in the line-outs, ably assisted by international star of the future, Brian Spillane but it was the Dooradoyle side who emerged triumphant. That season Ward also won an FAI Cup medal with Limerick, having played against Southampton in the UEFA cup earlier that season. However, others suggested that perhaps his season had been a failure:

"I remember taking part with Ollie in a Sunday sports programme on Radio One presented by Jimmy Magee. Jimmy concluded by saying: 'Well Ollie it's been a great year for you but Tony you must think the season was a bit of a nightmare.' I was slightly taken aback by that statement. I certainly would never consider winning a Munster Senior League Winners medal and an FAI Cup medal in the one season a failure!"

It's Not An April Fool

As Ward had absolutely no involvement with the Triple Crown winning side he was surprised to receive a letter from the IRFU. The

Ref RF/SMacS   1st April 1982
A.J.P Ward Esq
C/O Tony Ward Sport
48 Thomas Street
Limerick

Dear Tony,
    The question of your involvement on various radio and television programmes during this year's International series was discussed at a recent meeting of the IRFU General Purposes Committee.
    The President, Mr. John Moore advised the Committee that you had communicated with him, and of the contents of that telephone conversation on 5th January last.
    It appears that you did take part in various radio and television programmes, including the RTE current affairs programme, "Today Tonight".
    The items which you have discussed with the President would appear to be as follows:-
(a)   To participate with Carwyn James on a BBC TV production on coaching
(b)   To participate as a commentator on Radio or TV on the occasion of the Ireland v. Wales International.
(c)   To appear on the Radio programme, "Talking Sport".
    The President suggested to you that there might be some variation between what Carwyn James stated to you and to the IRFU, and that you should write to the IRFU setting out clearly what Mr. James required. Permission was not granted to you to undertake (b) above, but was granted by the President for (c), he having stated that in his opinion it would be in your best interest not to do so at that time.
    No permission was granted for you to appear on the "Today Tonight" programme.
    The Committee would be pleased to receive your comments on these matters at your convenience.

                        Yours sincerely,
                        R. Fitzgerald
                        Secretary

letter queried his participation in some television and radio programmes. Not for the first time Ward was forced to defend himself and set the record straight on a misrepresentation of his actions.

75, Shanganagh Vale,   7th July 1982
Loughlinstown,
Co. Dublin.

Dear Bob,
    Your letter of the 1st April duly received and, initially, I must apologise to you for not replying sooner. However, I feel sure you and the IRFU Committee will understand when I say I was particularly busy in recent months due to business commitments.
    With regard to your query re radio and television appearances, may I state that it was not and never has been my intention to contravene any IRFU regulations and I most certainly did not intentionally do so on the occasions to which you refer.
    I must stress that, I did not, participate as "a commentator" on either radio or TV on the occasion of the Ireland v Wales match. I watched that game from the upper deck of the West Stand. Just prior to the game I was asked to express a view on the likely outcome by a radio commentator and I answered one question for him and then took my seat in the stand. I am therefore at a loss to understand how anyone could possibly think I was involved as a commentator, even in the most tenuous manner.
    With regard to the "Today Tonight" programme, I most certainly did contribute to that programme, but in so doing did not think that I was contravening IRFU regulations. In that instance, I was not commentating on a specific game or contributing in a specific sense. However, I offer sincere apologies if, as seems apparent from your letter, I should have sought permission for appearing.
    I have always endeavoured to keep within the laws, the spirit and the letter, as evidenced by my approach to the president this season when I thought such a course necessary.
    In conclusion, may I express the hope that the IRFU committee will accept my explanations on the matters referred to by you and again my apologies for not replying at an earlier date.

                                         Yours sincerely,

                                         Tony Ward

Equal Lack Of Opportunities

In the close season Ward embarked on a three match tour of Romania with Munster. It was a real eye-opener for him:

"I didn't expect Romania to be anything like what it was. If it was equality for all it was equal poverty for all. To see children running

"A word in your ear"
Willie Duggan and Tony Ward with Big
Moss and Tony Doyle in the background.
England v Ireland, Twickenham 1984.

"Every face tells a story"
Ollie Campbell, Fergus Slattery
and Tony Ward.

"Emergency Ward"
Ollie Campbell going off, Tony Ward coming on. Also, in front row: Ginger McLoughlin,
Philip Orr and Ciaran Fitzgerald. Face in the crowd – Willie Anderson.

"El Syd"
Arriving at Jan Smuts Airport, Johanesburg, May 1980. Met by Syd Miller.
Note Ward's unofficial attire.

"Labour of love"
Dick Spring and Tony Ward concentrate on
Noisy's words of wisdom at an Irish squad
session.

"There is an Isle"
1978 Munster Cup Final.
Garryowen v Shannon,
Thomond Park.
Sequence of Tony Ward
scoring a try. Alas to no avail
– Shannon 16, Garryowen 10.

"Spot the Ball"
Ward kicks a penalty. Scotland v Ireland 1979.

"Three wise men?"
Willie John McBride and Willie Duggan in conversation. Ward awaits instructions.

"The man from Clare"
Irish captain, Shay Deering, introduces Tony Ward to President Paddy Hillary while
Colin Patterson waits next in line.

"The mighty men of Munster"
The munster team which defeated the All-Blacks. Oct 1978, Munster 12 – New Zealand 0.
Back row (l – r): John Cole (touchjudge), Gerry McLoughlin, Les White, Moss Keane,
Donal Spring, Colm Tucker, Pat Whelan, Brendan Foley, Corrie Thomas (referee),
Martin Walsh (touchjudge). Front row (l – r): Tony Ward, Christy Cantillon, Moss Finn,
Seamus Dennison, Donal Canniffe, Greg Barrett, Jimmy Bowen, Larry Moloney.

"The one that got away"
Final trial, Lansdowne Road, Dec 86. Harry Harbison and Philip Matthews left for dead as Ward dashes for the line.

"Holmes and away"
Ward eludes Southampton's Nick Holmes as Steve Moran looks on, UEFA CUP, 1981.

Limerick v Bohemians, 1982 Cup Final
Back row (l – r): Pat Nolan, Al Finucane, Des Kennedy, Ger Duggan, Kevin Fitzpatrick,
Brendan Storan, Eoin Hand, Willie Flaherty (physio).
Front row (l – r): Dave Mahedy (trainer), Tommy Gaynor, Jimmy Nodwell, Joe O'Mahony,
Tony Ward, Gary Holmes, Johnny Walsh.

Ward's first cap. Ireland v Scotland, 1978.
Stewart McKinney crosses for the only try of the game.

around half-naked in the streets was frightening and the filth of the country was something else. It is a country I would never wish to go back to unless there are fundamental changes.

"It was also a police state. At seven or eight o'clock everything stopped in the main cities because of a curfew. It was a very sad country. We got to know some of the players. I remember giving all of my gear, including rain gear, to one of the players and he couldn't believe how lucky he was.

"I remember going into the shops and really it was like going into a time warp and visiting another world in a different age. The shelves were practically empty. I went subsequently on a skiing trip to Bulgaria and both countries were so alike with the old weighing scales in the shops. It was mind-boggling stuff. It just made you appreciate how lucky you were."

Ward's happy memories from that trip are in the main connected with the exploits of a great Irish sporting institution, Maurice Ignatius Keane:

"We had to play three games in eight days and Mossy's career was nearing an end at that stage so it was felt that he would not be able to play in all three. After the first match Moss was told he would not be playing in the second game which meant he had a week off until his next match. Suffice to say he made the most of every minute.

"The Romanians were a bit in awe of Mossy. In the second match they asked him to do touchjudge. The problem was that Moss had enjoyed himself too much. I can still see him to this day with big red face, track-suit top, white shorts, pair of runners and ankle-socks like a scene from Fawlty Towers. Things were okay in the first half when Mossy was away from the crowd but in the second half they were not so good when he was right in front of the home mob. I remember them throwing things at him and he would turn around and growl back at them. It really was high comedy and a lovely memory.

"Mind you we got thrashed in that match. It was like playing against Young Munster or Shannon away. They were a very vociferous, hysterical, passionate, home-loving side but Mossy's performance put the whole thing in perspective.

"Mossy was a great tourist. He was great fun and always enjoyed himself on tour. Although he let his hair down, he never lost the head completely. He never complained though he had plenty of cause for complaint on that tour. Moss is a great guy – a big man, but a very gentle man with a soft heart. He is one of the guys it's been an honour and a privilege to know and share so many happy memories and moments with."

Voluntary Exile

The end of 1982 saw yet a further twist in the Campbell-Ward saga when, at the end of November, Ward asked not to be considered by the Irish selectors for selection for the Final Trial. This followed a poor performance for Munster against Ulster in the interprovincial championship. His decision took the rugby world by surprise. The fans had been looking forward to another Ward-Campbell confrontation but Ward has no doubts about the decision:

"It was pointless going into the final trial in that state of mind. My appetite and my thinking were not right and my confidence was gone. I was tired mentally and physically and probably made a big mistake playing in the number of matches I did at the start of that season. I think I played something like 14 games in September, including three for Munster on the Romanian tour. Perhaps my business commitments also had a bearing."

Nonetheless, although Campbell was very much the man in possession for the 1983 campaign when Ireland secured a share of the Five Nations Championship, Ward found himself back on the subs bench. When an injury to Campbell in the home match against England forced him to leave the pitch Ward replaced him for two minutes of international rugby. It was short but very sweet, particularly as the Lansdowne Road crowd gave him a huge ovation.

The Valentine's Day Message

In 1983 Ward received a message on Valentine's Day from the IRFU. The previous September he was one of four well-known sportsmen, one from each province, e.g., Wexford star hurler, Tony Doran represented Leinster etc., to sing the praises of CIE's train services on a radio advertising campaign. The IRFU were unhappy about Ward's involvement in this episode and wrote to him seeking information to determine whether he had breached his amateur status or not. The controversy generated a flood of correspondence. The following five letters give a flavour of what was involved.

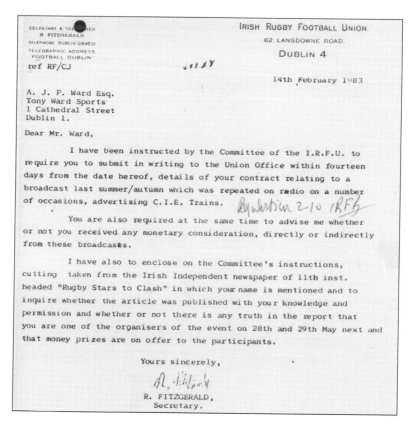

SECRETARY & TREASURER
R FITZGERALD
TELEPHONE DUBLIN 084601
TELEGRAPHIC ADDRESS
FOOTBALL, DUBLIN
ref RF/CJ

IRISH RUGBY FOOTBALL UNION.
62, LANSDOWNE ROAD.
DUBLIN 4

14th February 1983

A. J. P. Ward Esq.
Tony Ward Sports
1 Cathedral Street
Dublin 1.

Dear Mr. Ward,

    I have been instructed by the Committee of the I.R.F.U. to require you to submit in writing to the Union Office within fourteen days from the date hereof, details of your contract relating to a broadcast last summer/autumn which was repeated on radio on a number of occasions, advertising C.I.E. Trains.

    You are also required at the same time to advise me whether or not you received any monetary consideration, directly or indirectly from these broadcasts.

    I have also to enclose on the Committee's instructions, cutting taken from the Irish Independent newspaper of 11th inst. headed "Rugby Stars to Clash" in which your name is mentioned and to inquire whether the article was published with your knowledge and permission and whether or not there is any truth in the report that you are one of the organisers of the event on 28th and 29th May next and that money prizes are on offer to the participants.

    Yours sincerely,

R. FITZGERALD,
Secretary.

IRISH RUGBY FOOTBALL UNION.

SECRETARY & TREASURER
R. FITZGERALD
TELEPHONE DUBLIN 684601
TELEGRAPHIC ADDRESS,
"FOOTBALL DUBLIN"

62, LANSDOWNE ROAD.

DUBLIN. 4

ref RF/CJ

21st March 1983

A. J. P. Ward Esq.
Tony Ward Sports
1 Cathedral Street
Dublin 1

RECEIVED
22 APR 1983
KEVANS

Dear Tony,

     Thank you for your letter of 27th February last which has since been considered by the Union Committee.

     The Committee has asked me to convey to you its acceptance of your explanation regarding the article "Rugby Stars to Clash" published in the Irish Independent newspaper on 11th February last.

     The Committee noted that your letter did not advise whether or not you received any monetary consideration, directly or indirectly from the broadcasts advertising C.I.E. trains and I have been instructed to request you to let me have such information before the next Union Committee meeting on 22nd April 1983.

     Yours sincerely,

R. FITZGERALD,
Secretary.

IRISH RUGBY FOOTBALL UNION.

SECRETARY & TREASURER
R. FITZGERALD
TELEPHONE DUBLIN 684601
TELEGRAPHIC ADDRESS,
"FOOTBALL DUBLIN"

62, LANSDOWNE ROAD.

DUBLIN. 4

ref RF/SMacS

21st March 1983

P.A. Dargan Esq
Advertising Manager
CIE
35 Lower Abbey Street,
Dublin 1

RECEIVED
22 APR 1983
KEVANS

<u>re: Advertising - Limerick Train</u>

Dear Mr. Dargan,

     My Union Committee's attention was drawn to an RTE radio advertisment which was broadcast on a number of occasions last Summer/Autumn, and referred to travelling home on the Limerick train. The person named was Mr. Tony Ward who said, " Hi, I'm Tony Ward and I like a fast mover, so for the week-end I take the train. It's as quick as a scrum-half and the value is really good too. So whether you are playing at home or away, the train really scores".

     Mr. Ward was requested to submit details of his contract for the broadcast to this office for consideration by the Committee. He replied stating that "no contract exists or has ever existed between CIE and myself, so therefore, I am not in a position to forward details of a contract that does not exist. Should you wish to verify the truth of this statement , then you are free to contact CIE".

     On receipt of the above statement by Mr. Ward, my Committee decided to write to you to ascertain if a contract did nor does exist between Mr. Ward or his agent, if he has one, and CIE or any advertising agent that CIE may have appointed for the above mentioned broadcast.

     At the same time, please advise whether any remuneration in respect of the broadcast in question was paid by CIE or its agent to either Mr. Ward or his agent.

     Yours sincerely,

R.FITZGERALD
Secretary

Tony Ward Sport,
1 Cathedral Street,
Dublin 1.

Your Ref: RF/CJ   18th April 1983

Dear Sir,

I refer to your letter of the 21st March 1983 and am rather surprised that further explanation should be necessary relative to your queries in your communication of last February.

However, as obviously your committee is still not satisfied, I must make my position clear in the firm hope that I will be allowed to get on with my task of running my business.

As I stated in my letter of February 27th, I have not had a contract with CIE and do not have a contract with CIE. May I also make it abundantly clear no agent has ever acted on my behalf, nor do I have an agent, being an amateur sportsman.

I took part in an advertisement on behalf of Tony Ward Sport which, as I have already explained is made up of outlets in Limerick and in Dublin. CIE paid the sum of £100 to Tony Ward Sport as payment for my participation, as head of the firm, in the advertisement, which, as I have outlined was for the train facility between Limerick and Dublin.

This has nothing whatsoever to do with my functions as a rugby player, a position that had been clarified for me by my legal adviser, who has since reiterated that position.

I do hope that this will be the end of the matter. Quite frankly, I find it very strange and more than a little disconcerting that I am constantly being asked for explanations by your committee. It seems, however, that others are not being asked for explanations for similar matters.

As I stated at the outset, I would be very grateful if I am now allowed to get on with the task of earning my living through the medium of Tony Ward Sport, into which I have put everything I have and which involves me in 12 hours work each day and often more. I wonder would the members of your committee, who are constantly seeking explanations from me, be equally prepared to answer similar queries relative to their business interests or would they feel, as I now feel, that the point has reached the level of unwarranted interference.

Yours faithfully
Tony Ward

SECRETARY & TREASURER
R. FITZGERALD
TELEPHONE DUBLIN 684601
TELEGRAPHIC ADDRESS
"FOOTBALL, DUBLIN"

IRISH RUGBY FOOTBALL UNION.
62, LANSDOWNE ROAD.
DUBLIN. 4

ref RF/CJ

27th April 1983

A. J. P. Ward Esq.
Tony Ward Sports
1 Cathedral Street
Dublin 1

Dear Tony,

I acknowledge with thanks receipt of your letter of 18th inst., setting out the information requested in my letter of 21st March last.

The Committee has asked me to draw your attention to players' responsibility regarding the International Board's Regulations relating to Amateurism and the Laws of the I.R.F.U.

Yours sincerely,

R. FITZGERALD,
Secretary.

The upshot of the controversy was that Ward himself was forced to engage a firm of solicitors to establish that he had not contravened the laws of amateurism by proving that the money was paid to Tony Ward Sports and was related to his business in Dublin and Limerick and not to him in a personal capacity. To help them prove this he had to make available some of his own records and correspondence to the legal firm and take time off his business commitments and consult with his legal team in court.

Apart from the inconvenience and loss of his time Ward found himself out of pocket because of the incident. Tony Ward Sports had received a fee of £100 for his participation. However, Ward received the following bill from his solicitors for their work in the saga.

Bill of Costs

Paid Donal Seligman B.L. for Research and Consultation	£46.20
Plus V.A.T. at 23%	£10.63
Paid for Consultation Room	£5.00
Postage, Telephones and Photocopying	£10.00
Our Professional Fees to cover detailed Research, Briefing Counsel and Consultation	£105.00
Plus V.A.T. at 23% on £105.00	£26.45
Total	£203.28

Kickers At Twickers

After the highs of '82 and '83 Ireland came down to earth with a bang in '84 and were whitewashed in the championship. An illness to Ollie Campbell meant a recall for Ward for the England game at Twickenham. The news of his inclusion came like a bolt out of the blue to Ward himself.

"I was arriving at the Shelbourne Hotel and Ollie was leaving. We said hello but at that stage I had no idea that he was out and I was in. Of course because I had not been informed officially he was not in a position to tell me himself. I thought he was going for a walk, or something. Hearing I was back in the side was a complete shock. I had resigned myself to acting as a reserve. It was a great thrill, almost as big as when I won my first cap. Although I would have preferred to have got back on to the side in different circumstances my feet didn't touch the ground until I ran on to the pitch."

News of Ward's inclusion was greeted by the English squad's final training session at St Mary's Training College at Strawberry Hill with less than elation. English winger, John Carleton, remarked:

"God, Campbell's dropped out and who do they replace him with? Ward! He will take some controlling. He is one of the most exciting runners of the ball I have ever seen and he is desperately difficult to tackle."

Such praise was not what Ward wanted to hear at that juncture:

"I felt more nervous than I was when winning my first cap. The pressure on me was fantastic, especially coming back as a late replacement for Ollie Campbell. Ollie had been something of a goalkicking phenomenon. His success over the previous seasons certainly made him a hard act for me to follow. I knew my stomach would be churning a bit when I stood up to take my first place-kick."

When the moment came he responded to the challenge with ice-like nerve. On the half hour mark he was tackled so high by his opposite number, Les Cusworth, that there was a risk of decapitation. The penalty was deep and well to the right but he sweetly slotted the ball between the posts. His only other two penalties, one from 50 yards, also found the target. However, England won 12-9 courtesy of three penalties from Dusty Hare and a Les Cusworth drop goal.

Not for the first time the match was lost as much by Irish default as opponents' creation. The main problem was that penalties were given away with almost criminal negligence. On a positive note, new cap, Tony Doyle fitted in well at scrum-half.

Commenting on the game the following day Hugh McIlvaney wrote in *The Observer:* "Since aesthetic pleasure scarcely arrived in a flood it was natural to grab at emotional satisfaction and the performance of Tony Ward was certainly one of these." In the same paper Geoffrey Nicholson concluded: "Whatever else Ireland's problems may be, the only embarrassment at stand-off is one of riches."

Ward's own verdict was less prosaic:

"It was very disappointing to lose again especially after denying England a try. Our cover defence was fantastic and it had to be to stop the English backs after they had made some lovely moves. We knew England would play that way and, if we had the right possession, we intended to do the same. We had nothing to lose with the Triple Crown and the Championship gone.

"It took me a little time to get used to the pace which I found very fast early on but I managed to sort things out. I was very pleased for Tony Doyle. He had a great first game for Ireland and his service was first class. Willie Duggan's play was inspirational. Despite the 'Dad's army' tag our pack was still going well at the end.

"At the end of the previous season I had clocked up two minutes of international rugby as a replacement but I decided to work hard on my fitness in the close season and made myself a promise – international rugby or bust! Normally I would have taken a good rest and plenty of relaxation but having given quite a lot of thought to my future in rugby I decided to get down to work with the hardest of training and have at least one more fling at winning my place back on the Irish team.

"Although I was upset to hear about Ollie's viral infection I was glad I had made that decision the previous season. In just one moment all the lonely hours of training and hard work were worthwhile."

Although the game against England produced no tries the entertainment value was high with England running the ball to good effect. One of their stars was a young winger called Rory Underwood. Although his silken skills and running power were obvious from his debut none of the Irish fans could have foreseen that here was a man who would break their hearts so often in subsequent seasons.

Ward's three penalties brought his international total in 15 appearances to 98 points. And it also marked the sixth game in which he had scored all of Ireland's points in an international game.

There was considerable controversy before the game about the omission of Ciaran Fitzgerald from the Irish side. The official explanation was that he was unfit to play. However, while Ireland were losing to England, Fitzgerald was in Belfast helping St Mary's defeat Malone 12-7. The former Irish captain poured scorn on doubts about his fitness in the most effective way possible by breaking and running 20 yards to score a try.

Indecent Disposal

Campbell's continued injury problems meant that Ward duly found himself back in the number ten jersey for the next match, a home game against Scotland. He remembers the build-up to the game for all the wrong reasons:

"I had a lot of personal contact with Willie Duggan before the England game. He was captain and leading the forwards and I was leading the backs. It was important that we get the tactics right – particularly as it is fair to say that Willie John McBride, who was coach for just that season, was a big disappointment. We all had expected great things from him because of his record as captain of the Lions in 1974. Surprisingly, he had a very laid-back, softly-softly style which simply did not work at the highest level. Irish rugby teams need great motivating figures before matches. Tom Kiernan was one, Mick Doyle was one and of course Fitzy. Gerry Murphy is not but he has a great motivator at his side in Willie Anderson. Willie John did it his way but strange as it seems, it was not the Irish style.

"We gathered in the Constitution Room of the Shelbourne Hotel before the Scotland game for a team meeting. Willie Duggan was at the top table with Willie John and Roly Meates. The remaining selectors were all in the room. Duggan started to speak and suddenly he proceeded to lacerate me, and me alone, for a good five or six minutes. I mean he tore strips off me in front of everybody. He told me he wanted a display where there was no playing to the gallery. I can truthfully say, with hand on heart, that I never played to the gallery. He stressed that I was to come up on my man not like the way I had let Les Cusworth loose in the previous match. Cusworth did play well in that game but it was not because I gave him the freedom of the park as Willie Duggan claimed.

"It was a totally unexpected personalised attack. I came out of that room totally devastated. I can still remember that feeling of numbed shock and pain. Most, if not all, of the players came to me in private afterwards and said how disgusted they were about the episode. What really disappointed me was that not one of the selectors spoke up for me or said anything to me about it afterwards or indeed to this day.

"It totally shattered my confidence in the build-up to the game. That's something I can never forgive Willie Duggan for. My game is built on confidence and that was the very last thing I needed to hear. That game was to be Derek McGrath's first cap as a flanker and Duggan began his talk by welcoming him into the side and saying how well the senior players would look after him and then he launched into an attack on me.

"He lacked natural leadership – which, in my definition, is one who plays the game hard but has the sensitivity to approach individual players in a way that elicits the optimum performance. The great Irish captains, notably Fitzy, had the ability to get the best out of each individual player and knew how to deal with their diverse personalities on a one-to-one basis and then to press the team's collective button. Duggan knew just one way to deal with players – the way he liked to be dealt with himself. He and I are polar opposites. He thrived on being told he was useless and that if he didn't get his act together he was finished in an Irish jersey. Then he went out and played a blinder. If I was told that I had been playing poorly and was going to be written off then I was finished before I even went out on the field. If I was told how great I was I went out to show that I was even better. My game was built on confidence. I'm very sensitive. Duggan is not.

"As a player Willie Duggan was almost peerless. He was a great rugby player, the hardest I ever came across. When it came to taking punishment and laying his life on the line, only Shay Deering in my time compares with him, but as a role model and as a captain he left an awful lot to be desired.

"That year the leadership at the top was dreadful. Consequently the morale of the squad was appalling."

Ireland finished the season as they began it – with another defeat– and ended up with the wooden spoon. A rugby putsch saw Willie John deposed in favour of the more flamboyant Mick Doyle.

Church Or Chapel?

In his book, *A Patch of Glory*, Alan Richards refers to Welsh out-halves as being either High Church or Chapel. In this perspective Barry John and Gareth Davies belonged to the High Church while Cliff Morgan and Phil Bennett belonged to the Chapel.

The distinction was that the High Church type of number ten tended to play within himself exerting the minimum amount of effort to the maximum effect while the other relied much greater on physical activity. The theory was that when the intellect ruled the heart there was a more subtle, sophisticated approach. However, the "busy-busy" type need not be less effective.

In 1980 the former Welsh out-half, Carwyn James, who coached the Lions on their 1971 tour in New Zealand when they won the Test Series for the first time, applied the High Church and Chapel idea to Ward and Campbell. He argued that by nature and temperament Campbell was potentially High Church because of the sophistication of his game whereas Ward was a more direct player – influenced more by the immediacy of the surroundings, the occasion and the opposition.

His solution to the problem of two talented players for the one position was to play Campbell at out-half and Ward at full-back. His point was that full-back was the most exciting position on the field and that Phil Bennett played his best matches at full-back because coming into the threequarter line between centre and wing he had plenty of time to manoeuvre and to deploy his lethal side-steps. Such a move would not only be good for Ireland it would be good for Ward's future abilities as an out-half by helping him to discover the blind spots of the fly-half position.

The Mutual Admiration Society

On a Sunday afternoon in his Clontarf home, Ollie Campbell looks like rugby's Peter Pan. There seems not to be an ounce more on his body than in the glory days of '82 and he looks exactly the same as he used to on television all those years ago. He is the prototype of the "rugbyaholic". His passion for the game generates a force-field all of its own. His energy and vitality are evident even in his walk. Pleasantries completed, he is relaxed, gracious and attentive.

He talks about rugby with all the confidence and authority of a man universally acknowledged as a leading figure on the international stage. The irony of it all is that one suspects that he is a most unlikely and unwilling candidate for celebrity status on the grand scale; not the kind of man to have his head easily turned by adulation. He is the archetypal "reluctant star" with no time for the pretensions or arrogance that are often associated with star status. When probed he speaks in great detail about his own career, he is always willing to give great credit and praise to the other actors in the rugby cast.

Listening to him talk it is easy to feel overwhelmed by the sheer strength of his knowledge of the game. He speaks of little without betraying his love for the game, which appears to pervade every fibre of his soul. As the hours progressed I wondered if he ever steps down from this heightened plane of rugby existence to, as it were, the world of mere mortals? The question amuses him, without prompting the series of singular revelations half hoped for. He replies: "I'm nothing special." The supreme irony is that he really believes this to be the case. His eyes light up when asked about the man his name will always be associated with:

"The first time I came across and played against Tony was in a first round Senior Schools cup match in that mecca of boys' rugby, Donnybrook: St Mary's versus Belvedere in February of 1972. Little could two rather anonymous number ten's, or anyone else for that matter, realise that within seven short years the names would be forever linked.

"Heading out on the Irish tour to Australia in 1979 I was relatively anonymous but Tony was European Player of the Year. The events after I had been selected for the First Test side have been well documented. Suffice to say that life for both of us certainly changed after that.

"Having played in all four championship games in 1980, my next 'close encounter' with him was in South Africa during the summer of that year. With the First Test looming and with both out-halves, Gareth Davies and myself, out injured, a fit one was needed. Who was flown out but A.J.P. Ward. Not only did he play in the First Test but proceeded to score 18 points which was then, and remains, a Lions individual points scoring record in a Test match. Was there to be no escape from this guy?!

"The fulfilment of being on the Triple Crown winning side for me was heightened by the knowledge that I had put 'the Tony Ward issue' behind me – or so I thought.

"However, leaving Westport one beautiful morning some weeks afterwards, I picked up an oldish lady who, as it turned out, was visiting a friend in Castlebar Hospital. After our initial small talk the conversation went something like this:

Her: 'And what sports do you play? Do you play Gaelic?'

Me (As modestly as possible!): 'No, I play rugby.'

Long silence.

Her: 'Do you know there's one thing I'll never understand about rugby?'

Me (Again with all due modesty): 'What? I might be able to help.'

Short silence.

Her: 'The only thing I don't understand about rugby is why Tony Ward is not on the Irish team!'

"Since then Margaret McMenamin and I have become friends but she is still a 'Wardy fan'!

"At a more important level, Tony's career has been marked by his wonderful behaviour on the field, his sportsmanship and also his generous spirit – particularly towards myself. Our rivalry was always a purely sporting one and a healthy one at that."

Simply The Best

Now that the old saga is but a fading memory Ward can evaluate his great friend and rival from a position of some detachment:

"Where do I stand in relation to Ollie? Better? Similar? Or inferior? It's a question that has consumed rugby followers for years. First of all let me stress that I am not in any way bitter at having won only 19 caps (Ollie won 22) when no doubt the total would have been far more if it hadn't happened that I was playing in the same era as Ollie.

"I had the good fortune to play 19 times for my country, and made the Lions when so many of my friends and contemporaries never attained their ambition of winning even one cap. If you told me when I first started out as a rugby player that I would wear the green jersey 19 times, I would not have believed it.

"When I think of players like Rodney O'Donnell who had to retire from the game, I realise how fortunate I have been. Only a very few players make it to the top and I will always be grateful that I got a fair share of the limelight.

"I have no hang-up about Ollie, and no quibble with him for taking my place at out-half on the Irish team in Australia in 1979 and, in a way, ending my career to all intents and purposes as an Irish regular. Likewise, I have no hang-ups about Paul Dean. My crib is not with them. It is over the manner in which I felt I was treated when the selection was made for the First Test match in Australia. There was no feedback as to why I was dropped and the whole thing was handled in a very insensitive way.

"I feel both Ollie and myself could have been accommodated, as we were in the 1981 International Championship. The conclusion was generally drawn that the experiment was a failure. If someone can define clearly for me what 'success' or 'failure' means in that context I would be glad to know. I don't feel that those matches were a fair barometer to draw lasting conclusions.

"The reasons for the failure went deeper, and were not confined to the backs alone. At the same time, Ollie and myself were both specialist out-halves. At club level you can make the transfer from out-half to centre or vice-versa gradually; it's not as easy to step up to international level. The fact that Ollie fitted in so quickly speaks volumes about his ability.

"One of the big problems we have in Ireland is that we are extremely reluctant to try players in different positions. Whereas in New Zealand, for example, even though they have a bottomless pit of talent that is frightening, they are always trying different players in different positions. We have a much smaller pool of talent and should be trying different players in different positions. This lack of flexibility is something that really annoys me but is a real attitudinal problem in Irish rugby.

"Ollie was a more perceptive player, and thought more deeply about the game off the pitch than I did. I trained every bit as hard. But Ollie put a lot more into tactical concepts. He was marvellous at reading and analysing any given situation.

"I respond to situations much more intuitively and instinctively. Because of this, I might at times have gone too far with the ball on my own, leading to the valid criticism that I tended to run up a blind alley. But it was my style to have the instant reaction and when it worked everybody was happy and praise was heaped on my head. When it didn't, I knew what the wrath of supporters – and the media – could be like.

"Ollie Campbell is the best all-round out-half I have ever seen. He had a little bit of everything and a lot of everything necessary. He was a rounded player who had honed his game to the finest point at the peak of his career."

However, although Ward's admiration for Campbell as a player knows no bounds it pales in comparison with his respect for him as a man and as a friend. One of many incidents Ward considers to be typical of his great rival for the number ten jersey was a letter Campbell sent to him in 1989. Ollie organised a get-together for the players who had made the trip to Australia ten years earlier and wrote a letter to each player inviting them to attend the re-union. On his letter to Ward he added a little message saying that he understood that the re-union might evoke unhappy memories for Ward personally but he hoped he could make it nonetheless.

Ollie Campbell

HORTEX HOUSE,
5/7 UPPER ABBEY STREET, DUBLIN 1.

PHONE: 732500. 727922.
732356. 732478.

7th. June 1989.

Dear ____

I hope this letter finds you Healthy, Wealthy, and Wise.

As this Summer marks the 10th. Anniversary of our trip to Australia in '79 it has been decided to have an informal mixed re-union of the whole Squad, on Friday 30th. June '89.

We will be meeting in O'Donoghue's (where else!) from 6 o'clock followed by a meal in Stokers of Harcourt Street at 8.30 p.m. if we can drag ourselves away! (Rory O'Connor has indicated he will look after us like Royalty but bill us like Paupers).

Initial re-action to the idea has been very positive indeed, so to get some indication of how many will be attending, particularly for the meal, would you please let me know before the 23rd. June, if you will be able to join us or not.

If I am not available myself at any of the above numbers would you please just leave your answer with Kitty.

Please do your utmost to be there, a pleasant evening seems guaranteed.

Look forward to seeing you then.

Regards.

Yours sincerely,

Ollie.

P.S. Obviously Tony the will bring back memories of a different kind for you the we all - but I hope you can make it all the same.

PIERRE SANGAN.

7. Daylight Snobbery

"I know the major countries in the rugby world are in a mess but I felt it couldn't be as bad as that. I looked down on the that list of Lions and I thought: ' By damn. Some of those lads might have to play in a Test match.'"

This disparaging comment came from the undisputed star of the Lions' 1971 tour, Barry John, and was an attempt to justify his decision to put a bet on South Africa to win all four Test matches during the 1980 Lions' tour.

The squad he was reacting to comprised of the following players: Full-backs – Rodney O'Donnell (Ireland); Bruce Hay (Scotland); Wings – Andy Irvine (Scotland); Mike Slemen (England); John Carleton (England); Centres – Ray Gravell (Wales); David Richards (Wales); Jim Renwick (Scotland); Clive Woodward (England); Utility defender – Peter Morgan (Wales); Out-halves – Ollie Campbell (Ireland); Gareth Davies (Wales); Scrum-halves – Terry Holmes (Wales); Colin Patterson (Ireland); Props – Fran Cotton (England); Clive Williams (Wales); Graham Price (Wales); Phil Blakeway (England); Hookers – Alan Phillips (England); Peter Wheeler (England); Locks – Bill Beaumont (England); Maurice Colclough (England); Allan Martin (Wales); Alan Tomes (Scotland); Flankers – John O'Driscoll and Colm Tucker (both Ireland); Stuart Lane and Jeff Squire (both Wales); Number Eights – Derek Quinnell (Wales); John Beattie (Scotland).

A number of likely selections to the squad had declared themselves unavailable, notably Fergus Slattery, Steve Fenwick, Paul McNaughton, and Tony Neary – though Slattery and Neary had tentatively suggested that they might be available as replacements later in the tour.

Ireland's successes the previous year on the Australian tour had been a significant factor in the selection of Noel Murphy as coach of the touring Lions. In the light of his vast experience of South African rugby, which involved three Lions' tours, one of them as coach, Syd Miller was invited to manage the tour. The third member of the selection triumvirate was the English captain, William Blackledge Beaumont – not a universally popular choice as captain, but a universally popular man, which was a significant advantage. Moreover, he was known to be a conscientious guy.

Inevitably the tour attracted controversy because of the political ramifications of appearing to support apartheid. However, fortunately for the Lions, the controversy got a bit lost because of the huge furore about the morality of boycotting the Moscow Olympics after Russia's invasion of Afghanistan earlier that year.

The Casualty Ward

The composition of the side seemed to suggest a 10-man game. On a tour the difference between failure and success can be so thin you can hardly see it. In such circumstances a lot of responsibility and much of the media spotlight fell on the slim shoulders of Ollie Campbell. It was not the environment Campbell favoured.

Records and adulation meant little to the quietly-spoken fly-half, who would have rather melted into the background than be the centre of attention. A reluctant star, Campbell was far from the norm, with no time for the arrogance or pretensions associated with such a label. Off the field he tried to portray himself as an ordinary guy, on it he could not disguise his skill. Each score was executed with the minimum bother or fuss. For all his modesty he played with incredible confidence. When he kicked penalties he never looked as if the thoughts of missing had ever entered his mind. A tiny minority saw him solely as the man who had unfairly usurped Tony Ward the previous year. Such unfair criticism rankled and he was determined to put the record straight on the Lions tour.

However, hamstring problems meant he had to sit out the first two matches against Eastern Province, and a S.A.R.A. Invitation Team when the Lions won on scores of 28-16 and 28-6 respectively. In the very first match the second choice out-half, Gareth Davies, had been injured. The problem was exacerbated by the fact that Scotland's Andy Irvine had been injured and did not make the start of the tour, which meant that the Lions had no recognised place-kicker. A gamble was taken with Campbell for the third game against Natal. The Lions won 21-15 despite a below par performance, especially by the backs. Campbell kicked two penalties and a conversion. The selectors' disappointment with the Lions mediocrity on the field was more than offset by the relief that their star out-half had come through unscathed.

Their joy was short-lived. At the next training session Campbell's hamstring problem flared up again. There was only one possible course of action with just 12 days to the First Test and neither a fit out-half or place-kicker in sight – send for a replacement, particularly since the Lions would have to face, arguably, the most lethal goal-kicker the world had ever seen, Naas Botha.

There was really only one choice if the Lions were to amass the sort of points from kicks which their type of game required – Tony Ward. The problem was that Ward had not been put on hold as a standby player. He would have to extricate himself from all his business commitments. The advantage of this situation from Ward's point of view was that he was spared all the political elements of the tour before he travelled. Since nobody thought he was travelling no one had tried to persuade him not to go. He was on the plane before anybody really knew about it.

For reasons best-known to themselves the Lions' management refused to admit to the obvious and went through the ritual of saying that they had to wait to hear from the four Home Unions in London who the replacement would be. The charade continued even after the stage the Irish newspapers had declared not alone that Ward would be travelling but were able to disclose his travel arrangements.

The Irony And The Ecstasy

19 May 1980 was not a date Tony Ward would forget in a hurry, though his diary betrays none of the elation he must have felt:

> *Phone calls to Dave Mahedy from London Daily Mirror and Daily Mail. Rumour of call up to SA breaking through. Ronnie Dawson on – confirmation. Syd and Noel phoned from SA – to travel A.S.A.P.*

Nobody could have failed to appreciate the irony of the situation. It was the same three protagonists as twelve months earlier when Murphy told Ward he was out and Campbell was in. Now fate had decreed that a year later, it was Murphy who would tell Ward that he was in because Campbell was out. This time the gods had smiled favourably on Ward. Maybe they felt they owed him one.

The Accidental Tourist

One of South Africa's main newspapers, *The Rand Daily Mail* made Ward's dramatic summons to the touring party front page news, totally relegating a major political story of the day, a government decision to establish an industrial zone in Northern Transvaal, to a poor second place – a tribute to Ward's reputation but also evidence, if any were needed, of the extraordinary importance of rugby in South African society.

He did not arrive as a replacement but as an additional player. Under the regulations of the International Board a touring side was allowed to supplement its thirty players if individual players were injured. The cost of flying out supplementary players would be borne by the Four Home Unions while the tab for their stay would be picked up by the South African Rugby Board. At the time it was not clear how long Ward's stay would be. There were high hopes that Ollie Campbell would quickly regain fitness.

Having flown to London Ward boarded a flight to Jan Smuts Airport in Johannesburg. He got a pleasant surprise when he was told that the former South African captain, Jan Pickard had arranged four adjacent seats so he could stretch out and have a good sleep. He discovered that he was next to a rock and roll group called *Des Henley and the Fumbles* who were Bill Haley's backing group at the time:

"Later they arranged tickets for me to come and see Bill Haley in concert which is a lovely memory to have, to see one of the great legends of popular music."

He arrived in South Africa in reasonable physical condition having been playing an enormous amount of seven-a-side rugby, and the previous weekend helping Garryowen to finish second in a tournament in Amsterdam. It would only take him a week to get match fit. His biggest worry was that he had not practised goal-kicking for two months when he last played a hard match which Garryowen lost to Shannon in the first round of the Munster Cup. Had he been on standby he would have been practising constantly.

He has never forgotten his first few minutes in South Africa. Although his welcoming reception displayed nothing but amiable community Ward was not so duped by the camouflaged textures of the enthusiastic greeting not to risk a deeper look at the world around him:

"As I walked through customs I spotted those toilet signs, 'Black only toilets' and 'White only toilets'. At the other end I was astonished to be met by a battery of nearly 30 photographers. It was my first taste of the intensity of rugby in South Africa. But as the tour went on things just snowballed."

Ebony And Ivory

Ward candidly confesses that he had no hesitation about going to South Africa once the call came:

"I wanted to be a Lion and it was really as simple or as selfish as that. I offer no justification. I didn't even think – I simply went. However, was I in for a rude awakening? From the moment you enter the baggage area of Jan Smuts Airport in Johannesburg you are confronted by apartheid. To see this on television is akin to watching Cagney and Lacey or the Magic Roundabout. You say to yourself this can't really happen. But when the stark reality is but feet away from you, believe me it is frightening in the extreme."

However, over the next two months the experience would make a much deeper impression than he realised at the time. It was the slow dawning of an important realisation – of the type described by Thomas Kinsella:

There's no end to that which not understood
may yet be noted and hoarded in the imagination
in the yoke of one's being so to speak.

Ward was immediately 'debriefed' by Noel Murphy:

"He told me that there had been a lot of speculation in the press since my call-up was announced, to the effect that we didn't get on with each other because of what had happened in Australia the previous year. Naturally the two of us wanted to show to the world at large that there was no hostility between us. While Noel was one of the three people who dropped me we actually had no problem and we have got on better with each other with the passing of time."

Having arrived on a Friday he was selected to make his debut for the Lions the following Tuesday against the Proteas in the Dr Craven Stadium at Stellenbosch when he would renew his international partnership with Colin Patterson. It would be a big game for Ward – if he showed reasonable form despite his lack of match practice he would surely be chosen for the First Test instead of Gareth Davies, if only for his more reliable place-kicking. Ward's diary entry from the day of the game shows that he was all too aware of the high stakes:

May 27
Got up Late. Had lunch at 12.00. VERY NERVOUS. Game at 3.30. Very hot. Nervy throughout. Only kicked 3 out of 9. Got kick on Knee. Won 15-6.

Ward experienced mixed fortunes in a forgettable match. His place-kicking did not yield his normal success ratio. He succeeded with just one effort from six first-half attempts – a conversion of a John Carleton try. He kicked two penalty goals. His misses were all long range efforts apart from a kick from 30 yards. After that particular kick the Lions temporarily handed the kicking duties to centre, Clive Woodward, who had shown good form as the Lions' kicker in previous matches in the absence of Campbell and Davies. However, Woodward fluffed his kick completely and the Lions returned to Ward. He was striking the ball cleanly and getting the right distance but not with his customary radar-like precision, though none of his efforts were very far off the mark. Otherwise his line kicking and distribution were up to par and his handling was well timed.

The match provided a major scare for the Lions when the English prop, Fran Cotton, was assisted off the field with what appeared to be chest pains. Subsequently he was discovered to have suffered a minor heart attack. Inevitably his tour ended prematurely.

Ward's performance was enough to earn selection for the Test side. Almost 12 months to the day when he heard that he had been dropped from the Irish side to play in Australia in Brisbane the previous May, Ward got the news of his selection from the Lions. Fate's fickle hand had struck again.

However, Ward knew instinctively that he would have to fine-tune his place-kicking skills if he was to rise to the occasion. A feature of his place-kicking practice at the time was that Ollie Campbell always joined him despite his injury:

"Ollie could have been watching a movie or something but instead he always came and watched me training. It was something I always appreciated.

"It is an important psychological exercise for kickers to get in some practice the day before a game, particularly if you can get get on the pitch you are playing on. We were lucky on that trip because we had a great liaison officer, Choet Visser, a successful businessman from Bloemfontein. His chief concern was the welfare of all the Lions players and more than that you can't ask of anybody. He was certainly not your typical administrator and was ahead of his time in many ways. He was a rugby fanatic and had the most incredible rugby museum I have ever seen. His house was extraordinary – covered from top to bottom in rugby souvenirs. It was he who arranged the place-kicking practice for us."

However, his preparations for the game were handicapped by injury as his diary reveals:

May 28
Test Team announced. Training in Newlands at 10.30 a.m. Boiling Hot. Very tough Session. Leg Very Swollen and Sore. Went to Physio – Mrs Pilkington at 4.00 p.m.

May 29
Physio at 9.30 a.m. Training at 10.30 a.m. Could not Kick at all. Had lunch and spent evening in hotel room. Physio again at 4.00 p.m. Beginning to feel the pressure

May 30
Had late lunch then with Ollie and Phil Orr went training to Newlands. Disaster – Tore fibres in my thigh – Straight to Physio. There until 7.30 p.m. Team Meeting. No decision till the morning.

May 31
Physio at 9.30 a.m. Will have to risk injury with pain killing injection, tablets and strapping. Lunch at 12.00. Team Meeting Ground at 2.30 p.m. Treatment until 3.20 p.m. Lost 22-26.

Ward is still puzzled by such bizarre preparations for the vital confrontation in highly efficient and technical modern times:

"We started to tog out at 2.30 p.m. for the 3.30 p.m. kick-off but I spent the next 55 minutes getting cortisone injections and all sorts of treatment. I only saw the others as we were going onto the field. I had no warm-up at all. That is my most vivid memory of the game."

The crucial period in the match was the 15 minutes before half time when the Lions conceded 16 points and trailed 16-9 at half time. With his heavily bandaged right leg Ward kicked three penalties. Another 50 yard Ward penalty and a try from Graham Price levelled the scores before Ward kicked a drop goal with his left foot. The Lions' lead was short-lived with Gerry Germisheys scoring a fine try for South Africa which "Dead-eye Dick", Naas Botha, converted. However, Ward crowned a magnificent kicking performance to level the scores and in the process, set a new record, 18 points, for a Lion in a Test match – beating by one point the previous record of Tom Kiernan. With the scores tied at 22-22 a draw seemed inevitable until the little scrum-half Serfontein crossed the line for an unconverted try to give the Springboks a deserved victory – outscoring the Lions by five tries to one.

How does Ward react to the criticism after the game that he was responsible for two of the South African tries?

"Whatever about the first when a sliced diagonal kick led to a counter-attack by the Boks, there's no way I'll carry the can for the other. I kicked into the box, 75 yards from our line, and they ran it out of the defence. Poor tackling let them in for the score. I don't mind being judged by performances but it's a bit frustrating to hear people who never saw you play in a match pontificating about your alleged mistakes. I always felt sorry for Clive Woodward whom I considered the best back on the Lions tour. Woodward was accused of 'losing' the Third Test when he tapped the ball into touch and a Springbok threw it back in quickly to initiate the movement for the winning try."

John Hopkins of *The Sunday Times* said of Ward's performance: "The baggy-trousered general was simply magnificent". Despite his record score Ward was relegated to the 'Wednesday' team from then on. His next match would not be until 18 June when the Lions beat the Junior Springboks 17-6.

Four days earlier he was infuriated by the carry-on of some of the Lions' players:

"I can't stand this image of the irresponsible way rugby players behave when they are away on tour. I know Eamon Dunphy has written about this a number of times and I agree with him completely. For some reason, after the match against the Orange Free State, there was terrible messing with players throwing food about the place. I find this pre-school behaviour very hard to take. Thankfully you seldom, if ever, find that kind of carry-on in this country."

Tony The Barbarian Tamer

The King's Park, Durban, was the venue for the Lions' match with the South African Barbarians. The match was played in front of a near 40,000 crowd in a temperature in the high sixties under the dome of a cloudless blue sky. It was a rare opportunity for the peerless Argentinean, Hugo Porta, to display his mercurial talents on the big stage which his flair demanded. He grabbed the chance with both hands, creating possibilities out of the seemingly impossible. Despite the undoubted class of the inexperienced Errol Tobias, Porta was let down by those around him.

There was all-Irish pairing at half-back with John Robbie linking with Tony Ward. Both made a big impression. Robbie's passing was immaculate and although Ward kicked 13 points it was his running which was the outstanding feature of the Lions' game, regularly bringing centres, Peter Morgan and Jim Renwick and full-back, Andy Irvine into the action. The match was the first on the tour without any sign of tension with both sides determined to make it a running spectacle.

The Lions led by 19-6 at half-time courtesy of tries from Andy Irvine and Gareth Williams, three Ward penalty goals and a conversion of Williams' try. The Lions' only score in the second half was a try from Ward, following a good pass from Robbie, he swerved his way past a couple of defenders to breach the line for a try which he duly converted from out on the right. The Lions eventually won 25-14.

Ward's 17 points, particularly his brilliant try, seemed to tilt the balance in his favour for the outside-half berth for the Final Test, but as if to show that anything Ward could do he could do better, Campbell ran up 22 points a few days later, against Western Province to clinch the spot.

Near Fatal Distraction

The background to the game had been less than ideal for Ward. The previous day he had been relaxing with the Lions' players at the Umhalnga Rocks Indian Ocean resort north of Durban. He went for a swim but was washed out to the sea by the Northern Natal Coast Undercurrent. He had to be rescued by a lifeguard and was absolutely exhausted when he was dragged from the sea:

"It was the most frightening experience I ever had. I really thought I was going to drown. I am a poor swimmer but the undertow was very strong and carried me out and I was literally out of my depth. I started shouting and John O'Driscoll, who was a very strong swimmer, and the lifeguard rescued me.

"It was very funny to talk about afterwards and I got the nickname 'Flipper' but I can assure you it was anything but funny at the time."

However, there was good news to come that day, when Rodney O'Donnell rejoined the touring party at the team hotel after two weeks in intensive care. A fortnight earlier the "luck of the Irish" had turned badly sour in the match against the Junior Springboks when O'Donnell was seriously injured. Although he walked off the field, when he was examined in hospital it was discovered that he had dislocated his neck between the sixth and seventh vertebrae and that he had come within a fraction of an inch of being paralysed for life:

"Thanks to John O'Driscoll who was on hand, Rodney's neck was saved, perhaps from permanent paralysis. John is a great doctor and a lovely guy. The only problem was when he took a few drinks his personality changed completely – hence the nickname – 'O'Desperate' even though he's a consummate gentleman."

Ward's last game with the Lions was against Griquland West in the penultimate game of the tour when the Lions won 23-19 with Ward contributing a conversion and a penalty.

These Miss You Nights Are The Longest

As was the case with the Australian tour the previous year, from Ward's diary of the Lions' tour one can clearly hear two voices: that of a man struggling with the joys and tribulations of touring life and that of a man revitalised after phone calls from his wife and mother. Letters from friends also made a big difference to his morale.

At times Ward's diary from the tour reads like something written by Barry Norman. The touring party seemed to have seen a huge amount of films. Broadly speaking they seemed to fit into three categories: the good, the bad and the brutal.

One of the strangest aspects of the tour was the role of Steve Smith, the English scrum-half. Originally 30 players had been chosen for the 1980 tour. Altogether 38 eventually took part though the squad was reduced to 29 in the final days and the Lions were forced to send for Smith to sit on the replacements bench for the Final Test following a very serious injury to Colin Patterson which suggested that he might never play rugby again. Smith only trained once with the Lions but he was officially a fully qualified Lion and received his full regalia of Lions' blazer and playing kit – becoming the first player to be chosen as a British Lion and never to play one second of a game. It was the final chapter in a litany of injuries on the tour which began as early as the first minute of the opening match when the Welsh flanker, Stuart Lane, twisted his knee and was forced to withdraw from the tour. The pattern was set for an unprecedented series of injuries for a touring side.

While the Lions' forwards had acquitted themselves well on the tour, with enhanced reputations, a telling statistic was that Mike Slemen was the highest try scorer for the Lions with five tries and he had retired home shortly after the First Test when his wife, who was pregnant at the time, had been taken to hospital. This tally contrasted unfavourably with Tom Grace's achievement of 13 tries on the previous tour in 1974 – despite his failure to make the Test side. Moreover, it looked derisory when compared with Tony O'Reilly's total of 16 tries in South Africa in 1955 or his 22 in New Zealand/ Australia in 1959. The backs, particularly in the threequarter line, appeared to lack the requisite levels of skill and flair. Team captain, Bill Beaumont, pulled no punches in his assessment of the Lions' results:

"Ask any successful Football League team. Ask Brian Clough. Ask Bob Paisley. They will tell you that the game starts with defence, and ours just hasn't been good enough."

The Lions played 18, won 15, lost 3, scoring 401 points and conceding 244. The points were made up of 47 tries, 27 conversions, 45 penalty goals and 12 drop goals. The highest scorers were Ollie Campbell with 60 points (from 7 appearances and one substitute), Clive Woodward 53 points (from 11 appearances and 2 substitutes) and Tony Ward with 48 points (from 5 appearances) – an average of 8.4, 4.8, and 9.6 points per match respectively.

The Test match results were as follows:

One: South Africa 26, Lions 22 (Cape Town, Saturday, 31 May, 1980).
Scorers:
South Africa – Tries: Louw, W. du Plessis, van Heerden, Germishuys, Serfontein. Conversions: Botha (3).
Lions – Try: Price. Penalty goals: Ward (5). Drop goal: Ward.

Two: South Africa 26, Lions 19 (Bloemfontein, June 14).
Scorers:
South Africa – Tries: Louw, Stofberg, Germishuys, Pienaar. Conversions: Botha (2). Penalty goals: Botha (2)
Lions – Tries: O'Driscoll, Gravell. Conversions: Davies. Penalty goals: Davies (2), Irvine.

Three: South Africa 12, Lions 10 (Port Elizabeth, June 28)
Scorers:
South Africa – Try: Germishuys. Conversions: Botha. Penalty goals: Botha. Drop goal: Botha
Lions: Try: Hay. Pen: Campbell (2).

Four: South Africa 13, Lions 17 (Pretoria, July 12).
Scorers:
South Africa – Try: W. du Plessis. Pen: Botha, Pienaar (2).
Lions – Tries: Williams, Irvine, O'Driscoll. Conversions: Campbell. Penalty: Campbell.

Although Ward only played in the First Test he had a big scare in the Third Test in Port Elizabeth when he was a sub. As always he had prepared meticulously for the match and had his gear and boots in perfect order. To his horror he discovered in the dressing room that he had forgotten his boots. It was too late to retrieve them from the team hotel. His problem was exacerbated by the fact that nobody had a spare pair of boots to lend him. He consoled himself with the thought that he probably wouldn't need them.

The seating arrangements for the subs that day were bizarre to say the least. They were to sit on the very top row of the stadium. As the match began Ward was making the long journey up countless flights of stairs with John Robbie, continually being passed out by frantic latecomers to see the match, when he heard somebody shouting for him. Ward chills visibly at the memory:

"What had happened was that Ollie Campbell had been injured in the very first minute of the match and they wanted me to go on for him. It was panic stations all round. In his eagerness to help me John Robbie got a pair of boots from a ball boy for me to wear. At size nine they were too big for me but an even more serious problem was that the studs were moulded. The pitch was waterlogged that day and even if they had been the right size they would have been a disaster in the conditions but they were all I had at the time. As I stood at the sideline I could see that Ollie was covered in blood. It was the most frightening experience I ever had in rugby – all my worst nightmares rolled into one. Fortunately, Ollie was able to play on but I never want to have to go through an experience like that again.

"On a more positive note one very happy memory I have of the trip occurred on the 9 June when the Lions went on a procession through Pretoria. We arrived at 11.30 a.m. and from about noon there was a welcoming procession to take us on to the city hall. We travelled in open-decked vintage cars, two Lions in each car. There were dancing girls, and bands and there were seemingly hundreds of thousands of people lining the streets. I've never come across anything like it. It was beyond belief, the real highlight of the tour for each of us – not so much like winning the World Cup as winning a World War. That day will stay in our minds forever. It was nothing short of incredible.

"Another sweet memory was the flight home from South Africa to London. Colin Patterson had sustained a bad injury on the tour which effectively ended his career. He was seated at the very front of the plane with his leg in plaster to give him all the room he needed. I sat with him. We were joined by Dave Sexton, Steve Heighway and Viv Anderson who had been over to give a soccer clinic, as well as by Phil Bennett, Barry John and Steve Smith. We had an extraordinary conversation or debate about the vexed question of coaching versus flair. Steve Heighway and Dave Sexton were stressing the coaching side of things while Barry John was stressing flair. Barry's famous comment in his playing days when he formed perhaps the greatest half-back pairing of all time with Gareth Edwards was: 'You throw it Gar, I'll catch it.' In otherwards, he would have the skill to cope with any ball. I liked Phil Bennett's approach best of all. He was very much in favour of coaching techniques but not at the expense of skill.

"The one thing I was not prepared for though when I got home was how big a downer it was to return to normal living. After the hype and excitement, not to mention the five-star hotels and red-carpet treatment, you certainly have to come down to earth with a bang when you go back to work."

A Tale Of Two Countries

Although rugby preoccupied Ward's attention, he was not immune to the socio-political environment. His first glimpse of how many of South Africa's blacks live was gleaned from a visit with Colin Patterson and some friends to a black township outside Bloemfontein. It left a powerful legacy:

"We drove around slowly in the car with Colin snapping off pictures from the back seat. We were afraid even to stop and get out. I found it absolutely horrific. The shacks were made of tin, there seemed to be thousands upon thousands of them. If they had toilets it was just a barrel at the back, and one thing that struck me was the number of cars they had – old bangers, mind you. I understand under law they couldn't buy their houses so they bought these cars instead. It was a real horror story. I was sickened."

His mind is a theatre of memories of the trip – the memory bank of his instincts have displaced the casual paraphenalia of rugby statistics to their rightful place. At a later stage in the tour, Ward and a group of players and journalists tried to visit the New Brighton black township close to Port Elizabeth. The authorities had been gravely upset by the reporting on other townships earlier in the tour. They decided to make a preemptive strike in Port Elizabeth because there was a huge international press corps in attendance for the Third Test. All 11 entrances to the township were sealed off by armed police with a convoy of land-rovers. Ward shakes his head at the memory of the closet of secrecy. His peculiarly intense gaze, tinged with grief, suggests he is still clearly angered by the deception:

"We were warned off and told that there was rioting going on. Quite clearly the place was totally quiet. We could see right down into it."

All the Lions' players were puzzled by the attitude of the blacks to them:

"They all wanted us to win. We all found this quite extraordinary. After all they were South Africans too. Yet everywhere we went we met blacks who told us, 'Go man, beat the Boks'."

The energy cell of his personality was quite clearly singed by his own perceptions of their serfdom – at once in sympathy with those in suffering he is ruthlessly objective in his critique of the system which makes them suffer.

The agonising tyranny of the plight of the majority struck him forcefully on a visit to the paradisal world of a golf course in Bloemfontein on an excursion with John Robbie, Paul Dodge and Clive Woodward. There, the diet of half-formed truths which he had been fed about the advances in racial integration vanished into thin air. The riches of the imagination had caused him to hope for the best but after that day he could never be naïve again because the deliberately detached distance between the rugby players and the reality of the unjust society around them was painfully breached:

"On the course we were surrounded by about 30 black youngsters – about late teens and all literally dressed in rags. They wanted to caddy for us. 'Masta . . . Masta' they called me. This was the bit I could never take – people calling me master. We selected two kids at random and I took them aside and said this is John and Paul and I am Tony, but after that they didn't call us anything at all. It really confused them.

"They explained that they were allowed to play golf only on a Monday morning and had to pay handsomely for the privilege. The cost was way beyond the two Rand they received for the average two or three-hour caddy. Tipping was forbidden but we left them thinking they were millionaires. But all these little inequalities, they were simply everywhere."

Ward was involved in two incidents where poisonous hatred was shown towards them by the natives. The first was at Capetown University, when he and Ollie Campbell went for some kicking practice, a large crowd of blacks gathered and began a barrage of abuse. They called them racists, and in no uncertain terms told them to go back to their homes. Their practice had to be abandoned.

A bizzare incident, which to this day still puzzles him, occurred in the team's hotel lobby when a white soccer team who were also staying in the hotel booed and jeered at them, taunting them with chants of 'racists'. The incident, all the more powerful for its stunning simplicity which sums up the treatment of blacks for Ward, occurred in the hotel lift:

"A group of us were coming down for breakfast. A black chambermaid entered the lift laden down with a tray of glasses. Seeing her the manager roared at her to get out and walk down. We were all deeply affected."

Another disquieting experience for Ward was visiting a school with Clive Woodward and Billy Beaumont:
"What particularly distressed me was their chilling assembly song. It was sung in Afrikaans and I found it to be very intimidating especially as it was pumped out with gusto. Obviously I didn't understand the words but I vividly recall the effect it had on me. I can still hear the voices now and it inspired nothing in me but terror."

It was a highly stratified, paternalistic society without even a notion of *noblesse oblige*. It seemed that the lot of the blacks was to live frugally on the crumbs from the whites' tables. The badly faded memory of two lines he had learned in school from a poem by Yeats came to Ward as he saw the living conditions which black people existed in.

For the world is more full of weeping
than you can understand.

Hard Times

Without a shadow of a doubt the most formative influence on Ward's subsequent attitude to tours in South Africa occurred when he, Bill Beaumont and some other players went to visit the Watson brothers. Both Cheeky Watson and one of his brothers, who lived in Port Elizabeth, had decided some years previously to play rugby with a non-racial team in the New Brighton township rather than to continue to play with a whites-only club. 'Cheeky' was a top class rugby player and had even won a Springboks' trial.

"They were both renounced by their white friends because they were playing with a black club. Cheeky's marriage broke up. He's been arrested numerous times for breaking the law by entering the black township without a permit. They explained in great depth the set-up in South African rugby and they told us in unequivocal terms that we shouldn't have come at all. Looking back now I guess that afternoon was in many ways a unique occasion, a debate about South African rugby among rugby players.

"They made no bones about the damage we were doing just by being there at all and I remember that this seemed to have a strong effect on Bill Beaumont. As Lions' captain he was of course in a difficult position but as we drove back in the car I spoke to him about it and he seemed both deeply impressed and depressed at what he had heard."

Their final impression of the visit to the Watsons was of a shaft of light illuminating the monstrous barbarism of apartheid – two noble natures stoically enduring the exclusion they had to suffer for standing up for their principles. Preserving that cherished image remains important to Ward.

As the Lions' tour progressed the players became more sensitive to the racial mix that was going on all around them – the factional and racial closenesses and distances which is the reality of South Africa. However, events approached boiling point after the game against Transvaal in Johannesburg:

"We noticed that among the huge crowd of approximately one thousand people there was not one black to be seen. Then for some strange reason we were refused entry into the members-only bar at the Springboks' ground. To add insult to injury, in his after-dinner speech the local dignitary cracked a most inappropriate joke. Its punchline had to do with a coloured television. I can't remember the actual joke but it was clearly a racist one and all the Lions in the room felt very uneasy."

If Ward ever needed further demystification and dismantling of the idealising message he had been given about the position of blacks in South Africa and of the dangerous Messianic arrogance of some whites it was provided by an acutely suggestive discussion with a number of wealthy women after the Second Test match in Bloemfontein:

"This was a real eye-opener for me in terms of the attitudes of whites to blacks. The women talked about the black problem and boasted about the number of servants they had. The way they were talking about them you would think these people were the scum of the earth. They really believed this but I couldn't figure where this attitude came from. It just sickened me."

Crime Without Punishment

The best analogy Ward can find for the Lions' 1980 tour is a war:

"The pressure from the Afrikaners to beat us was enormous. The midweek teams were loaded with quality players which meant no easy matches.

"The day they had won the Test Series I remember in the papers, 'SPRINGBOKS – WORLD CHAMPIONS.' There was an awful lot more than rugby at stake in that tour, for the South Africans."

One of Ward's fondest memories of the tour was of a friendship he formed with one of the most exciting talents in South Africa, Errol Tobias:

"I suppose because we were both out-halves we developed a special bond. He told me that he owed everything he had to rugby. He could become the first black player to play for the Springboks. But he had his feelings too and when we were talking together he was always very careful in case anybody was listening. I knew he wanted to speak his mind but couldn't."

On the final visit to Capetown, Ward was one of a number of players brought to visit a children's hospital by former Irish scrum-half, Dr Roger Young. It was a harrowing experience to see so many seriously disabled children but for Ward what compounded their tragedy was that even in the wards there was segregation between whites, blacks and coloureds.

"It was a hospital similar to Harcourt Street or Our Lady's, Crumlin, full of sick children. Some very serious, some not so serious yet within that children's hospital there was the black children's wing and that for the whites. It was unbelievable. I found it the saddest sight I had ever seen. For me that was as much as I could take and the sad feeling of that moment will stay with me forever."

Ward's most treasured moment from that tour was a card presented to him by a girl on that visit to the hospital. The girl wrote the card using her mouth because her arms had been amputated.

When Conscience Does Not Make Cowards Of Us All

With an Irish tour to South Africa in the offing for the following summer, Ward decided on the day he returned from the Lions' tour that he would not travel. It was a clear-cut ethical decision though it did cause him to revise his expressed beliefs in his college years:

"When I left South Africa in June of that year, I did so, certainly enriched for my rugby experiences, certainly content to have achieved the personal honour of Lions' status, but overall I was deflated and deeply hurt by what I had seen, heard and experienced.

"So when 12 months later, Ireland were to tour South Africa I had no decision to make. My mind – no, my conscience – said: 'No – never again'.

"I remember when I was in college, I did a paper arguing that sport and politics don't mix. But really when you boil it down, by representing your country you are playing for a political entity for starters."

Towards the end of January 1981, 44 Irish rugby players were written to by the IRFU, requesting that they indicate to them if they would be available for the Irish short tour of South Africa in May-June. The letters went out amidst a welter of controversy as political, clerical and media people objected to the notion of Ireland having sporting contact with South Africa. Six Irish players declared themselves unavailable immediately. On foot of a tour of South Africa with London-Irish in 1977, Donal Spring went on television to explain why he would not be travelling. Moss Keane, like Ward in a more low key way declined to travel on 'a point of principle'. Business commitments ruled out Paul McNaughton and Mick Fitzpatrick. Ciaran Fitzgerald, then an army captain, had been informed by his superiors that he would be refused permission to travel.

In South Africa, rugby offered a consolidating factor, a means of bearing and informing the central values of white society. It was, at the time, a conservative force, in the true sense of the term, a keeper of the old, a continuer and a cohesive element. Rugby has been the tuning fork which the white majority strikes in order to conduct the whole orchestra of supremacy:

"I had no doubt whatsoever that politics and sport were one and the same in South Africa. To my mind rugby was used as a political weapon and that is why I refused to go on the tour. My view was that rugby was so important to the Afrikaaner that if we refused to tour he would be forced to confront the question: 'Why is this happening'?

"I felt I owed something to those black players in South Africa. I love the game and feel that everyone must have the opportunity, at the very least, to develop their own game to the best of their ability. The South Africans were arguing that the blacks were not good enough to play at all levels, but that was a catch 22 situation. How can they be good enough if they are not given an equal opportunity. And responsibility lies on the shoulders of all rugby players to ensure that it comes about.

"When I played a game anywhere else in the world we all went for a drink afterwards. If I played a game with a black in South Africa that was not possible. I could go to the bar and he would have to go home to his township. That is neither rugby nor sport and most of all it's certainly not right or moral."

In later years the former leader of the Labour Party in Britain, Neil Kinnock, himself a keen rugby enthusiast would cite this comment from Ward as a refutation that South Africa had got its integration policies right.

Ends And Means

Although Ward has no quibble with the players who did travel, he retains a special admiration for one emerging player at the time:

"My decision was my own personal one and I respect the rights of others to make up their own minds. However, I must say that the bravest decision of all was taken by Hugo MacNeill who was just establishing his place at the time. It was remarkable moral courage for an emerging star to turn down his first overseas tour with his country.

"I refused to go to South Africa on three subsequent occasions, the most recent one being 1987, just after the World Cup, when Jim Glennon and I were invited by Sir Arthur Jennings, to tour South Africa with a South Sea Barbarians Fifteen comprising mainly Fijians."

Although Ward is happy to stand over his decisions he does have misgivings about aspects of the campaigns which were waged at the time:

"I was picked for a match to mark the centenary of the Welsh Rugby Union when a Home Countries XV played a World XV. The anti-apartheid lobby put pressure on me not to play in the game because there were a number of South Africans playing as individuals. I was afraid of being considered a hypocrite and acceded to their request but I remember thinking at the time that they had overstepped the mark on this occasion.

"I remember in 1981 a lot of politicians jumped on the bandwagon and there was huge pressure put on players not to go. One incident remains stuck in my mind. I was flying over that year with Dave Mahedy for the FA Cup final between Spurs and Manchester City and I met Ginger McLoughlin on the plane. He was not wearing official gear, just 'civvies'. That was sad. As soon as the tour commenced many of the politicians who had been so vociferous went back into the woodwork when there was no more cheap publicity for them. The Irish players were forced to sneak out of their own country. We were acting like the regime we were objecting to. These players had the freedom to make up their own mind one way or another but yet Ginger was leaving the country in such a furtive way.

"People are fully entitled to make their own decisions. If we are the democracy we are supposed to be, we should allow people make use of their decision-making faculties.

"As the years went on, having seen the changes made in South Africa my views have changed. I have learned since that a total break down in communications is not the answer.

"I remember one private chat I had with Noel Murphy at a meal one evening and I told him how disturbed I was about some of the things I had seen. Noisy wasn't trying to play it down but he told me that although things were still very bad for the blacks they had nonetheless improved significantly from the first time he had toured there in '68. I, though, had no prior frame of reference to judge it by."

He has no illusions or delusions about the importance of his decision:

"Not for one moment did I believe that by me, Tony Ward, not going to South Africa to play rugby, would the system crumble. It was purely that my conscience dictated it and did the three times I was invited back subsequently. However, I did believe in 1981 that by depriving the South Africans of their international rugby it would enforce change.

"Unfortunately this was a most naïve and mistaken belief. And I must further add that I do see much merit in the theory of bridge building leading to gradual change. I do not believe that rugby should be the whipping boy for other sports and rugby owes athletics nothing! That was one particular argument that really vexed me down through the years – when athletes complained about 'selfish' rugby players who might deny them the right to compete in the Olympics because of tours to South Africa.

"South Africa was a great place to tour from a number of points of view – the rugby is so hard, the pitches are perfect, the quality of stadia and training facilities are fantastic and there is so much beauty in the country. I certainly have visited no more beautiful city than Capetown, and Durban would not have been far behind it. Turning down an invitation to tour there was not easy particularly in 1981 when I was turning my back on two possible caps.

"However, when all is said and done, for me it came down to the fundamental issue as to what do those most sinned against want. How could we best help those deprived of the most basic human rights – by this vile system? They told us not to come, that said it all for me, it was, to coin a phrase, the bottom line."

If Only

Ward retains a huge file of correspondence from the Irish anti-apartheid movement as well as more personal letters from its chairman, Kadar Asmal (complete with a number of insightful comments on the topical issues of the day) – initially urging him to refuse in advance, any invitation for selection for the tour which would: ". . . provide a life-line to racialist sport in South Africa." After the tour came a further series of letters complimenting him on his principled decision to boycott the tour. Following a lengthy interview he gave to *The Sunday Tribune* on his reasons for boycotting the tour he received a flood of correspondence complimenting him for taking a stand against apartheid.

Despite the public response, he remained unsure if his decision made the slightest difference or not. Two little incidents years later gave him food for thought:

"I was introduced one night to Olivia O'Leary. Apparently she is known for her lack of interest in sport. She was asked if she knew me or not. She said: 'I know nothing about sport but one sports personality I do know is Tony Ward because he refused to go on tour to South Africa.' The other episode occurred in 1985 when I was presented with an award for being the first N.C.E.A. graduate to play for Ireland. The award was presented to me by the former Government Minister, Justin Keating. He told me he knew little about sport but he admired me because I had declined to tour South Africa."

Along with Donal Spring, Hugo MacNeill and Moss Keane, Ward was awarded Honorary Life Membership of Brunel University Students' Union in England.

As a result of his stand against apartheid in 1982 Ward received a telegram from the UN headquarters in New York inviting him to speak at a special conference on sport in South Africa.

It is indicative of the pace of Ward's life at the time that he put the telegram away and forgot about it. He was getting such a continuous volume of requests for appearances, signed photographs and jerseys that he barely noticed it at the time. It was years later that he came across it again when the pace of his life had slowed down. Only then did he appreciate the magnitude of the honour that had been given him and the opportunity he had lost.

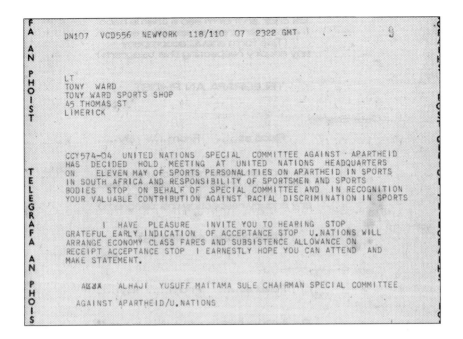

On the left margin, reading vertically: FAAN PHOTOIST — TELEGRAFA — AANPHOIS

```
DN107  VCD556  NEWYORK  118/110  07  2322 GMT

LT
TONY WARD
TONY WARD SPORTS SHOP
45 THOMAS ST
LIMERICK


CCY574-04 UNITED NATIONS SPECIAL COMMITTEE AGAINST APARTHEID
HAS DECIDED HOLD MEETING AT UNITED NATIONS HEADQUARTERS
ON    ELEVEN MAY OF SPORTS PERSONALITIES ON APARTHEID IN SPORTS
IN SOUTH AFRICA AND RESPONSIBILITY OF SPORTSMEN AND SPORTS
BODIES STOP ON BEHALF OF SPECIAL COMMITTEE AND IN RECOGNITION
YOUR VALUABLE CONTRIBUTION AGAINST RACIAL DISCRIMINATION IN SPORTS

        I HAVE PLEASURE  INVITE YOU TO HEARING  STOP
GRATEFUL EARLY INDICATION OF ACCEPTANCE STOP  U.NATIONS WILL
ARRANGE ECONOMY CLASS FARES AND SUBSISTENCE ALLOWANCE ON
RECEIPT ACCEPTANCE STOP  I EARNESTLY HOPE YOU CAN ATTEND  AND
MAKE STATEMENT.

    AAAA  ALHAJI  YUSUFF MAITAMA SULE CHAIRMAN SPECIAL COMMITTEE
AGAINST APARTHEID/U.NATIONS
```

Cry Freedom

In 1990 Ward was rewarded for his principled opposition to touring in South Africa when he was invited with fellow former internationals to a special meeting with Nelson Mandela during his visit to receive the freedom of the city of Dublin. Mandela wanted to thank them personally for their courageous stand. It was an honour which touched Ward as much, if not more, than many he had received as a player:

"It was a great thrill to be able to meet him. I had been really impressed a few months earlier with the spontaneous reaction of all those present at the Mandela concert in Wembley. I don't know how long the standing ovation went on for, but it was touching and terrific, it was fantastic.

"He's been so mythical in many ways, a fictional character who doesn't exist. We had all heard about this man who has been locked away for 26 years, and then suddenly he appears. I met him and his then wife, Winnie, with Donal Spring and the Dunnes Stores' workers when he received the freedom of Dublin in 1990. He just shook hands and thanked us. It is a memory I will always treasure.

"I've been thinking about my tour to South Africa recently, following an article by John Robbie in the October '93 issue of *Rugby World* magazine. John resigned his job with Guinness on a point of principle when he was refused permission by the company to travel on that Ireland tour in 1981 and subsequently he emigrated to South Africa. Twelve years on he wrote:

'Isn't it the supreme irony that during the obscene days of apartheid rule, rugby supported South Africa? Ireland came in 1981 and England in '84. Both decisions were misguided, damaging and potentially disastrous for players, fans and ordinary people alike. Many of us realise that now and will forever have to carry the shame of participation.'"

8. Elation Once Again

The ultimate measure of a man is not where he stands in moments of comfort and convenience, but where he stands at times of challenge and controversy.

Martin Luther King

After Ireland's whitewashing in the international championship in 1984, team manager, Willie John McBride, was deposed after just one season in an unprecedented move. Tragically, Ollie Campbell was forced to retire from representative rugby. Campbell's tragedy would surely be Ward's opportunity. The popular expectation was that Ward would logically fit straight into Campbell's shoes, particularly as he was the only kicker in Campbell's class. The man who would make the decision about Ward's future was McBride's successor, Mick Doyle, awarded the job on foot of his achievements as coach to Leinster.

Condemned Without Trial

Ireland's first match under Doyle was against Australia. It was a match Ward hoped to use as a platform to win back and secure his old place on the Irish team. It was not to be.

Ward felt that it was a straight contest between himself and Mick Quinn to replace Ollie Campbell. The issue would be decided on interprovincial displays the weekend before the Australia match. On the Saturday, Leinster lost badly to Ulster which seemed ominous for Mick Quinn. Meanwhile on the Sunday, Ward, despite not having one of his better games, helped to secure a victory for Munster in Limerick. The team would be announced the following day. He was not in as strong a position as he would have wished but he felt he was holding the aces.

Ward stayed overnight in Limerick to see Garryowen play Young Munster the following day. It was a bank holiday Monday. On his way home he tuned in eagerly to hear the teatime Sports Report like nervous students collecting their Leaving Cert results. The opening announcement was the last thing he wanted to hear:

Good evening. There's no place for Tony Ward in Ireland's rugby team to play Australia. Ward has been replaced by club-mate Paul Dean.

On this occasion it was a long way from Limerick:

"The team had been announced at lunch-time but I had not heard anything about it. The one thing I had noticed after the match was that a lot of people were congratulating Willie Sexton who had been selected for his first cap. That should have told me something. I had watched the match from the 'Popular' side of Thomond Park but nobody said anything to me about the team selection – presumably out of embarrassment."

In Australia in 1979 he had known the loneliness of a crowded room. In 1984 he was to experience the numbing loneliness of the long-distance driver. This time though he was better able for it. It was a severe blow but the world had not collapsed around his shoulders. Older and wiser, he was better able to cope with the disappointment.

It was important that he should feel wounded – otherwise he had no chance of summoning up the courage to pick up the pieces again. Five years later Martina Navratilova would articulate a sentiment that is at the very heart of successful sporting personalities' make-up: "Losing still hurts, but that's good. When it stops hurting, that's when I stop playing."

Paul Dean was chosen at out-half and in the absence of a specialist kicker, Moss Finn, was given the place-kicking duties, though Michael Kiernan took over from him during the match itself. Ciaran Fitzgerald was recalled as captain. Four new caps were selected: Michael Bradley at scrum-half, Willie Anderson in the second row and Philip Matthews and Willie Sexton on the flanks. No less than nine changes were made from the last Irish side to play an international game – against Scotland the previous March.

One of the many colourful phrases which Mick Doyle has contributed to future research students of the linguistics of rugby speak was the colourful: "The age of Biggles is dead" – an apparent reference, or so Ward thought at the time, to the fact that with the retirement of Ollie Campbell and Ward's fall from grace there would be no more superstars in Irish rugby. The phrase rankled with Ward as much for the apparent slur on Campbell's contribution as any reflection on himself:

"In a recent conversation with Doyler I asked him for the first time what he meant by that phrase. He explained that with his game plan for the Irish side the out-half would be just one player among all the rest. The team would not be built around him. Instead his job would be much more about bringing the other backs into the game than had been the case in previous years. Knowing Mick's philosophy of the game I appreciate the point he was making. If only I had known then that the last thing he intended was to hurt Ollie or me."

The game ended in an Irish defeat and left a lot of unanswered questions. Although Dean moved the ball well, was his tactical kicking, and in particular his line kicking, up to the required standard? Could Ireland really afford to go into the Championship without a recognised penalty taker in the belief that they would win matches by scoring tries alone? What changes would be made to bolster the pack, particularly in the back row? The selection of the teams for the Final Trial was eagerly awaited to get an idea as to the way the selectors were thinking.

When the teams were announced one thing was crystal clear – the selectors did not want Tony Ward. Not alone was he omitted from the two teams – Paul Dean and Ralph Keyes were chosen instead – he was not even listed among the substitutes, where Mick Quinn and Ian Burns were chosen as the replacement out-halves. The implication was that Ward was not even Ireland's fourth choice at out-half at best. The words of the late Carwyn James seemed even more appropriate than normal: "Ward should have been born a Welsh man."

The Australian captain, Andrew Slack, who led his side to a clean sweep in all four Test matches commented: "I cannot understand the Irish attitude to Ward. With Ollie Campbell out of action I would have thought that he was the obvious choice for out-half. Certainly, he did well for Munster against us. I know there has been criticism that he tends to run across the field and this sometimes tends to be the case but there are too many positive elements in Ward's game to dwell on that."

Deano

Having lived in Ollie Campbell's shadow for so long it seemed that Ward was going to come out on the losing side in another saga: 'Wardy and Deano'. Ward himself has great respect for his other great rival's abilities:

"An injury I sustained in a Leinster League game on a dark autumn afternoon in 1984 opened the way for Paul Dean to become Ireland's out-half after Ollie's retirement, displacing me in the process.

"Mary's were playing Monkstown in Sydney Parade. I was to travel to Cork that night to play for an Irish selection against a Highfield selection in an exhibition match the next day. The injury meant that I had to ring Mick Cuddy in the Imperial Hotel and tell him I was out – but that Deano was ready to travel in my place.

"So Paul Dean played out-half to Mick Bradley and the rest of the back-line comprised Brendan Mullin and Michael Kiernan in the centre, Trevor Ringland and Keith Crossan on the wings and Hugo MacNeill at full-back. They went to town against the Highfield selection, inspired by the brilliance of Dean, a back-line that was to help subsequently to win the Triple Crown and win it in style.

"Both my working life and my playing career overlapped with Dean's progression from exceptional brilliance as a schools player to wearing the green jersey at international level.

"When he was in sixth year in St Mary's College, I was on the staff. And when John Moloney and myself – the St Mary's club partnership – were the half-back pairing for Ireland, Philip McDonnell and Paul Dean formed the half-back combination on the Irish Schools international team. In fact Deano had the distinction of being a schools international both in fifth year and in sixth year.

"When I returned to St Mary's from Garryowen, the problem arose as to which of us would play at out-half. We talked it over and Paul agreed to switch to first centre. Ironically I think it helped his game immensely that he played first centre to me at this time.

"By that I mean I had a particular fault in my game – namely the tendency to drift across the pitch once I took a pass from the scrum-half. But Paul was the best player I have known to straighten a line. He was able to run incredibly straight. It came so naturally to him.

"I know that once he moved to out-half and made the number 10 shirt his own, the general consensus was that he was much more effective at stand-off than in the centre. But I am convinced that he was a better inside centre than out-half. If he could have been first centre to himself at out-half, he would have been sheer dynamite.

"Deano was a beautifully-balanced runner with an outstanding hip movement which he used to great effect in beating the opposition. He created space for those outside him. But he needed space to produce the full array of his talents as a runner.

"My team of the eighties would have Ollie at out-half with Deano as first centre and I would bank on the qualities of both of these together against any opposition.

"Deano had magnificent hands. You rarely, if ever, saw him dropping a pass. He was also an exceptionally good tackler. If he had a weakness it was in matching as a tactical kicker the other supreme qualities of his play. There were times, of course, when he got in great kicks, but it was for the lack of consistency in this aspect of his game that he was justifiably faulted. But then even the greatest players have faults. It is difficult to combine all the attributes that go to make up an ideal player. Paul Dean came near to it."

In support of Dean's selection he took attention off his centres more effectively than Ward, his back-line alignment and speed of delivery were superior to Ward. However, Ward's most vocal critics claimed that the reason he was dropped from the side was that he was a selfish player. This suggestion is completely dismissed by Ward himself:

"I have never in my life gone out to play a game of rugby thinking primarily about myself, and if I was going to make a few breaks on a particular day or whatever. I played the game as it arose. I think the biggest asset I always had as a rugby player was my own unpredictability, in the sense that I never knew what I was going to do myself. I didn't. And therefore the opposition couldn't have known either, and no, neither did my teammates. But I think if you weighed it up over the years it worked out on the plus side by and large."

Should I Stay Or Should I Go?

Principally for personal reasons, the end of '84, beginning of '85 was the low point of Ward's life. His self-confidence was drained and he was profoundly unhappy. He knew he had to take drastic measures to turn his life around before it was too late. He now sees 1985 as the crucial turning point in his life.

"I remember sitting down one night on my own that spring and thinking about where I was going with my life. My worst nightmare had come through when my marriage failed. It was, perhaps, the real crossroads in my life. I made three big decisions that year. I was going to change my job, change the physical layout of my house and I had already changed my rugby club. The shops were going well at the time but I decided I needed to move out and make a new circle of friends. When I lived in Limerick I had spent a lot of time coaching kids in St Munchin's and Glenstal and when I moved back to Dublin in '82 I was involved in a coaching capacity with St Gerard's in Bray. By pure fluke about two weeks later in early May, I happened to read *The Irish Times* one Saturday, and saw a job advertised for a PE teacher in St Andrew's College I applied for and got it.

"I'm happy to say I have never looked back. It's a marvellous school – a co-educational, multidenominational and international, with every kind of race, skin-colour and belief. A large number of the children of the Diplomatic Corps attend also. I believe it to be a fantastic educational environment. My two eldest children, Richie and Lynn, are going to the junior school now and will attend the senior school when they are old enough, while Nikki is registered to enter in 1995.

"I get tremendous satisfaction at the school – nobody is in teaching for the money. When I applied, the principal was Jimmy Duke and he was succeeded by a friend of mine and rugby foe (the hooker on the High School team) from my secondary school days, Arthur Godsil. Both Jimmy and Arthur have been very supportive to me and encouraged me to pursue my journalistic activities – provided of course they didn't conflict with my teaching duties. St Andrew's has been very good to me from day one. I will always be grateful to Jimmy for the support he gave me in my time of crisis after my marriage broke up.

"I changed my house substantially. I know it might seem a trivial thing to some people but believe me, it meant an incredible difference to me in psychological terms – just to keep my sanity.

"I also moved to Greystones which had a huge impact on my rugby because I began to really enjoy it all again. I was made to feel welcome from the very start. Moving to a new club gave me the impetus to get up and start making a serious claim for my place back in the Irish side, should the occasion arise."

On 4 January, 1985 Ward received a letter from Ken Ging inviting him to join Greystones, which included three promises:

1. Senior rugby at *out-half.*
2. A brand of football to suit your talents.
3. A warm and sincere welcome.

For Ward the joy at settling in at the new club was dampened when he discovered that he was ineligible to play for Greystones in the Leinster Senior Cup in his first season there because he had played for St Mary's in the Leinster Senior League. However, although the powers that be did not know it at the time for once they were doing him a favour:

"It suited me at the time because I needed to be physically at home as much as possible since I had to raise my daughter, Lynn, as a single parent then."

Moreover, he seemed to put a jinx on his new club. They were on a run of eleven consecutive victories when he lined out to make his debut against Shannon in Limerick on 12 January, 1985. Virtually every other rugby game in the country was called off that day because of dreadful climatic conditions but Shannon realised the crowd-pulling potential of their game and went ahead with it. Greystones lost and proceeded to lose their next six games. It was a difficult introduction for Ward and such a dampener on his morale was the last thing he needed at the lowest point of his personal life.

The decision to join Greystones was unintentionally shrouded in controversy when all kinds of stories were in circulation about the motives for his move. Paul Dean always preferred to play at out-half but, when Ward returned to Mary's from Garryowen in 1982, Dean was moved to the centre and Ward went in at number 10 as it seemed to make the best use of Mary's resources. When Dean was selected to play for Ireland against Australia at out-half, Mary's were put in a difficult predicament because Ward had been their fly-half for three years and was still the Munster out-half. The club felt certain that both players would be chosen at out-half for the final trial in '84, but when Ward was not even on the replacement panel their problems were magnified.

Both players wanted to play at fly-half but two into one won't go. After Ward had agreed to alternate with Dean during matches he was dropped for the game against Dolphin. It was suggested that he make himself unavailable for a few weeks (through phone calls from Tony Hickie and Terry Kennedy), to see how things would go but he asked that it be announced that he had been dropped. Ward is philosophical about the whole situation:

"I fully understood Paul's position and the club's position. Paul was Ireland's out-half and it was only natural that he wanted to play his club rugby in that position. What possible use was there in me postponing my decision for another few weeks. The same position would have applied then and the following season the same problem would still have been there. That was why I decided to move, plain and simply because I wanted to play senior rugby at out-half.

"Greystones restored my self-belief, my pride and my sanity. Greystones are Leinster's Garryowen and for me, Jack McVitty and Ken Ging are Hogan/Whelan equivalents."

Ward's primary concern when he joined Greystones was to ensure that he didn't have a detrimental effect on team spirit there. In particular, he didn't want to tread on the incumbent out-half Jerome O'Brien's position. Before he joined the club he had a meeting one Saturday in Clontarf Castle with O'Brien and the Wicklow club's officials – Ken Ging, Sonny Kenny and Seanie Fitzpatrick – to ensure that his arrival would not ruffle any feathers. He was assured that he would be welcomed by everyone at Dr Hickey Park:

"Rugby has become so professional in everything except the purely monetary sense that it became a very serious business. But there is a beautiful attitude to the game in Greystones. The whole community is involved and I was never happier playing my rugby than I was there.

Wardy

"I believe the club had a big part to play in me being recalled out of the blue to play for Ireland against Scotland in 1986. My interest had gone and rugby had become a chore for me until I went to Greystones. There my appetite for the game was rekindled. The spirit of Greystones is summed up for me in the words of my former team mate there, Johnny Murphy: 'We may not be a winning team, but we're sure as hell a happy one.'

"There is no more scenic ground to play in than Dr Hickey Park in Greystones. When I would travel down to train, through the Glen of the Downs, I felt as if I was entering a different world. My mind switched off and all tension left me.

In autumn 1986 I was selected to play for the first time for Leinster against Canada. It was no big deal save for the fact that the Leinster team consisted of five Greystones' backs which was unprecedented, John Murphy, Paul McNaughton, Hubie Gallagher, Tony Doyle and I – but as it turned out it was a terrible game. But when I arrived at the dressing-room in Lansdowne Road there was a telegram of congratulations waiting for me from guess who? Ollie Campbell. That, to me, is what rugby is all about."

Ward's view on the importance of rugby friendships is shared by the English international Mike Teague: "I have always thought that the friendship you get out of rugby is the only thing money cannot buy."

What Becomes Of The Broken-Hearted?

Ward was disappointed to have to transfer his allegiance to Leinster. His official explanation at the time was:

"It was a decision I took with regret but one forced on me by circumstances. Were I a member of the Munster panel it would have meant travelling at weekends and midweek for training sessions. My domestic circumstances and my business commitments were such that I just could not. I saw little point in taking an approach that would have been unfair to Munster."

PHONOGRAM (INLAND)

C 29   No.   A 60

Rec'd by	Subscriber's No		Charge	Sent	Date Stamp
				At	DUBLIN 1 - OCT 1986 PHONOGRAMS
Prefix	Office of Origin	No. of Words	Date	Handing in time	To
X	Dublin 1	34/33	01	0939	By

TO: Tony Ward
c/o Leinster Branch I.R.F.U.
Old Wesley Rugby Club
Donnybrook
Dublin 4

You have played with distinction in various shades of blue before — hope it continues!

Ollie

However, this was only part of the story. The reality was otherwise. Ward is almost choking with emotion as he recounts the events which led to his departure from Munster. His words cannot do justice to the piercing, almost overwhelming, sadness in his voice that the memory of these events triggers off for him.

He became disillusioned in 1985 with the leadership structure of the Munster team. He was dropped for Munster's opening match in the interprovincial series having declined to play in the Munster trial, where he had been selected as captain of the Possibles. The trial clashed with Greystones' League match against Lansdowne which offered Ward the chance to play his first competitive game for Stones because of the ban on him the previous season. He chose club before province and paid the penalty.

Munster lost badly in their opening match, the selectors panicked and he was asked to take part in a squad session. He agreed but the episode does not bring back happy memories for him:

"I remember standing in Thomond Park at 11.30 on a Sunday morning in November wondering what in the name of God I was doing there. I had left home at eight, having played a game the day before. Eventually somebody brought out two sets of grotty jerseys, blue and white, and I discovered they were going to have a form of trial – one of those freeze sessions where the match was stopped when something went wrong and the error was pointed out. Here were amateur players shown so little respect and I had travelled down to Limerick for this! There was no squad session and I ended up playing in a mickey mouse match, Mickey Mouse with capital Ms. I spoke to no one and nobody said anything to me, least of all John Moroney and Jim Kiernan who were calling the shots at that time. When we were finished I just drove off into the sunset, literally and metaphorically. I decided there and then I was finished with Munster – seven years after, almost to the day, we had beaten the All-Blacks. It was a sad ending because I had taken such pride wearing the red jersey.

"I had a particularly good season with Greystones but the next season was going to be vital for me because of the build-up to the World Cup. It would be important for me to be involved in representative rugby if I was to make the touring party. It was not an easy decision to declare for Leinster, but the decision was made easy for me because of the events that day in Thomond."

Paradise Regained

The 'give-it-a-lash' philosophy which brought Ireland the Triple Crown in 1985 did not bring the same results the following season – with Ireland's final game of the season against Scotland offering the last opportunity to avoid a whitewash. Injuries to Paul Dean and

Ralph Keyes meant that Ward, the now third choice out-half, was given a recall. It is ironic that the only two seasons in his eleven year career as an international player, that Ward never had the slightest involvement with the Irish team, even as a sub, were the two years Ireland won the Triple Crowns. Ward comments: "Highly significant perhaps!"

The man with his future behind him was back. The morning of the match, *The Irish Press* thought his recall of such importance that they devoted their editorial to it – pointing out that the Ward-Campbell argument had assumed the proportions of the Dempsey versus Tunney political debate.

Although it was to be a salvage operation, the match began on a high note with Phil Orr leading out the Irish side to a tremendous ovation on the occasion of his 50th cap. Throughout the game the crowd had much to cheer about in an exhilarating match with Ireland playing some splendid running rugby only to lose 10-9. Defeat seemed unthinkable in the 79th minute when Michael Kiernan stepped up to take a 20 metre penalty. The previous year, in the final match against England, in one of the great moments in Irish sport, Kiernan had added the now legendary drop goal to secure the Triple Crown for Ireland. However, on this occasion his kick drifted across the face of the posts. It seemed a travesty of justice for Ireland to suffer the indignity of a whitewash despite so much quality play.

For Ward it was very much paradise regained, reviving memories of the heady days of '78 and '79 and nailing the lie that he was not a team player as he regularly brought his three-quarters into the game. Back from the wilderness Ward was faced by the celebrated John Rutherford, a duel that the Irish man was to win emphatically – moving his line speedily, creating room and space with a series of incisive breaks and staying on his feet and keeping the ball alive in seemingly impossible circumstances.

Ireland's only try came from Trevor Ringland, his third in consecutive international games, and was scant reward for Ireland's fine show, with Kiernan adding the conversion and a penalty goal. Ringland and Keith Crossan's performances suggested that the Irish had the finest wingers in Europe. Michael Bradley, Brendan Mullin, Michael Kiernan and Hugo MacNeill also shone. The forwards had their best game of the season with Nigel Carr giving yet another five star performance.

Scotland's points came from a try by Roy Laidlaw and two penalties from Gavin Hastings, one a wind-backed effort from the centre of the field – earning himself a place in Scottish history with a total for the season of 52 points. The result was good enough to give Scotland a share in the Championship with France.

The Return Of Biggles

Much had changed in the eight years since Ward had played his first international for Ireland against the same opposition but, just like the old times, it was Ward who dominated the post-match interviews and analysis. The Scottish were perplexed as to Ward's failure to win a regular place on the Irish team and both sides were almost falling over each other in praising him.

The Scottish skipper, Colin Deans, observed: "He was splendid. He was like a youngster out there the way he mixed his game and moved that backline in such a way as to give his backs so much scope."

The Scottish coach, Derick Grant, remarked: "Ward controlled what amounted to the best backline we played all year, other than the French."

Mick Doyle mused: "I would give last year's Triple Crown back to see one more performance from Ireland like this one. I don't believe I have ever seen the Irish backs get so many opportunities to perform so well . . . Ward's skills, craft and general know-how have truly not deserted him and he proved this in the manner he returned to the international scene to play so well."

Irish captain, Ciaran Fitzgerald added his thoughts: "Today our performance reminded me of the Irish teams of old and Ward, who relished so much being back with the likes of Brendan Mullin and Michael Kiernan, fitted in so well."

The public showed their feelings for him in the flood of messages he received on his recall:

"The response was unbelievable. The telegrams, telephone calls and personal messages I received were far in excess of when I got my first cap. I found it very touching and I was flattered. I was never more nervous going onto the field than for that game. I really sensed that the public wanted me to do well.

"That remains my most memorable game for Ireland. My marriage had failed, I had changed clubs, Greystones having restored my belief in humanity and my game had been put back together. I was delighted to be back and joining such a well organised Irish side where the parameters of the game were set for us by the coach. Doyler put the onus on the team to help me and not vice versa. I felt very comfortable in that set-up because Mick handled me and the whole team so competently that weekend and I know I played well."

Whatever the various Irish selectors saw lacking in his game the fans had no doubts. Other players were greatly admired and respected – Ward was loved. They had no inhibitions about showing it. From the first kick to his final break the crowd embraced him like a long lost love.

Ward's special charisma was never more in evidence than in that match. He had that rare gift to stir the hearts of the crowd to the extent that every time he got the ball there was a buzz of anticipation – building up to a crescendo as the promise was delivered. George Best had it. Barry John had it. Maradona had it. On that day Ward displayed the breadth and depth of his repertoire – the magical little shuffle, the acceleration and jinking run, the skyscraper of a garryowen, the delicate chip, the testing screwkick and the calm cover. The crowd's reaction was simple – adulation. The Sunday papers the following day were the stuff to induce deep blushes for rugby's lost sheep. Ward must have wondered was he dreaming. The notices were ecstatic but the performance which inspired them had been remarkable.

Reports of Biggles' death had been greatly exaggerated!

A Spanner In The Works

After returning to the international arena, albeit for only one match in 1986, Ward set himself one goal – to be selected on the Irish squad for the inaugural World Cup the following year. However, he was unwittingly embroiled in controversy in the autumn of '86 and early months of '87. He feared that this might jeopardise his chances of making it onto the squad.

The problem arose when he was asked by an organisation called "Rugbyclass" to be involved in a summer coaching course for boys aged between 8 and 18 which was to be run in Blackrock College, at a fee which even underprivileged kids could afford. The venture was to be run in the four "Home Countries". Bill Beaumont was to be involved in the English equivalent, Andy Irvine in the Scottish one and Phil Bennett in the Welsh.

It is almost standard practice for PE teachers to be involved in summer camps during their long summer holidays and Ward agreed to participate. Moreover, he agreed to lend his name to the venture. In order not to contravene his amateur status Ward refused to accept his fee for this. Instead he asked that the money he should have received go to two places for underprivileged boys. However, the IRFU though intervened. Once again Ward was swept away in a cycle of letters and responses to letters of which the following are only a sample.

Ward capitulated to the IRFU's demands without so much as a whimper even though it flew in the face of all his principles. He felt that the principle behind the coaching course was only marginally different from a summer camp, which as a PE teacher, would have been a perfectly legitimate way to supplement his salary.

Having an exceptional insight into the vagaries of the Irish selection process he knew that if he fell foul of the rugby authorities for any reason he would be shooting himself in the foot in terms of making the trip to the World Cup. Although something deep inside him rebelled against it, he bit his tongue and meekly complied with the IRFU's decree. The '87 Ward was a very different model to the '79 version and he knew that honesty is not always the best policy in courting favour with the selectors. Slightly the worse but a good deal the wiser from his trials and tribulations, Ward knew now how to play the game off the field. Discretion was the better part of valour.

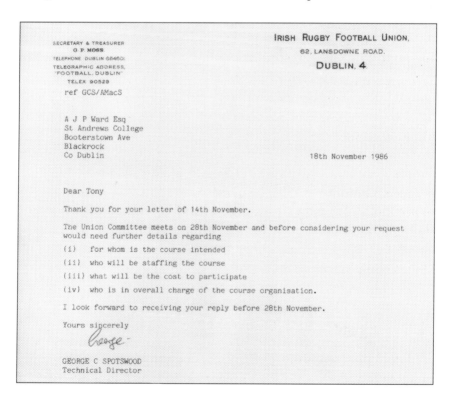

SECRETARY & TREASURER
G P MOSS
TELEPHONE DUBLIN 684501
TELEGRAPHIC ADDRESS,
'FOOTBALL, DUBLIN'
TELEX 90529

ref GCS/AMacS

IRISH RUGBY FOOTBALL UNION,
62, LANSDOWNE ROAD.
DUBLIN, 4

A J P Ward Esq
St Andrews College
Booterstown Ave
Blackrock
Co Dublin

18th November 1986

Dear Tony

Thank you for your letter of 14th November.

The Union Committee meets on 28th November and before considering your request would need further details regarding

(i)   for whom is the course intended
(ii)   who will be staffing the course
(iii) what will be the cost to participate
(iv)   who is in overall charge of the course organisation.

I look forward to receiving your reply before 28th November.

Yours sincerely

George

GEORGE C SPOTSWOOD
Technical Director

R GBYCLASS
RUGBY COACHING CENTRES

Mr G Spotswood
Irish Rugby Football Union
62 Lansdowne Road
Dublin 4
Eire   7 January 1987

Dear Mr Spotswood
I wanted to thank you for your interest in our Rugby Coaching Course
in Ireland and am writing to let you know a bit more about our Courses.
We have operated Rugby Coaching Courses for several years now and
currently operate in England, Scotland, Wales and Ireland. As you
can see from our brochure, many of the leading players and coaches
have been involved with our coaching and our aim is not just to improve
the standard of play but to increase the enjoyment and interest in the
game.
Most of the home Unions offer coaching courses to the most promising
players and we are not in any way trying to compete with this. What
we are trying to offer is a rugby based holiday which will appeal to
boys of any ability. The majority of their days will be spent being
coached but they will have a chance to try their hand at many different
sports in late afternoon and there will be a full evening entertainment
programme with lots of varied activities. Tony Ward has very kindly
agreed to lend his name to the Course in order to stimulate as much
interest in the Course as possible but, obviously, we are not able to
pay him any fee for doing this. What we would like to do, in lieu of
the fee, is to offer the Irish Rugby Football Union two free places
on the Course, for the Union to give to any two boys which they consider
deserving. I know that Tony's own feelings are that the places should
go to boys who would not normally be able to afford any sort of residential
coaching but I would leave that entirely up to you.
If there are any other questions that you would like to ask about the
Course, please do not hesitate to contact me and I look forward to
hearing from you with the names and addresses of the two boys. Once
again, thank you for your interest in the Course.

Yours sincerely

SIMON COHEN
MANAGING DIRECTOR

IRISH RUGBY FOOTBALL UNION,
62, LANSDOWNE ROAD.
DUBLIN. 4

SECRETARY & TREASURER
G P MOSS
TELEPHONE DUBLIN 684601
TELEGRAPHIC ADDRESS
"FOOTBALL DUBLIN"
TELEX 90929

ref GPM/AMacS
A J P Ward Esq
St Andrews College
Booterstown Ave
Blackrock
Co Dublin   21st January 1987

Dear Tony
I refer to your letter of 14th November requesting permission to organise a
coaching course in Blackrock College in August 1987 and your letter of 4th
December in reply to George Spotswood's letter of 18th November.
It is noted that the course is being administered by Rugbyclass Ltd and that
your are head coach.
The Committee of the Union considered your request at the meeting on 2nd
January. It disapproved of the fact that the details of the course had been
circulated to schools when approval for the course had not been given by the
Union. It further noted that the brochure sent to schools and subsequent
newspaper advertisements use your name, and, in the case of the brochure, your
photograph, which is in contravention of Law 19 (2) of the Irish Rugby Football
Union. A copy of Law 19 is enclosed.
Further, the Committee of the Union is not satisfied that the coaching school
to be organised by Rugbyclass at Blackrock College will conform to the
Regulations of the International Rugby Football Board relating to Amateurism
and therefore it disapproves of the involvement of any Irish players or
coaches in the coaching school in which you propose to participate. It does
not believe that such courses run on a commercial basis are in the best
interests of the Game in Ireland.
The Committee of the Union is advising its Branches, Clubs and Schools not to
participate in the course organised by Rugbyclass and advertised as the Tony
Ward School of Rugby.
The Committee further requests that you give an immediate explanation in
writing as to why, as a current player, you allowed your name to be used in
advertising a course which is being run as a commercial venture.

Yours sincerely

G P MOSS
Secretary

Telephone:
Headmaster } 882785
Bursar
Staff 882290
Pupils 888169

St. Andrew's College,
Booterstown Avenue,
Blackrock, Co. Dublin

28th January, 1987

Mr. G.P. Moss,
Secretary,
I.R.F.U.,
62 Lansdowne Road,
Dublin 4.

Dear Mr. Moss,
I refer to your letter of the 21st January in relation to the coaching
course in Blackrock College in August, 1987 and wish to advise you that
I had absolutely <u>no</u> idea that my consenting to that course was in
contravention of the Law 19 (2) of the I.R.F.U. I presumed that as
P.E. teaching is my full time livelihood that such a course would be
regarded as part of my work, i.e. in much the same way as Summer Sports
Camps are viewed etc.
As you have now pointed out to me that this is not the case and as I
do not wish in any way to infringe my amateur status, I will therefore
unreservedly withdraw my name from this course. I await your advice
as to how this should be done and will act upon that advice when
received.

Yours sincerely,

Tony Ward.

SECRETARY & TREASURER
G. P. MOSS
TELEPHONE DUBLIN 684501
TELEGRAPHIC ADDRESS:
"FOOTBALL, DUBLIN"
TELEX 90528

IRISH RUGBY FOOTBALL UNION.
62, LANSDOWNE ROAD.
DUBLIN. 4

ref GPM/AMacS

A J P Ward Esq
St Andrews College
Booterstown Ave
Blackrock
Co Dublin

2nd February 1987

Dear Tony
Thank you for your letter of 28th January. The Union Committee accepts your
explanation regarding the use of your name by Rugby Class Ltd in advertising
their course and is pleased at the decision conveyed in your letter to
unreservedly withdraw your name from the course.
The Union has replied to a letter which it received from Mr S Cohen of
Rugbyclass and has informed him of your decision and requested him to cease
using your name in the promotion of the course. A copy of this letter
is enclosed as is a copy of the Press statement released by the Union on
29th January.
There may be merit in your communicating directly with Mr Cohen to inform
him of your decision to withdraw your name from the course and to instruct
him that he must not use your name to advertise the School of Sport in
Blackrock College.
Finally I am grateful to you for co-operation with this office concerning
this matter and commend you on your common sense approach. Should you
require further assistance or advice do not hesitate to contact me.

Yours sincerely

G P MOSS
Secretary

PRESS STATEMENT

The Irigh Rugby Football Union has today written to its four Branches and to all Clubs and Schools affiliated to the Union to inform them that the Union disapproves of the proposed course for schoolboys to be held in Blackrock College in August 1987 which is being organised by Rugbyclass Ltd. The Course has been advertised as the Tony Ward School of Sport which is in contravention of the Laws of the IRFU. Tony Ward, on being advised of this, has unreservedly withdrawn his name from the course.

The Union is not satisfied that this course will be run in accordance with the Regulations of the International Rugby Football Board relating to Amateurism. It does not believe that coaching courses run on a commercial basis are in the best interests of the Game in Ireland and it has therefore advised its Branches, Clubs and Schools not to involve themselves in any way in this course or other courses of a similar nature.

GP Moss
Secretary

Mr. G.P. Moss,
Irish Rugby Football Union,
62 Lansdowne Road,
Dublin 4.

Rugby Class,
16 Chestergate,
Macclesfield,
Cheshire.

Dear Mr Moss,

Thank you for you letter of January 28, 1987.

While I do not, in any way, dispute the right of the IRFU to form its own opinion of rugby coaching holidays, I do feel that the way the Union has acted, arbitrarily and without consultation, has not been in the best interests of the game.

My prime concern is that two completely innocent parties, Tony Ward and Blackrock College have been treated in a way that their service to Irish rugby does not deserve. It is ironic that this should happen because they, unlike the IRFU, had taken the trouble to find out exactly what Rugbyclass was all about.

Rugbyclass offer rugby based activity holidays for children. These holidays are intended to stimulate an interest in rugby for boys who are either not keen enough to go on an intensive coaching course or who would otherwise be on a football holiday or ponytrecking holiday. This means that the Rugbyclass holidays do not, in any way, conflict with the intensive courses that the IRFU run and are, most certainly, in the best interests of the game. I would be interested to know how the IRFU would explain the fact that the holiday in Ireland was only set up as a direct response to Irish boys and parents who had come on holidays in England and Wales and wanted a rugby holiday nearer home.

Tony Ward, therefore, felt that putting his name to the holiday was one way that he could put something back into the game without the pressure that an intensive coaching would entail. He felt that, as there was no question of any fee being involved, that he would not be jeopardising his amateur status. Blackrock College also felt that by hosting rugby based activity holidays they were contributing to an expansion of interest in the game. They are in the business of letting their facilities and it seems ironic that the IRFU seem to be saying that it would be better for the game in Ireland if Blackrock College had let their facilities to a football holiday concern.

The IRFU has said in its statement that it is not satisfied that the holiday will be run in accordance with the International Rugby Football Board regulations to amateurism. I would be interested to know how the IRFU have come to this conclusion when they have no knowledge, whatsoever, of the financial workings of Rugbyclass and have not taken the trouble to contact Rugbyclass or anyone who has helped in previous years.

The result of this is that Tony Ward and Blackrock College have been made to appear as though they are supporting some sort of professional rugby coaching. As has been shown, not only is the original allegation totally unfounded, but the interference does a great disservice to two of Irish rugby's most loyal supporters.

It may well be that the IRFU feel that they have tried to halt a commercial coaching course, but the main losers if the holiday was not to operate, would be the boys who had chosen to go on a rugby holiday instead of, for instance, with their families abroad. The under-privileged children who were offered places in lieu of Tony Ward's fee would also be missing out on their one chance of a holiday.

In view of the arbitrary manner in which the IRFU has dealt with this whole manner, it would seem unlikely that the truth is one of their main priorities, but if they were genuinely interested in the undivided future of the game then they would have no hesitation in issuing a statement which not only mentions the above points, but which establishes that Tony Ward and Blackrock College were innocent of any attempt, as alleged by the IRFU, to harm the interests of the game in Ireland.

I, myself would welcome any discussion with the IRFU regarding the points raised in this letter and I, therefore look forward to hearing from you.

Yours sincerely,
Simon Cohen
Managing Director

Horses For Courses

In a phone-in to Radio One's *Sport Around Seven* before the World
Cup, Mick Doyle was confronted with a series of questions about
Ireland's preparation. One question concerned the possibility of
Ward playing a role in the World Cup. Doyle talked about "horses for
courses" and suggested that the selectors might consider playing Paul
Dean for one game and Ward for another – pointing out that the
attributes of the two of them worked in different ways for the team.

He went on to say that in his opinion Dean, on form, was the best
mover of the ball in the business, in any country. His verdict on Ward
was that he was not as good a team player as Dean, though he could
have been, but through his involvement with Greystones and Leinster
he had improved significantly in that respect.

A few months earlier in the October '86 issue of *Rugby World,* in an
interview entirely devoted to Ward's possible role on the Irish team,
Doyle had claimed that although Ward was a superb handler and a
superlative line kicker, he tended to treat beating opponents as
almost an end in itself. Consequently, in the past, the three-quarters
didn't feel they would get the ball because he wasn't any good at
linking. The main weaknesses in his game were considered to be that
he didn't come up quickly enough on his immediate opponent in
defence and he didn't link with his fellow backs very well.

The More Things Change . . .

When Ward started the 1987 Five Nations campaign on the Irish
reserves bench he had every reason to feel confident that he would
make the touring party for the World Cup, particularly as his club
form was good and he handled the 'Rugbyclass affair' without
ruffling any feathers in the IRFU. Moreover, he had played well in the
final trial. He subbed in Ireland's home victory to England and in the
defeat away to Scotland.

Ward was quickly to face another irritation when he was one of the players who was asked to play in a trial between the Combined Provinces and the Rest of Ireland. None of the Irish team who had played against Scotland was requested to participate – only the subs. The trial proved as inconclusive as the topical debate at the time about the greater or lesser merits of Ward and Dean. If, as was believed to be the case by some observers, the main issue was to decide the reserve out-half berth for the World Cup between Ralph Keyes or Ward the trial was meaningless with Keyes clashing heads with Ward after only 19 minutes and being forced to make his exit from the game. Ward played on.

The match was played on a Wednesday in Ravenhill under floodlights, which meant Ward had to take a day off school, travel by coach from Dublin at noon, play the match that night and then return home with Tony Doyle and Ciaran Fitzgerald. It was a major inconvenience for such a meaningless fixture. Then the selectors, as they seemed to make a habit of doing in his case, made a decision which appeared to fly in the face of all known logic. The incredulous look on Ward's face six years on as he recalls the nadir of his rugby career tells its own story:

"Unquestionably the biggest disappointment of my career, bigger even than Australia, if not as traumatic or as long-lasting, was being dropped from the reserves bench for Ireland's match against France in the '87 season. After the Scottish defeat Nigel Carr was dropped for Brian Spillane on the flank with Willie Anderson at number eight and Jim Glennon in the second row and I was dropped from the reserves in favour of Ralph Keyes. I would have thought I could have done nothing wrong from the bench! That was the ultimate low point for me.

"I had always managed to put my disappointments behind me up to that point but I felt I could take no more after that and made up my mind to retire from representative rugby. However, a phone call from Syd Millar caused me to change my mind but boy did I need convincing! I've had a good relationship with Syd down through the years and his advice was rock-solid. He said that if I bit my tongue and did nothing hasty everything would work out okay. Ned Van Esbeck offered the same whole-hearted encouragement. They were both proved right and I was recalled to the bench for the next international, which in itself was unfair to Ralph Keyes and highlighted the lack of logic in selection decisions. Happily I later made the squad to New Zealand.

"That was the nearest I came to calling it a day. I had dedicated everything to winning a place in the World Cup squad and trained very hard for it. To be treated this way really stank to the high heavens."

In an article in *The London Times* at the time, George Ace commented that: "The bench in Irish rugby is as dangerous as the trapdoor on a scaffold – you can disappear into oblivion mighty quickly."

Ward shrugs his shoulders when asked the reason for the selectors machinations at that time:

"Obviously I was not privy to the selectors' decisions or what went on at their meetings. It was suggested to me that Jim Kiernan might have a vested interest in me not making the trip but I am in no position to comment on the veracity of that belief. I certainly know he was no fan of mine and that there was something going on which could not have had much to do with rugby, otherwise I would not have been dropped from the bench. It was very hard to take.

"The other side of the coin was flying into Sydney Harbour in June of that year, my first time since 1979, and listening to U2 on the earphones. It was a truly marvellous feeling. I remember thinking to myself that it really was worth all the hassle, disappointment and effort that had gone before.

"I have little respect for the system of selection we have, which is supposedly an example of rugby democracy at its best, that is to have five selectors. Up to recent times the coach was not even one of them, at least now that situation has been rectified. I believe the less people who have a say in selection the better. Ultimately I would like to see a situation where we would have just one man in charge à la Jack Charlton in soccer. Knowing Irish rugby as I do I can never see that situation coming about but I can envisage a time when we will have only three selectors – the coach, the manager and one other.

"I have no respect for the selection system we have now or what existed before because of the trading that went on and the politics – where selectors from the various provinces had to be seen to have players from their province on the team. Despite the lip-service about always picking the best team, human nature being what it is, their job is to do the best they can for their province. The sooner we do away with this system the better because, to the best of my knowledge, we are the only country in the modern game that have the old system of five selectors still in place.

"Over the years there have been a number of selectors who took great satisfaction in expressing their views for public consumption – views that should have been left in the selection room and by that I mean, for example, the amount of feedback I got from Myles Breen's pub in Limerick, about comments made there about me from people in selectorial positions, was extraordinary.

"I also firmly believe that selectors should not be in a position where they are considering players who are in any way, shape or form related to them for a place on the team. It is not the player's fault when this situation arises but otherwise the finger of suspicion is pointed at them that they are not in the side on merit alone."

The Number Ten Who Came In From The Cold

As Mick Doyle conceded subsequently, Ireland made a major blunder in the build-up to the World Cup by trying to wrap up their players in cotton wool and not allowing them to play any club matches after March, whereas the Welsh players were involved in club rugby right up to the first half of May. Ireland looked very battle-weary in that opening match while Wales were sharp and incisive. The match is as much remembered for an incident before the game as for the action on the field. Ward was as taken aback by it as everybody else:

"I will never forget the version of the Rose of Tralee which the band played before the game instead of the Irish national anthem. It was horrendous. I love James Last's version of that song but this was excruciatingly painful and embarrassing to us all."

After the 13-6 defeat against Wales in the opening match in Wellington changes were inevitable. Ward was recalled at out-half in place of Paul Dean – who came in for a lot of criticism for not using the strong wind in Wellington against the Welsh. Somewhat surprisingly, Ward was not delegated to take the place kicks, Michael Kiernan retained that role. The other two changes were in the forwards. Malone's John McDonald, the Ulster hooker, who arrived as a replacement for the injured Harry Harbison, was chosen as hooker instead of Terry Kingston and Lansdowne's Paul Collins was chosen on the flank instead of Derek McGrath.

Ward was delighted with the news of his recall:

"There was a time in the earlier part of my career that I tended, perhaps, to take my place on the Irish team a bit for granted. But I gradually learned that nobody has a divine right to play for Ireland. So after many ups and downs I was delighted to be back."

Although Ireland beat Canada 46-19 the result was very misleading. It was only a late flurry which yielded 27 points to the boys in green and for long periods in the match Ireland's dream looked in danger of perishing. The turning point of the game was a try in the 70th minute from Keith Crossan with the scores tied at 19-19. Crossan had scored a try earlier, along with Michael Bradley. Late in the game Brian Spillane scored a try and in injury time Trevor

Ringland and Hugo MacNeill scored tries. Michael Kiernan, in splendid kicking form in an otherwise undistinguished performance, kicked 19 points and Ward added a drop goal. It was not the type of performance that would induce anything other than high blood pressure.

Ireland secured a quarter-final place with a 32-9 victory over Tonga. Two new caps were selected, both from Blackrock: prop, Job Langbroek and second row, Neil Francis. David Irwin replaced Michael Kiernan in the centre. The day before the game Ward trained in Ballymore with Ollie Campbell, who habitually made his holidays into rugby pilgrimages. He hoped it would be a good omen as it was the first time they had trained together since 1980 on the Lions' tour in Capetown-Newlands. Campbell also reminded him that it was the eighth anniversary of Ireland's game against Australia in Ballymore that very day.

It was a game when Ireland chose their tactics to counter the strengths of the opposition and above all to secure victory. The pack laid the foundation for Ireland's victory with Donal Lenihan, Neil Francis, Willie Anderson and Philip Matthews dominating the line-out. At half-back, Ward formed a good partnership with Michael Bradley, keeping the ball in front of his forwards and kicking to put the Tongans under pressure.

It was a particularly happy day for Brendan Mullin who scored three tries equalling the then record for an Irish player in an international. Hugo MacNeill scored two tries and Ward kicked two penalties and three conversions.

The Tongans had brought only two sets of jerseys with them to the World Cup and were unable to swop them with their opponents in their previous matches. After the defeat against Ireland they were free to do a swop. Their hour had come and gone.

In reaching the quarter final the Irish had justified their seeding and went to face Australia with history in their favour – Ireland had never lost a test to Australia in Australia with three wins there in 1967 and two in 1979.

Despite his contribution to Ireland's victory over Tonga, Ward was dropped for the quarter-final and replaced by Paul Dean. Michael Kiernan returned in the centre in place of the hard-tackling David Irwin, and Phil Orr and Des Fitzgerald replaced Jim McCoy and Job Langbroek. Ward shakes his head more in sorrow than anger as he recounts the circumstances of hearing about his demotion:

"The team was to be announced to us at 9 a.m. At 8.20 that morning I rang home to my mother to check on Lynn. The first thing she said to me was: 'Are you very disappointed?' 'Disappointed with what?' I replied. 'With being dropped of course!' 'What do you mean? The team hasn't even be announced yet.' 'I don't know what is happening out there but the team was announced back here on the radio last night and all the papers this morning are saying you are dropped.'

"Of course, as I learned half an hour later, she was absolutely right. It was so typical that I should hear such disappointing news in such a freakish way."

Ireland were comprehensively beaten and soon on the plane home.

Although Ireland had not really impressed in any of their games, ironically one of the greatest stars in the tournament, New Zealand stylish fullback John Gallagher, was eligible to play for Ireland by virtue of the fact that his London based mother came from that great rugby shrine – Limerick. John had played for London-Irish before emigrating to New Zealand. He was 'one that got away' from the Irish selectors.

In the cool of a summer's evening six years on, Ward's memories of the World Cup are positive in the main.

"The defeat to Wales put us under tremendous pressure straight away, even against Tonga and Canada. It might have made a big difference to have played one of them first. Also our travel arrangements meant an awful lot of flying: between arrival and departure we had 14 flights within the two countries. For example, we played Canada in Dunedin on the Saturday, flew to Christchurch on the Sunday, flew to Brisbane via Sydney on the Monday; had the Tuesday off and then played Tonga on the Wednesday.

"There was one incident in the Irish camp which disappointed me greatly. It was a symptom of an unsavoury trend which developed after Ireland's Triple Crown win in 1985 when a clique developed amongst four of the Irish backs comprising Hugo MacNeill, Michael Kiernan, Paul Dean and Michael Bradley – Keith Crossan and Trevor Ringland were inseparable and Brendan Mullin was always his own man. The event which epitomised this for me arose the morning of Ireland's opening match against Wales. Hugo and Michael Kiernan came down together to breakfast as we were all eating together in the Terrace Regency Hotel in Wellington. Each of them had a few postcards. The convention on tours like that is that when you are sending postcards home you get every player in the squad to sign their name – from number one to twenty-six or whatever. Hugo and Michael though had their cards numbered from one to fifteen only. Those of us who were not in the first fifteen were only too delighted not to be signing autographs. It was much nicer to be able to enjoy breakfast without distractions but everybody noted the symbolism of the gesture – the first fifteen and the rest rather than all for one and one for all. It was a very insensitive act but I'm afraid it said a lot about the clique of four within the squad.

"My opinions about this trend were confirmed some time later in a chat with Moss Finn. Moss is one of the easiest guys to get along with that ever graced any dressing-room. Moss came into the team for one match in Doyler's reign after '85 but he told me he found it a very uncomfortable experience because he felt he was intruding into someone else's backline because of the clique that was there. If Moss was having problems getting on with the rest I can't imagine how difficult it would have been for anybody else.

"Otherwise, the World Cup itself was marvellous for the game. The semi-finals were an ideal advertisement for Rugby Union. The France-Australia match had everything you could ask for while the All-Blacks' performance against Wales' was a purist's dream."

Asked for his impressions of Mick Doyle's influence on the tour Ward speaks with typical candour:

"I've got to know Mick particularly well in recent times. I know he could have had an immense influence on my career if he had worked with me earlier. He's a great thinker about the game, has great ideas and was a great man manager. I think he could have been a positive influence on my game if we had been closer when I was in my prime.

"I never knew him when I was a player, nor he me, and it's one of my great regrets that we only got to know each other in the last few years through broadcasting and I know he has the same feelings about me. Furthermore, I know there is a perception abroad that he is a very arrogant, opinionated man but I can tell you that is most certainly not the case. Opinionated, yes – but arrogant never.

"On the downside he sometimes got so wound up before a match that he overstepped the mark. I remember one incident from the World Cup in '87. Rugby facilities in New Zealand, astonishingly for the so-called 'rugby-country', were poor. We are streets ahead of them in that respect in Ireland. Before one of the games in Athletic Park in Wellington I was a sub for the team and we were changing in the dressing-room but, because it was such a tight area, the subs had to go down the steps and change in the shower room. At one stage Jim Glennon went up into the dressing-room to get a strapping for his leg from Joe Doran. Doyler blew up and roared at him – telling him in no uncertain terms to get out. The irony was that Jim went on as a sub very early in that game.

"Although Doyler didn't mean it as it sounded, if that had been me, because of my sensitivity, I would have wanted to have been on the first plane home. Jim was made of stronger stuff than me and took it on the chin. I was rooming with him at the time and I know how much it did hurt him but as he said: 'Doyler is Doyler'. Rooming with Jim was a great experience for me because he's such great fun to be with. I always say life took on a whole new meaning after rooming with him. He's one of the real characters of the game.

"One of Doyler's strange comments about that World Cup was after Ireland got trounced by Australia. He said at the time and I've heard him repeating it since: 'We won the second half.' But so what. The Australians had the game so well won at half-time they could afford to go to sleep. All they were interested in doing in the second half was saving themselves for the semi-final and, as they mistakenly thought at the time, the final. They could have moved up a few gears in the second half any time they wished but why bother when they had the game so well won already. It reflects little credit on Ireland that we were not massacred in that second half.

"The downside of the World Cup is that you never knew when you would be finished. Obviously you hoped you still would be involved up to the final but I remember sitting with Jim Glennon on the subs bench for the Australian match and both of us knew long before half time that we would be on the plane home after that match."

All I Want For Christmas Is . . .

After the World Cup a new coach took over the fortunes of the Irish international side – Jimmy Davidson, who came to the post with an impressive pedigree having brought great success in Ulster. His first big test was scheduled for 16 January 1988 when Ireland faced Scotland in Lansdowne Road. For those who wanted to secure a place on that side a key fixture would be the final trial on 19 December.

For Ward in particular it would be his last chance to wrestle the number ten shirt from Paul Dean. He needed to pull something special out of the hat to achieve the perfect Christmas present – a recall to the Irish side. It was all or nothing.

The pre-Christmas Saturday was a mild, though slightly blustery, day. There was to be no Christmas miracle. He went into the game hampered by a thigh injury and was forced to withdraw 20 minutes into the second half. The spectators generously applauded him as he left the pitch. It was an afternoon when the hallowed stadium could have done with floodlights. Dusk was descending as Ward walked off. The curtain had finally come down on a glorious career. Ward had blown his chances of a recall.

Coach, Jim Davidson, put his arm around Ward. There was a slightly farcical element to the proceedings, appropriate to the pantomime season, when Ward had to take off his blue jersey and hand it to Ralph Keyes. The gesture said it all.

There was a poignant moment when he put on a green jersey before he trotted alone, a disconsolate figure, down the tunnel to the dressing-room. In his heart of hearts he knew that Paul Dean had won a decisive triumph, particularly because of his involvement in a classic movement which culminated in a try for Hugo MacNeill near the corner flag just before the interval. In the event Ward would not play in a championship match again. There was a curious irony that his championship career which had began in a blaze of glory ten years earlier and which down through the years had produced enough column inches to destroy ten rainforests could end in such a low key way. It defied belief that Ward could go out with a whimper. Yet again, fate intervened and decreed that he would go out with a bang. Nobody could have foreseen it – the omens were so unfavourable.

Ward has no qualms about his demotion but was irate at the treatment of Ciaran Fitzgerald at the time:

"Fitzy had all but retired prior to the World Cup and was not in the squad for the campaign down under. He had just won a Leinster Cup medal with Mary's and was delighted to be leaving on a high note.

But then he was coaxed back into making himself available for selection. However, he was completely ignored by the selectors the following season. It was such a travesty of justice that a player of his stature should be dumped in this way. What does this kind of behaviour say about the selectors?"

Omega Point

The 1988 Championship season began badly for Ireland and drifted deeper into chaos, culminating in two humiliating defeats against England, the first in Twickenham and the second in Lansdowne Road, a once-off fixture to coincide with Dublin's Millennium celebrations. Again there was no place for Ward in any of the matches. After the Millennium mismatch misery and the earlier 35-3 defeat to England, Ireland headed off on a close season tour to France with heavy hearts and a severely depleted squad which included only a handful of experienced, senior players including Willie Anderson, Jim McCoy and Mike Gibson. Initially Ward's instinct had been not to travel with the squad:

"Everybody seemed to be crying off and I was not too pushed about making the trip myself. It was the end of the academic year and I said to the principal of our school at the time, Jim Duke, that I had little interest in travelling. He thought it would be good for the school and a nice way to finish my career. Happily he was right and it was a very rewarding trip."

However, Ward was taken aback by the training regime before the tour:

"Jimmy Davidson said at the very beginning of his reign that he wanted players who were 'Bigger, leaner and fitter'. At one of his first training sessions in charge of the Irish squad he had gone as far as to demonstrate the correct way to do a press-up! I remember Trevor Ringland, for one, being less than impressed at the time. Also the mere thoughts of the sort of physical activity that such a regime involved had played a decisive role in Phil Orr's decision to retire after the World Cup.

"Before we went to France we had a two-day squad training session on the back pitch at Lansdowne. For one of the sessions Jimmy told us to take off our tops. He videoed the session and showed it back to us. He wanted to show us the differing body types, but, for guys who have the metabolism to put on weight and are very self-conscious about it, this was the last thing we needed. The more I think back on it the more I realise how degrading and insensitive it was.

"Ironically I played one of my best ever games for Ireland on that tour and I was really delighted I had travelled but that type of incident had me asking why we do it. It was the first introduction to an Irish squad for players like Michael Galwey, Nick Popplewell and Nicky Barry who was just out of school and they were put through this!!

"Jimmy had an admirable vision for Irish rugby. He wanted it put on a par with the rest of the world but he was in the wrong position as national coach to implement all his plans and ideals. He was trying to change things from the top down whereas, as far as I am concerned, what is required more so is change from the bottom up. He was aware of that but as coach he was in no position to do anything about it. In short he was in the wrong position with the right ideas. I think he could do a brilliant job as the IRFU game development officer. His great legacy to the Irish game is the changed attitude to fitness. There is no doubt about that."

The key match of the four game tour was the third, a full-blooded international in Auch, France, between Ireland and France in all but name. Ireland got off to a flying start when Neil Francis, superb in the lineout throughout, scored a try in the second minute. The French pack responded with the less edifying side to their game but the Irish side did not yield to their intimidation. Camberabero and Lafond kicked penalties for France before Ward kicked a 50 yards penalty effort to leave Ireland leading 7-6 at the interval.

In the second half, Ward kicked a drop goal before Rodriquez snatched France's only try which Camberabero converted. Lafond kicked another penalty to leave France leading 18-13 with only six minutes remaining. Then, after a move which involved a number of players and was more typical of French flair than anything else, Ward completed the move he had initiated himself to score a try. It was all down to the conversion from way out on the right. Ward faced the kick to a chorus of boos and answered the unsporting behaviour in the most effective way possible by adding the two points.

It was a victory for Irish pride and passion, the first win by an Irish international combination on French soil since 1972. One astonishing statistic was that Ireland won the lineouts 25-13. Nobody could remember when that happened before.

The Irish manager, Ken Reid summed it up when he said: "I have never in my life been as proud of Irish rugby as on this occasion. They stood up to everything." The other IRFU officials echoed similar sentiments like: "This was the best performance I've ever seen from an Irish team, bearing in mind the circumstances."

The display was all the more memorable in the light of the inept efforts over the previous season – Ireland's *annus horribilis*.

Although it was a fantastic team performance there was absolutely no doubt that Ward was the star of the game as he ran the game like a masterful conductor. Apart from scoring the whole range – a try, a conversion, two penalty goals and a drop goal, his running and tactical kicking teased and tantalised the French to the point of sheer frustration. The French coach, Jacques Fouroux, singled out Ward's contribution as the difference between the two sides. Ward recalls:

"It was an unbelievable performance. We were really up against it but we played with such fire in our bellies the French just couldn't handle us. Because of the adverse circumstances I don't think I've ever been as happy with a result. I cried in the dressing room afterwards because we had won in such a turn up for the books. It was the only time I ever cried after a game but it's difficult to explain to anybody who wasn't actually there what a magnificent performance it actually was.

"That was the only time I ever remember Ned Van Esbeck coming in to a dressing-room after a match. All the Irish journalists covering the game came in to congratulate us which was unprecedented and said a lot about the magnitude of our achievement."

The Irish team on duty that day was: P. Danaher (Lansdowne); J. Sexton (Trinity); V. Cunningham (St Mary's); P. Clinch (Lansdowne); P. Purcell (Lansdowne); T. Ward (Greystones); F. Aherne (Dolphin); T. Clancy (Lansdowne); S. Smith (Ballymena); J. McCoy (Ballymena); N. Francis (Blackrock College); W. Anderson (Dungannon); Capt; D. Whittle (Bangor); M. Gibson (London-Irish); D. McBride (Malone). Replacement – P. O' Hara (Sunday's Well) for Whittle (45 mins).

Ireland were unable to finish their tour on a winning note in a match that marked Ward's last appearance in the green jersey when they lost to a star-laden French Barbarians' team, 41-26 at La Rochelle. The match was played in alien conditions for an Irish side – the temperature touched 90 degrees and the surface was hard as concrete. Moreover, the Irish pack were deprived of the lineout expertise of Neil Francis and Michael Gibson. The star of the show was the French wing, Jean Baptiste Lafond, who scored a whopping 29 points.

Despite the heat and their depleted side, the Irish showed the same never-say-die spirit as they had shown in Auch. To their credit they managed to score five tries – two each for Rab Brady and Peter Purcell and one from Mick Galwey. Ward kicked three conversions. In the immediate aftermath of Ireland's nightmare season, in particular the shambles against England, the tour was an astonishing success. Ward credits much of the reversal in Ireland's fortunes to the inspiration of Willie Anderson:

"In a conversation in the Westbury Hotel just before we left for France, Willie told me that what he wanted to achieve most of all during the tour was to put the spirit back into Irish rugby. And he did restore pride in the green jersey after the setbacks of the 87-88 season, instilling on the field of play the passion, fire and tigerish commitment that has been an integral part of the make-up of the greatest Irish teams.

"Ireland are best with their backs to the wall. They found themselves written off as no-hopers when they left for France but Anderson first of all worked on team spirit off the field and then succeeded in transmitting a tremendous sense of harmony on the field of play, leading to that famous victory at Auch.

"At that time Irish rugby was in a state of flux. The playing ethos that remained from the 1985 Triple Crown winning side and whose philosophy continued to dominate, though it had been overtaken by events on the world stage, was broken down.

"Ask me to come down to essentials and put my finger on what went wrong in the '88 season before the French tour, to spell out the reasons why there was what appeared to be a failure of spirit, especially at Twickenham, and my reply is that it cannot be taken in isolation from 1985 and even before.

"The 1982 Triple Crown and Championship success was fully deserved. The attainment of the Crown and Championship again in '85 was another marvellous moment for Irish rugby but it has to be admitted, in retrospect, that the bounce of the ball favoured us through the season although the rugby we played was a joy to behold. I am afraid that the '85 success was understandably blown out of all proportion and it took all of '86 to introduce a note of realism. Then it was all borne out that the 'give it a lash' philosophy just would not continue to work. The two push-over tries and one penalty try at Twickenham made people wake up to the problem in the scrum.

"But there had been problems in the scrum since '84. The Triple Crown and Championship success of '85 disguised to an extent that which would emerge with clarity in '86.

"Ireland won in '82 with a strong, experienced pack – John O'Driscoll, Willie Duggan and Fergus Slattery in the back row, Moss Keane and Donal Lenihan in the second row and Phil Orr, Ciaran Fitzgerald and Gerry McLoughlin forming the front row. It was basically an immobile pack and it must be remembered that Slattery, who earlier in his career was a rampaging world-class wing forward, was at the end of his career.

"In 1985 Ireland had a completely different pack. Now the back row was comprised of three very mobile players in Phil Matthews, Brian Spillane and Nigel Carr while Willie Anderson in the second row was also comparatively quick. The policy now was to move the ball wide which was perfectly understandable and fully justified.

"Everything was geared to second-phase possession. Mick Doyle spoke of the scrum as 'a means of restarting the game'. I think he was misrepresented.

"Doyle saw an Irish pack that was lighter than that of '82, one which could not afford to engage in hand-to-hand battle, so to speak, in the set scrums and he cut his cloth accordingly.

"Nigel Carr was a key figure in the whole set-up, as good an open-side wing forward as ever wore the green jersey. Usually he was the first to arrive to the break-down and what many people seemed to overlook about his play was that, not alone was he tremendously mobile but also very strong and he was able to hold on to the ball until the other forwards were up to form the ruck or maul. And it was from second-phase play that much of the damage was done to the opposition during that '85 season.

"It was unique then in a sense, a special season in a way because Ireland were playing to the strengths of a particular kind of pack. But we did not do ourselves justice in the World Cup, morale was poor on the Irish team's return and what Jim Davidson took over was, to all intents and purposes, an uphill struggle. The wonderful philosophy that Mick Doyle expounded created in the minds of the public an aura of invincibility. Caution could be thrown to the wind, the running game would succeed every time. It's not as simple as that. The philosophy of the hard core persisted right up to the Millennium debacle against England when finally reality dawned.

"One of our biggest problems is that we have had no overall coaching policy. I played under at least six different national coaches and I must confess that there was never a sense of continuity, no pattern overlapping from one to the next. Dramatic differences occur as one coach gives way to the next. We have much to learn from New Zealand habits.

"Looking back on it there could not have been a greater contrast between Doyler and Jimmy D in terms of coaching philosophy. There is of course much to be said for the scientific approach but not when it is taken over the top. The downside is that you lose out on the fire and guts side. There was a lot more to Mick Doyle than just 'give-it-a-lash'. You have to know how to give it a lash in the first place and he did.

"'This is another area where I agree with Doyle a million per cent. Who cares how many times you push the scrum-machine around the pitch or how many press-ups you can do? Provided you have the required standard of fitness, what matters is the heart, the do or die, traditional Irish fighting spirit."

Apart from his displeasure with a pure scientific approach Ward is also unhappy about the way modern players talk so much about commitment:

"Throughout my career I trained as hard as anybody. One of the things that bugs me about the modern game is to hear some players boasting about their commitment. They may have to play more games but there are no more hours in the week to train in."

After the tour and approaching his 34th birthday, Ward announced his retirement from representative rugby though he pledged to continue playing for Greystones.

The announcement of his retirement prompted a flood of tributes. Bill Beaumont reacted with surprise: "But why? – he proved he was at the top of his form on your tour to France. It is rare that a country can produce two such players as Tony Ward and Ollie Campbell in the same era. Tony has been missed by Ireland in the last few years. I can't understand how they left him on the sidelines. At least he had the satisfaction of proving them all wrong by the manner he went on the tour of France and performed so well. I don't think he should be retiring – he still has a place in international football."

While Ward was touched by the praise of his peers and journalists the outstanding memory he retains from that time is the number of letters he received from fans who had never met him but still thought of him as a friend. Typical of these letters was from a man in Waterford:

"It is with a tear in my eye that I write this brief note. I read today of your retirement from representative rugby and I just wish to add my voice to many others in wishing you every happiness and good health in your retirement. I'm sure we haven't heard the last of you yet.

I have never met you and perhaps never will but I have enjoyed your successes along with many others . . . Through your sporting career you have enjoyed your honours and borne your share of crosses with dignity and have been a shining light to all who believe in fair play and sporting behaviour. Good on you and thank you for brightening our lives.

God bless you and yours."

There are incredible variations in the letters in terms of length, literary elegance and formality but the one common thread is a tone of genuine sadness at the passing of a playing great.

Quote Unquote

Ward's announcement of his decision to retire was marked extensively at the end of 1988 in many of the "Sports Quotes of the

Year" compilations. The most favoured comment about him was that of Gareth Edwards:

"We have always believed that if he'd been a Welshman he would have played far more internationals than he did for Ireland. We sometimes couldn't credit it that he wasn't in the Irish team."

Other interesting items in the same feature were Jack O'Shea's remark on his Munster final provocation by Cork's Conor Counihan: "He grabbed me right between the legs – and I can tell you I felt it."

Don't Pick Wardy

The more objective of Ward's fans could understand why he was not chosen ahead of Ollie Campbell, a minority could even see the logic of choosing Paul Dean before him but even non-Ward fans could not fathom why, in the post-Campbell years, he seemed to be shunted to the very back of the queue.

There were a number of jokes doing the rounds about selection policy and the Irish team. Typical of the type were:

"I'm going to play out-half for Ireland this season!"

"But sure you don't play rugby."

"What's that got to do with it? My credentials are impeccable. Okay, I have never played at out-half before and okay so I have never even played rugby before but most importantly, my name is not Tony Ward."

"How do the Irish selectors pick their out-half?"

"They pick the best man for the job. Hang on, that can't be right. I don't know."

"They go to the telephone directory and tear out the Ws and stick a pin into one of the pages."

Ward became one of the few famous Irish sporting personalities who had a song written about them, joining an elite group, which included such greats as John Joe O'Reilly, when Dermot Morgan penned a song which resonated deeply with many Irish rugby fans

entitled: 'Don't Pick Wardie'. The lyrics were not number one
material but had a ring of outlandish truth to them:

You can pick Joe
with the broken toe
but don't pick Wardie.
You can pick Dean
or any human being
 but don't pick Wardie.
Wardie always went too far
he behaved like a superstar . . .
he appeared in his swimming trunks. . .
He's not my choice mister
he is not even a bloody solicitor.
You can pick mother, A.N. Other
but leave Wardie off the team.
You can go for our Hugo
but don't pick Wardie.
He'll never get my vote,
he doesn't even wear a sheepskin coat.
You can pick Trevor
it doesn't matter whoever
Wardie's not my style.
You know I am no knocker
but he used to play soccer.
It makes me sick
he's far too slick
let's bring back Jack Kyle.
We don't mind Mick Kiernan on
we knew his dad and his uncle Tom
but it makes me histrionic
Wardie doesn't even drink gin and tonic . . .
You can pick a one-legged midget

but leave Wardie off the team.
My wife said it shocked her
to hear that he wasn't even a doctor. . . . .

Morgan also displayed his comic talents in the way he organised celebrity soccer matches. His communication about games differed radically in style from what Ward had been used to from the IRFU. Typical of his style was the following letter sent to Ward about an upcoming charity game:

> "*Dear Tony,*
> *Next Sunday we face a crucial challenge to our unrivalled football dominance, from Denis Waterman's XI. A schedule of events is enclosed for your inspection:*
> *Saturday 22nd 11.00 p.m. – Meet and intimidate opposition at Flamingos. Wives or girlfriends or both welcome.*
> *Sunday: Lunch for players only. Perhaps 'her indoors' would drop you in the Peppermint gardens at Parkes.*
> *Mon: Morning – Alka Seltzer.*"

The Unsolved Mystery

An evaluation of Ward's career is fraught with pitfalls. He induced such extreme emotions and such conflicting opinions that it is virtually, if not totally, impossible to chart a middle ground. More than any other character in Irish rugby, Ward touched people at the level of the gut. You were either for him or against him. There was no middle ground.

From his first senior game Ward had star quality. He always exuded a sense of grand opera – robust, thick-thighed, the craftsman in midfield, the magician on the run, with the physical poise of a touch player in an era when jinking around defenders was not in fashion but kicking over their heads was the norm. It was cut and thrust, without the use of a blunt instrument; push and run, without the head-down mentality, claiming the final honours by virtue of clinical finishing – a heady blend of pace, aggression and artistry. His burning desire to please the eye, while remaining combative and competitive, earned him as many friends as points. How the public adored it.

Sport can represent what we are and what we have failed to be. There was something special about Ward that struck a deep chord with the masses. He loved to win in style and in pursuit of this objective was prepared to play on the game's edge. This meant trying the unexpected, the daring, even occasionally the foolhardy. This was heartstopping for his teammates and the fans, but when it worked, and it did more often than not, it was magic. When it failed it was easy to say: "He should have . . ." To the cautious he was anathema. They knew he could win games but they feared that he might lose some too.

Such was Ward's charisma that his legend extended far beyond the confines of a rugby pitch. Arguably Ward achieved a revolutionary change in Irish rugby dragging it away from its elitist, however unjustified, image to a more popular acceptance. Some saw that as a point in his favour – others saw it as a weakness.

To the international rugby community his 19 caps seemed scant reward for his talent. Such a record for one so talented is redolent of waste. In the contemporary sporting world the only parallel is David Gower, a cricketer of extraordinary class, yet inexplicably shunned by the English selectors despite their obvious paucity of talent. As was the case with Ward, when reflecting on the selectors' decisions in his case, a paraphrase of Winston Churchill comes to mind: "Never did the decisions of so few puzzle so many so often."

Bill Beaumont often said: "Ward was the one Irish man we feared." In Wales there was nothing short of disbelief that he could have played so rarely for his country. Had he had an abrasive personality it would have been easy to understand how he could have aroused such polarised opinions. This is the heart of the Ward enigma. He inspired a breathless array of controversy, irony, glory, begrudgery, idolatry, jealousy, agony, ecstasy, achievement and failure. The pieces refused to weave together into the nice, neat tapestry that everybody wanted. The one certainty was that if Ward was to be judged under the headings of integrity, dignity in adversity and honesty, nobody could fault him.

Thanks to the miracle of video the memory of Ward's magical skills will always be secure. And yet the most remarkable quality about Ward, which not even his most ardent detractor can take away from him, is his resilience. All his young life he had dreamed of playing for Ireland and by the age of 24, he had become the first among equals, Europe's number one. In sport, ambition is not constant. Tennis reveals this better than most sports, witness the early retirement of Bjorn Borg and Mats Wilander. However, Ward's ambition to play at the highest level never wavered even when it seemed that nobody wanted him.

Spurned in '79 he returned from the wilderness in spectacular fashion just 12 months later. In '84 and '86 he arose like Lazarus from the rugby dead, after hauling himself off the floor when his world crumbled to bits following the break-up of his marriage. The fire still burned inside him. When Irish rugby was at its lowest following two matches against England in 1988 which ended in abject humiliation he would return again, tempered with maturity, with a flourish. One thing is certain, Irish rugby will never see his like again.

Every time he was written off he came back. The phenomenal place-kicking and famous jinking runs pale into insignificance when compared with his mental toughness. He persevered and put in countless hours of lonely practice so that if the call ever came he would be ready to answer it.

International caps were the icing on the cake – not the substance of Ward's evaluation of his own rugby career. There is conviction in his voice as he looks back with the benefit of a mature perspective on the vicissitudes of his extraordinary rugby career:

"I have few regrets about my rugby career and I carry very few grudges – and that is genuine."

9. The Boys In Green

Form is temporary. Class is permanent.

What makes a great player? In Ward's opinion this is the wrong question. The proper question, since the different positions on a rugby team require such specialised skills, is what are the characteristics that make a great player in a particular position? However, Ward contends that there is one quality common to all top international players – big match temperament:

"I need go back no further to illustrate this point than the 1993 season and the dramatic arrival onto the Irish team of Eric Ellwood. Here was a player who had not exactly set the club scene alight but once he got his chance on the big stage he played like a master."

A bizarre illustration of the importance of self-confidence to a player is the case of Ray Gravell, the Welsh centre. He consistently required reassurance on the field about his performance. This was used against him by his international colleagues when they were playing against him in club matches. A typical ploy was to approach him early in a match and ask him was he feeling okay. Gravell would be thrown into panic straight away and enquire what prompted the question. He would be told in a most concerned voice that although he had looked the picture of health the previous week when he played so well for Wales now he looked very sickly indeed. As a result his confidence would go to pieces and he would be totally ineffective until some of his Llanelli teammates reassured him he was in the prime of health.

An incident which revealed his insecurity came on the 1980 Lions' tour when he was sharing a room with Ireland's John O'Driscoll. One morning O'Driscoll said with a flourish: "I slept really well." Gravell's response was made in tones of hushed anxiety: "I slept all right, too, didn't I?"

Another famous case of nervous-induced Gravellspeak came on the same tour at a team meeting when he said in his typically earnest way to the great amusement of his colleagues: "I like to get in one really good tackle early in the game, even if it is late . . ."

Ward's abiding memory of Grav on the tour was his reaction to praise after games:

"I would say to him on the Lions' tour in 1980: 'Well played Grav.' Normally when you congratulate a player for his performance after a match he just says: 'Thanks very much.' Grav though would always ask: 'Do you really think so? Did I play well?' in a voice riddled with insecurity. It was extraordinary that such a great player, who was so highly thought of by his peers, could need so much reassuring about his game."

In his long career Ward played with and against many great players. To pay a tribute to some of the greats he decided to select his own greatest Irish team of players who either played with or against him.

Iron Toe And The Prince

As was the case with all positions Ward was spoilt for choice at full-back. He began by considering some of the great players who played with and against him as schoolboys like John Cronin who had everything a great player needed when he played for Terenure College. At club level there were many great full-backs also like Tony Hickie, an outstanding player for St Mary's. Hickie is remembered with particular admiration because he was equally at home with both feet, an unusual accomplishment for any player. He cites Ralph Keyes as the only other example of a player in the modern game with a similar talent. He digresses slightly to confidently predict that Hickie's son, Denis, an Irish schoolboys' international, will one day play for

Ireland. He recalls two very talented players in this position who never made it to the Irish side – Collegians' Roy Palmer, and UCC and Munster's John Barry. Philip Rainey, "Chipper", who finally made it onto the Irish side in 1989 also earned his respect.

However, the eventual choice settled down to five players, John Murphy, Larry Moloney, Tony Ensor, Rodney O'Donnell and Hugo MacNeill. He began by considering the finest attacking full-back he has ever seen to wear an Irish shirt – Larry Moloney:

"Larry's nickname was 'the Prince' and he came from de Valera country, Bruree in county Limerick. He looked anything but a rugby player. He was all skin and bone and looked downright unhealthy when he was playing. He didn't carry himself very well, but what a talent! When he hit the line you knew he was there. In the modern game where the full-back is so important, particularly with the new rules because the mid-field is so cluttered, it is great to have a full-back like that. Witness the way New Zealand struggled after John Gallagher went over to Rugby League.

"Unfortunately, Larry didn't fulfil his true potential when he played for Ireland. His best games were probably on the New Zealand tour in 1976. He had little interest in training. The biggest joke in Munster was that in training sessions, whenever either Larry or Barry McGann was in charge, their warm-up consisted of leaning up against the post and blowing their hands. When it came to physical work they were not overly interested.

"I remember in the '70s when we used go to Sunday training sessions with the Irish squad during Noel Murphy's reign, we would train in the morning, have lunch in the Mount Herbert hotel across the road and have another training session in the afternoon. The way Noisy planned it was that we would have a tactical session in the morning and a tough physical session in the afternoon. At lunch-time Larry, being from a country background, could not resist the spuds, cabbage and bacon. In every single session we had after lunch Larry would be in the bushes throwing up.

"It could justifiably be argued that if he had dedicated himself fully to the task of making it to the top, he would have achieved it. Having said that, if you asked anyone in Garryowen, Limerick or Munster to name their all-time great full-back, I don't think many would go beyond 'the Prince'.

"Johnny Murphy or 'Iron Toe' was a bit like Larry in so many ways. Many remember Johnny from the famous photograph of him going away with David O'Leary, Frank Stapleton and Liam Brady to join Arsenal. Johnny came home almost immediately. I remember I was with Rovers at the time and Louis Kilcoyne brought him to our training session one night. To the best of my knowledge Johnny never played for Rovers.

"I only really got to know him well when I joined Greystones though I have a very clear memory of him in a schools junior game in the semi-final of the Cup between Presentation Bray and Mary's. My great memory of that game is that there were two hulks on the field that day who were way bigger physically than anybody else, Johnny and Rodney O'Donnell. Pres hammered Mary's that day and I went to see them playing Blackrock College in the final. Blackrock won 3-0. This time it was Johnny and Hugo MacNeill who clashed. I remember Pres throwing everything into attack to get a try to win the game and they came in wave after wave of attack but 15-year-old Hugo would tackle Johnny every time.

"I don't believe that Johnny ever fulfilled his full potential and I think he would now be the first to admit that himself. Had he achieved the full level of fitness he might have realised his enormous potential. That's where I have to take my hat off to Hugo MacNeill whose career coincided with Johnny's but Hugo maximised his potential to the fullest whereas Johnny ended up with only three caps . . . A poor return for such an outstanding talent.

"Johnny was the backbone of Greystones for many years. He was a very strong all-round player and very well-built. He captained club and province in his own inimitable style. His after-dinner speeches became almost legendary. It didn't matter who was in the audience – he said it as he saw it no matter whose toes he was treading on. One of the few classics that is printable goes back to a Leinster-Connacht match. Johnny's opening sentence was: "Mr President of Leinster, Mr President of Connacht, players and the rest of youse hangers on.' Only he could get away with it. He was tremendously popular as a player.

"I only played a few games with Tony Ensor. We stayed in the Hampton Court hotel, near Twickenham, before playing England in 1978 and I remember going for a walk with him shortly before the game, at around 12.45 when he said to me: 'Wardy, the hard work is done now.' I knew immediately what he meant. The morning of a match is mental hell and I got a headache after almost every international match. What he was saying in effect was let's work at this, get it over with. Then once we get on the pitch we can start to enjoy ourselves. It was his last game for Ireland.

"I remember him when he was a schoolboy with Gonzaga. He was a great attacking player, the best I have seen as a counter-attacker. He was also a great reader of the game, especially in the one to one overlapping situation.

"Hugo MacNeill's record speaks for itself and he would have to be a very strong candidate for the best ever Irish full-back, but the man I have chosen for that position on my team is Rodney O'Donnell. I knew Rodney since he was knee-high to a grasshopper because he was two years behind me in St Mary's. Much later, his one Test game for the Lions was the same as mine, though it is not a game either of us remember as being one of our best.

"As most people know he sustained a horrific injury on that tour. I was playing with him against the Junior Springboks in Transvaal. Danny Gerber, who went on to become a great centre with the Springboks, stepped off his right foot and Rodney came to tackle him diagonally, as a full-back would do naturally. Rodney stuck out his arm and shoulder to try and take him on the inside, but in the process his neck was knocked back by Gerber's hips. Rodney was in trouble straight away. John O'Driscoll, who is a particularly close friend of Rodney's, sensed something was wrong immediately and was up to him like a shot and would not let anybody go near him because he knew it was a serious injury. When we eventually returned from the tour, surgeons had to graft a piece of bone from his hip and insert it into his neck. It was a sad end to a potentially great career. I genuinely believe he could have been the greatest Irish full-back ever, ahead of George Norton, Tom Kiernan and Hugo MacNeill. Hugo won a huge number of caps but I don't believe he would have got a fraction of them had Rodney been around.

"Rodney's greatest asset was his presence under a high ball. He seldom missed his touch. He was good in the tackle, though like Hugo and Johnny Murphy he was not particularly fast. When he hit the line he was very hard to take down with his low centre of gravity and perfect timing.

"When he graduated to club rugby his nickname in St Mary's was 'Odd Bod' and it was most appropriate. In my final year in Mary's he was big into motorbikes. I was captain of the school team that year and it was part of my brief to get the players to training. Although we trained right beside his house in Kenilworth Square, Rodney was the hardest player to get to train because he always wanted to be working on his motorbike and 'dicing' (racing) with his classmates and fellow rugby players, Declan ('Skinny') Howard and Paul (Hoppy) Oppermann. Only for his mother I would never have managed to drag him along."

Rodney's middle name could have been 'Superstition'. He had a huge fear of anything connected with the number 13. On tour, he refused to stay in a room numbered 13, or 213, or a room on the 13th floor, which was bad enough, but he would not even room in a room in which the numbers added up to 13 like 274.

His pet hate was going out on the pitch more than twice before a match. If he went out to inspect the pitch he would not go on the field again before running out to play if at all possible. Whenever he was forced to commit this unpardonable transgression – chiefly for a team photograph, he was wont to wear the same sort of doleful expression favoured by Alex Ferguson at the end of the 1991-2 season as Manchester United let the first division championship slip through their fingers.

He had an interesting theory about the psychology of the rugby ball. When an opponent had kicked a goal against his team he felt much better if the ball came down in such a way that he was able to throw it back over the crossbar, his theory being that the next time, the ball was either unsure where to go, or would lose the habit of travelling in the right direction.

When he believed in something there could be no deviation. He always insisted on being the last man on the team bus and would patiently wait for every one to assemble on the bus regardless of the climatic conditions. Not surprisingly he refused to step over a line. On a stone pavement he would make the most bizarre movements to avoid treading on one. Such an event could only trigger tragedies of apocalyptic proportions. With all this practice some of his fellow players said he could have been world champion at hopscotch!

Yet another ritual was preparing to tog out before games. He had to put on his togs in such a way that the material did not touch his skin on the way up. Should such a calamity occur he would begin the whole process again – and if necessary again and again until he got it exactly right. The second part of this operation was that he would never button up his togs until he was literally running onto the field.

He was preoccupied with exactitudes to the point that he went around every room adjusting pictures so that they hung straight on the walls. This tendency was dramatically illustrated on Ireland's tour to Australia in 1979. In the middle of Noel Murphy's team talk he jumped up to the astonishment of all present to adjust the position of the telephone.

One of his most famous idiosyncrasies was his desire to get into bed each night without touching the bottom sheet. The task had to be executed with military like precision. If he failed the first time he tried, he kept trying, until he got it exactly right. Only then did he allow himself to relax. Some of the wags on the Irish touring party in Australia had great fun speculating how he might cope on his wedding night!

Ratskinski

Ward began his search for a right winger for his 'ideal' imaginary team with a player who played with distinction on the Lions' tour in 1974:

"Tom Grace's last game for Ireland was my debut. He had lost the captaincy to Johnny Moloney that day which I suppose was ominous. He was a great winger and I have many fond memories of watching him score tries for Ireland, particularly the famous one when he beat Joe Karam to the ball late in the game to give Ireland a 10-10 draw with the mighty All-Blacks. Gracer had a good sense of humour and was a great slagger. He wasn't as good at taking it as he was at dishing it out. He was a great servant of Mary's, Leinster and Ireland.

"He gave me a really solid piece of advice after I was selected for my first cap. Tradition had it at the time, though sadly it has been changed since, that after the final trial both teams went to the Punch Bowl in Booterstown for a few drinks and later back to the Shelbourne Hotel and the team for our first match in the Five Nations Championship was announced.

I can't describe the euphoria I felt when I heard I had been selected for Ireland. Gracer congratulated me but added a note of caution: 'Over the next two weeks people will be slapping you on the back because you have been picked for Ireland. Remember you have still got to go out there and do the business. When you do that you feel pleased with yourself but not until then.' It was a warning I heeded right up to my debut because the fear of being a one cap wonder was very great.

"Terry Kennedy was in the same class as me from second class up. I find it extraordinary to think of what he achieved. While soccer was my chief love at the time I nearly always made the school team whereas Terry was too small to make the first team at any level. He was always captain or vice-captain of the seconds with Patrick Shaffrey (who went on to play full-back for the Irish Universities). When it came to side-stepping Terry was almost peerless. He was so small and slight, as he remains to this day, but his timing in defence was immaculate. He had an amazing ability to take man and ball for such a physically small player.

"He was very talented and I loved playing with him, especially in sevens, because he had the same philosophy of letting the ball go as I. I suppose it was because we were brought up in the same environment that we could reach each other's play so well.

"Terry's nickname is 'the Rat'. Everybody in rugby knows this but very few know its origin. On St Mary's tour to Russia in 1977, J.B. Sweeney, who is a great stalwart of the club, christened Terry, 'Ratskinski' and it was then abbreviated. Hence 'the Rat'.

"Of more recent vintage is Richard Wallace who compares in many respects with Gracer and Trevor Ringland. There are many things about his game that I like though I don't think anyone can deny his defensive play leaves a little to be desired. He is very much a route one man. He only knows the one way – the shortest to the line.

"However, my choice for right wing on my 'ideal' team would be Trevor Ringland, only slightly less of a route one man than Richard Wallace. I well remember the first time I saw him playing. It was before he played for Ireland and we were playing together for the Wolfhounds against Bective Rangers. He was playing on the wing and we had an injury to a forward who had to be replaced by a back. Straight away Trevor volunteered to go into the pack and I think that says it all about the way he played the game – a winger volunteering to go wing forward, especially in such elite company, with top class internationals in the scrum that day like Robert Norster of Wales. He was deceptively fast without having blistering pace and scored some fantastic tries for Ireland.

"I had a clash with him in the World Cup in 1987. Trevor played with Paul Dean in the international side in Doyler's years. Paul's outstanding gift was his ability to straighten the line and release the ball quickly. Trevor was spoilt by that and my style was different to Deano's. After losing our opening game against Wales, I was brought back into the side and Deano was left out for the second game against Canada. We were in the middle of a training session before the game when Trevor said something to me like: 'Straighten up'. I remember losing the head completely with him which I seldom do. It was a big enough ordeal coming into the side unexpectedly without hearing a comment like that. Trevor believed in straight talking. Later that night he came and apologised for the incident and explained what he meant, naturally I understood.

Fab Vinny

"Again there were some great players on the left wing whom I played with and against. One was Vinny Becker. He played scrum-half when he was at school. He had a great physique and low centre of gravity. Although he was not the greatest footballing winger ever, he was very difficult to take down. He was not an out and out route one merchant but a great man to sniff out an opening – like a striker in soccer. The most obvious quality he had was his competitiveness.

"There are two incidents which really illustrated this for me. He took part in the early years of the RTE *Superstars* competition. He would query almost everything, not just about his own results but about other competitors as well. Needless to say this did not do much for his own popularity but it summed up his competitiveness.

"He played in my first ever final trial. The backs were meeting to plan their defence before the game. The full-back and wingers had to decide which system they would use and who would take which player and when. Invariably it depended on the full-back, this time we had decided that our full-back would take the last man which meant that Vinny would most likely have to take the opposing full-back. We discussed this at length with Tom Grace and Tony Ensor doing most of the talking and we thought we had agreed when Vinny interrupted to say: 'I don't care what system you use but once my man comes I'm going to take him and if anybody here thinks I am going to step off my wing and take the full-back and let my man score a try on my side with those assholes (the selectors) watching from the stand – see that happening and think it is my fault, they have another thing coming'. Okay some people might say it was a very selfish attitude but that was the nature of the man to be so competitive that he was not going to give his opposite number any chance to shine. In the context of a final trial his behaviour was understandable. He was nicknamed 'the Red Rocket' for obvious reasons.

"An outstanding attacker for Ireland on the left wing was Freddie McLennan. He was a very talented player, though not the greatest defensively and quite the opposite, physically, to Vinny. He now lives in South Africa. He always seemed to have problems with his hamstring and while most of us would be getting our boots ready before a game and attending to the minor details he would be sprinting up the hotel corridors, warming and stretching his hamstrings. The biggest prankster in the squad was Mick Quinn and he told Freddie that all the great players had a cold bath before every game so Freddie and 'the Rat' always had an ice cold bath. Mind you Quinny used to have one himself.

"However, my choice in this position would have to be Keith Crossan or 'the Gremlin' as he was affectionately known. Keith too was a great attacker but what was special about him was that he was such a competitor, as much at home in defence as attack. Like Trevor Ringland he was fast without being blisteringly so. Keith was the type of player that, if you were going to war and digging deep into the trenches, you would want to have him with you. He was the complete winger, good in timing the tackle and cornerflagging an opponent on the other side as he put in a last ditch try-saving tackle, which he did so often for Instonians, Ulster and Ireland. He had great hands and was a good kicker, competitive in defence but also great in attack and scored many tries for Ireland."

The Men In The Middle

No discussion on great Irish centres could fail to consider Mike Gibson but because Ward played with him at the tail end of his career he did not see him in his prime and therefore was not considered for a place in the imaginary side. However, Ward retains vivid memories of Gibson, particularly from his debut game:

"When you are starting in international rugby you have no idea of the right or wrong way to prepare for such an event. Obviously when I was in school Mike Gibson was *the* player so when I made my debut I was going to do everything as he did. Normally I ate very little before a game but I saw him and Willie Duggan drinking a couple of glasses of a concoction of raw eggs, honey, sherry and cream. Well, I thought, if it was good enough for Mike Gibson it was good enough for me so I had a glass! After I drank it I felt a bit queasy and light-headed. I thought I was going to be tipsy but it was all in the mind and thankfully I was fine for the game. Gibson was arguably the best all round player to play for Ireland and his record speaks for itself.

"One centre I had a lot of time for was Ray Finn, now a doctor in Letterkenny. He and John Brennan were two great centres for Belvedere. They were two huge players at school level. Ray is central to my understanding of the depth of feeling for rugby in Wales. He was a sub and touchjudge in my first ever representative game for the Wolfhounds against Cardiff in their centenary at Cardiff Arms Park in 1975. At one stage the ball was kicked into touch and went out of the stadium over the stand. Ray kicked a spare ball across to the other sideline with a spiral or torpedo kick. There was a huge crowd there that day and the entire stand burst into spontaneous applause at the skill of the kick. To this day I can hear the applause ringing in my ears and it really drove home the depth of passion that there is for the game in Wales my favourite rugby playing country.

"I have said already that Paul Dean was a brilliant centre. He was very fast off the mark, had good hands, good distribution, regularly intercepted opponents' passes more often than not and was a great centre for Ireland in '82.

"Another great St Mary's player was Paul Andreucetti. He was a big bustling centre who went straight from the school side into the first team which was very unusual. Our mentor in Mary's, Fr Kennedy, often pointed out the speed with which he put the ball through his big hands. He made the Irish touring party to Australia in '79 but never got a cap.

"Perhaps the most physically competitive centre I've ever come across was David Irwin. Everybody dreaded playing against him. Seldom do you get a player who would get as physically involved as he. He had a never-say-die attitude which was central to Ulster's success in the '80s. In many ways he was an underrated player in attack because he was so physically good in defence.

"Michael Kiernan was a very talented player. He played on the right wing in our match against Romania in Bucharest in 1982 and had a fantastic game. I was convinced then that he was going to spend his representative career on the right wing. Having said that, the best centre combination I ever saw play for Ireland was Michael and Brendan Mullin. Neither were the best defensively but they organised their lines so well that they covered any deficiencies in that area.

Michael was a very talented natural footballer, a footballing three-quarter with all the bits.

"I remember Mick Doyle's first game against Australia. I was dropped from the panel initially but brought in as a sub. Michael and Moss Finn were the centres. We had a training session in the Suttonians' club. Before the game nobody knew who was going to be place-kicker not even Doyler himself. The feeling was that it would be Moss because he had a bit of experience with his club and at that stage Michael had, really, no experience. I watched them for about 20 minutes and Doyler asked me what I thought and I said: 'Does it matter? You probably have your mind made up already.' He said: 'Yeah, Moss Finn'. I said: 'I think you are making a big mistake because Michael is a far more natural kicker of the ball'. Moss started as kicker against Australia but Michael took over early on when it wasn't working out and the rest is history.

"Paul McNaughton was a player I loved playing with. Macker, Terry Kennedy and myself would run the ball from anywhere in exhibition matches.

"I remember one of a million different interviews carried out at the height of the Ward/Campbell controversy being done by one P.P. McNaughton. Macker was asked for his tuppence worth on the relative merits of each and in a nutshell came down quite emphatically on the side of Seamus Oliver! Tempting though it is to even the score now, I will resist temptation. When it comes to quality in the centre, Macker was a class apart and one of the most under-rated players, even at the highest level of the game. He had the lot. Good hands, strong in the tackle, exceptional in the air, elusive on the break and most importantly the out and out arrogance to 'go for it' from anywhere. He, more than anyone, put Greystones on the international map.

"Brendan Mullin was an outstanding schoolboy talent. Blackrock has provided three of them in recent times – Hugo MacNeill,

Brendan and Neil Francis. Brendan fulfilled his potential though many would argue that he never fully fulfilled it and I for one believe he should be adding to his reputation still because I feel he retired prematurely. Like Michael Kiernan he was an athlete in the strictest sense of the word. That is one reason why they complemented each other so well and put pressure on the opposition. Brendan was a brilliant attacker and reader of the game, whenever you would make a half-break Brendan was always at your shoulder.

"It's always nice to feel you have a guardian angel and I was blessed when I started with Garryowen to have two such guardian angels – Seamus Dennison on my outside and Shay Deering on the inside. Phil Bennett told me about how important Ray Gravell was to him as a minder and Seamus did that kind of a job for me. He won caps for Ireland on the wing but none in the centre which I find extraordinary.

"He didn't look the slick, macho type but he was a great footballer. Nobody who saw it will ever forget his tackle on Stu Wilson in Munster's victory over the All-Blacks in 1978 which summed him up. I remember after that when we played for Garryowen opposing centres would be eyeing him up and he would say: 'Here's another gunslinger'. Everyone wanted to take him on and hit him with a tackle like he hit Stu Wilson. After the game he would say: 'There's another notch on the belt', when he won the duel, as he invariably did. He too was a very under-rated player, very skilful, with a brilliant dummy, a very good tackler, good runner and very fit.

"It was a pleasure and an honour to play with Seamus, Brennie and Macker and it was a struggle to select my final two. I would pick Seamus without hesitation and I would have to favour Brendan over Paul, for his sheer class and pace.

"Another player I have to mention at this juncture is Moss Finn. Both Moss and I played our first final trial together. We were staying in the Shelbourne Hotel and I was sitting with him and Tom Grace at lunch and he was telling us how good he was feeling. It was possibly his first trip to Dublin and he went on to say that he had been out for a lovely walk in front of the hotel to see the ducks in the Phoenix Park. He had of course been to Stephens' Green but he genuinely thought it was the Phoenix Park. Of course the worst possible person to make a mistake like that in front of was Gracer who needless to say had a good laugh and never let him forget it. The great thing about Moss, and to a large part the reason he was so popular in the dressing-room, was that he always made himself the butt of his jokes.

"I would have to have Moss as my utility reserve back because he could play in any position. I argued for many years his best position would be full-back because he had such great pace and strength in joining the line. Coincidentally I have long felt the same about Nicky Barry as a possible full-back or outside centre. Moss is best remembered for his tries in '82 especially the two against Wales. He was a great character in the dressing-room."

The Good, The Bad And Ollie

Ward began his consideration of contenders for the out-half position with another former soccer player like himself, Barry McGann, a former Shelbourne player:

"When it came to tactical kicking Barry McGann was without peer, though he was not the fastest in the world. The main memories I have of him go back to my own schooldays in Mary's and Fr Kennedy telling us that when you got within 10 or 15 yards of the opposing line it was sacrilege to kick the ball away. Then I would watch Barry playing for Ireland and see the amount of tries he would set up from that position with his little grubber kicks for Alan 'Dixie' Duggan to run on to and score. I must confess, I listened to Fr Kennedy and now preach the same message to my pupils in school.

"Barry had great physical presence and was a wonderful team player. He could kick onto the proverbial sixpence. I remember

playing for Munster against Ulster in Thomond Park in 1976 and
Johnny McDonnell, who was playing in the centre for us, had to leave
the field. McGann came on with 10 minutes to go, I passed to him
and straight away he thumped an almighty ball into the air and it
came down with snow on it – so whether it was out-half, centre or
prop forward he was born to kick."

Another contender was Mick Quinn:

"Quinny was an outstanding schools player who won the Leinster
Cup with Newbridge College in 1970. He had a massive boot of the
ball and loved physical contact. He was a non-stop chatterbox and the
biggest difficulty I had playing against him was trying to ignore his
chat.

"He is an awful prankster. The way I would sum up Mick Quinn is
to say that he is 41 going on 21. He is a great man for the nicknames.
Mick was a great servant of Leinster and I think his return of caps for
Ireland was a fair reflection of his talent.

"I have one of many memories of him from 1990 when we played a
golden oldies games in Anglesea Road against the Welsh side the
morning of the corresponding international between the countries.
There was about 4,000 people there, Quinny was organising the
whole thing in his own inimitable style. He does a lot of great fund-
raising work for the Childrens' Hospital in Crumlin. Before the
match he came into the dressing-room and said: 'Wardy there's some
auld fella outside and he wants a word with you.' I hadn't played for
over a year, I was in dreadful physical condition and I just wanted to
prepare for the match and get it over with. I said: 'Don't be annoying
me' or a more colourful variation of it. Eventually I agreed to go out
but with some trepidation because you never know what to expect
with Quinny. Who was waiting for me but Neil Kinnock and his son. I
didn't know what to say. The reason he was there was just to meet me.
It was a great boost for my ego, particularly as it seemed at the time
that he would be the next prime minister. He was reminiscing about

games I had played in Cardiff. He told me how he had brought his son to those matches when he was only a boy and that he had liked my style of play. It meant a lot to me to know that he had gone to all that trouble just to shake my hand.

"Ralph Keyes was a great all-round player. In fact, as is well documented at this stage, I found it extraordinary that the selectors would choose Brian Smith ahead of him for the Irish team. Nobody compares to Ralph as a two-footed player. His kicking and all round play was superb. I was delighted to see him doing so well in the '91 World Cup when he was at last recognised as the class player he assuredly was.

"I remember him when I was playing with Munster and he was an outstanding player at under-20 level. I was starting to wonder would it happen for him. He wasn't the greatest trainer. Probably if he had worked harder at his game he would have been an even better player but that's Ralph. I'm sorry he has retired. It's ironic that he and Michael Bradley never played for Ireland together.

"Paul Dean was an outstanding schoolboy player from the St Mary's backline conveyor belt. When it comes to a running, 15-man game he was the tops but he didn't influence the game as much as Ollie even though he was a great player in his own right. When I am picking my schoolboy teams I always like to have a player like Deano as out-half on my side."

However, there was never any doubt as to who Ward would have as out-half on his 'ideal' team – Seamus Oliver Campbell:

"Ollie was by far the outstanding out-half. He had all the little bits and pieces that make up a great player. Defensively he was a workaholic. He acted like a third wing forward. Ollie maximised his potential to the fullest. I worked very hard at my game but so too did Ollie. He lived, drank and slept the game. He was the sweetest striker of the ball I have ever seen, from his hands or off the ground, and again this was something he worked hard on."

We're Forty Minutes From Immortality

As the rain lashes incessantly on the window on an Irish summer's day Ward rhymes off the players who caught his eye in the scrum-half position. He began with a somewhat surprising selection:

"Not many people might remember Danno Heaslip but he was a great scrum-half for Galwegians. He was the heart of the team for so many years. Games between himself and another great scrum-half, Liam Hall, were a great battle of wit, in every sense of the term.

"Fergus Aherne is an outstanding reader of the game. If he has a weakness in his game it is that he attempts to break too often. He is a beautiful passer of the ball off either hand, a lovely, balanced runner who runs on his toes and has a lovely chip kick. He is very competitive and is the traditional, nippy scrum-half.

"When I was playing for Garryowen, Liam Hall retired at the end of my first season with them. The club went through a hard time finding an adequate replacement so when I played with Munster it was a particular joy to link up with Donal Caniffe. With his long arms the pass he could throw out was a joy. Like Johnny Moloney and, to a lesser extent, Tony Doyle he was not the model build for a scrum-half. The classic number nine is a small, nippy Jacques Fouroux type player. Donal was captain of the Munster team that beat the All-Blacks. My fondest memory of him from that game was when we gathered around at half-time leading 9-0. There was an eerie silence because the crowd could not cope with a shock of such massive proportions. To keep us all fired up all Donal said was: 'We're 40 minutes from immortality. . . . believe it!'

"Robbie McGrath was scrum-half on the 1982 Triple Crown side and deservedly so. He had a great all-round game and was an incredible servant to Wanderers' club into the bargain. He was arguably the most rounded scrum-half of this era in that he had all the skills.

"If I had to pick the best club scrum-half that I played with, at club-level, it would be Tony Doyle. Tony's weakness is his physique. He is so thin and light and often rides competitively as a jockey. He didn't break as often as he could but when it comes to passing and twisting his body to find his man, he was the best and I know that other out-halves, Mick Quinn for one, agree with me wholeheartedly.

"As he has shown in 1993, in difficult circumstances, Michael Bradley is an excellent player. His strengths are his organisational qualities, his work rate, his tackling, and working close-in linking the back-row and his leadership. He is like a third wing forward. His Achilles heel is the consistency of his passing.

"John Robbie was the classical scrum-half, if ever there was one. He was a brilliant passer, a lovely kicker of the ball and a great captain and leader. He is now a radio chat show host in South Africa. We toured together with the Lions in 1980. It was an unusual occurrence because we had four Irish half-backs on that tour, John, Colin Patterson, Ollie and I. Robbie, or 'JR', was responsible for the biggest disappointment of my career when he scored the winning try for the High School side that beat us 10-9 in the Leinster Cup semi-final in '73.

"Although in 1976 when he was first capped for Ireland he was playing with Trinity, JR has had a huge influence on Greystones club. John is from Greystones and played his underage rugby there until he went to college. He was at the heart of their rise to the big time in Irish rugby before he emigrated to South Africa.

"John Moloney was a most under-rated player even though he won 27 caps for Ireland. He was the ultimate third wing forward. With his athletic build, his work rate around the field and ability to read the game his impact was phenomenal. Tony Doyle was the best passing scrum-half I played with but Johnny Moloney was the best all round tactical scrum-half I ever played with. There was no finer reader of the game. To summarise Johnny, he was a combination of John Robbie, Donal Canniffe and Michael Bradley. When I was in first year in Mary's he was a special hero for me. It was such a thrill to play with him for St Mary's and Ireland years later.

"Overall though, the outstanding scrum-half I played with was without doubt, Colin Patterson. I will never forget playing with him in South Africa the day he sustained the injury that ended his career. He passed the ball to me and as I ran on he was tackled. Next I heard a groan of pain and the play broke down and I rushed straight back to him because I knew immediately it was a serious injury. He wrecked his medial ligaments. We played a few exhibition games afterwards when he played with a brace on his knee.

"Colin had everything. The media at the time went on a lot about Robbie's pass being vastly superior to Patterson's but they forgot to ask those who mattered most – those at the receiving end. It is significant that the best years of my career coincided with Patty's pass. He had the chirpy personality and arrogance that is so needed. It wasn't just self-confidence, it was an arrogance, which I was particularly fond of. He is a great friend and was a great scrum-half and if he had not got injured he would have been shown, like Rodney O'Donnell, to be one of the all time greats – which in my opinion he is anyway.

"Had he not got that injury, he had arranged to go out and play in Australia for a season. In fact he already had his ticket bought. Possibly he would have gone on to play for Australia and not returned.

"I bumped into Colin recently at Terry Kennedy's wedding. Colin is now coach to the Irish Colleges' side and he was raving about Niall Hogan – a scrum-half from Terenure who will play for Ireland sooner rather than later. I asked him if he still remembered the National Anthem and I was delighted to hear he does but now he rounds it off with a verse from the Sash just to give it political balance!"

The Stuff Of Legend

One of Ward's most difficult selections was the number eight position. He began his recollections by recalling two number eights who were unfortunate not to play for Ireland, St Mary's Declan Fanning and Connacht's Mick Casserly. There were two serious rivals for the final selection but he also gave serious consideration to Mike Gibson the younger:

"Mike Gibson played at full-back when he was at school and many would argue that he played there as a number eight! He was a very under-rated player whose best years at the highest level coincided with mine. One of my happiest memories in the green shirt was in Auch in 1988 when he gave one of the the best displays of number eight rugby that I have ever seen. He was brilliant. Gibbo that night took the game by the scruff of the neck and was physically involved, which was an aspect of the game he was often accused of avoiding. He and Willie Duggan were in many ways, in the rugby context, polar opposites with Donal Spring somewhere in between.

"When Gibbo got stuck in he was a great player. He was seen by some as a bit of a glamour boy. He was very good in the loose and the line-out. His weakness was that he was a little loose all round as a number eight.

"Donal Spring will, I believe, one day coach the Irish team. If he doesn't it will be a crying shame. He is one of the few genuinely gifted people we possess in this country to read a game and to be a coach at the highest level.

"His return in terms of caps was pretty poor. I remember walking with Johnny Moloney in Paris in 1978 the night before we played France and he said that of all the young players he had seen and from the attitude he had shown on his debut, Donal would be the backbone of the Irish team for the next ten years. He had made his debut in the same game as me two weeks previously but missed the trip to Paris because he injured himself falling down the stairs in

Trinity. Sadly, for many reasons, not least of which was injury, Johnny's prediction never came to pass.

"What he had above the majority of other number eights was the ability to read a game. He was a real thinking man's player. He was a great strategist and liaised so well with the defence.

"Willie Duggan was one of those players, like Keith Crossan, that you wouldn't go to war without. He had such a physical presence and was so competitive. I found it hard to choose between himself and Donal but in the end Willie would have to be my final choice."

Legend and myth have built up around Willie Duggan. One story dates back to 1978 when Willie was playing for the Lions against a Maori team in a very physical contest. At one stage he was trapped at the bottom of a ruck when a few players kicked him on his head. True to form he got up and carried on. After the game he was asked did he remember about the pounding on his head. His reply was vintage Dugganesque: "I do. I heard it."

How true are these stories?

"I had heard stories about him smoking in the dressing-room before international matches but didn't really believe it. My first time to play with him for Ireland was my debut and I remember going on a nerves induced visit to the toilet before the match and sure enough there was Willie smoking away. I found that unbelievable at the time.

"He hadn't a great interest in the theoretical side of the game. I remember him falling asleep during a team talk in Sydney in 1979. Willie's attitude was that he was prepared to dish out punishment and take it in equal amounts. He certainly was the toughest forward I have ever seen with only Shay Deering coming close. He wallowed in a rough-tough game. He seldom went into a ruck without the ball coming out on his side.

"On the downside his discipline left an awful lot to be desired. The classic story told about him in this respect is that in the '70s when he was finding it difficult to turn up for training with his club team,

Blackrock in Dublin. It was agreed, at John Cantrell's suggestion, that one Sunday the entire squad would go down to Kilkenny Rugby Club to facilitate Willie because he lived there. That morning they were all there apart from guess who? Willie! Somebody had to go and wake him because he had slept it out.

"He would not be my type of player or I his – yet at the end of the day he would most definitely be in my side."

The Magnificent Sevens

As was the case for the number eight position there were two outstanding candidates for the open-sided wing-forward position though Ward noted the talents of Derek McGrath, Alan McLean and Willie Sexton. Not surprisingly he retains a soft spot for Christy Cantillon the player who scored Munster's try in their victory over the All-Blacks:

"He was one player I was always conscious of when I played against him. He loved playing against me and I enjoyed playing against him. He was as fair as they came and a real character into the bargain. Mind you, he had a bit of a devilish streak in him too. One night during our Australian tour in '79, himself and Pa Whelan stripped the then rugby correspondent of *The Irish Press*, Bob Messenger, naked in the hotel elevator and left him there. There was a big fuss about it the following day following an official complaint."

However, the choice was between two quite outstanding players, Fergus Slattery and Nigel Carr:

"Nigel looked for a long time as if he was always going to be the bridesmaid never the bride, until he got his first cap. In my view he was the most important piece in Mick Doyle's jigsaw in 1985. It was he who brought continuity into that game plan. He was one of the best I played with or against.

"I will never forget hearing the news of the horrific bombing that gave him the injury that ended his career. We were having a squad session in Merrion Road when Syd Miller broke the news to us. I remember our anxiety for him and also for Philip Rainey and David Irwin. It was the first time the Northern troubles ever impinged on me and it really brought home to me the mindlessness and barbarity of the violence.

"Without doubt the greatest open-sided flanker I ever saw in an Irish jersey was Fergus Slattery. Slatts was never a particular fan of mine but the reverse is not the case. He simply never gave up. Slatts at his best was the best and that is recognised worldwide. What he had was presence on the field in the opposing out-half's mind. He was always first to the break-down and first to the out-half but it was the angle of his running that gave him so many options. Only three players ever attempted to put me off when I was taking 22 drop-outs by talking to me, Willie Burns, an outstanding hooker who would have made it all the way to the top were it not for injury, Ciaran Fitzgerald and Slatts."

The classic story about Fergus Slattery goes back to an African trip. After a British Lions' tour fixture in Rhodesia in 1974, there was a celebratory dinner organised. The then Rhodesian Prime Minister, Ian Smith, arrived to make a speech. Shortly after, two Irish players, Dick Miliken, and Slattery decided to return to their hotel. Having consumed beverages stronger than orange juice they were feeling particularly adventurous. As they walked out they noticed, just outside the entrance to the club, a beautiful Cadillac with black-tinted windows. They decided to borrow the car and go for a drive. After driving around for a few minutes, the partition behind the front seats slid across and the Prime Minister said: "Are you gentlemen looking for a job?"

Six Of The Best

Yet another position where Ward had many options was blind side wing forward. On his initial list were Noel McCarthy (St Mary's and

Connacht), Paul Collins (UCC and London-Irish) Ian Crowe (City of Derry) and Malone's Willie Duncan. Then he cut his list down to six, beginning with Pat O'Hara:

"Pat was a revelation on the tour of France in 1988. He was the sort of guy you would take to the Alamo. He never complained and always had a smile on his face despite his injuries. He is the outstanding character in the Irish squad at the moment.

"Another great character, one of the greatest I have come across, was Stuart McKinney. He was a great player and had many party pieces, the best-known being his ability to eat all the flowers on the table at a rugby dinner. He was constantly requested to do so and generally obliged.

"John O'Driscoll made his debut in the same game as me. He was a tremendous back row player and complimented perhaps Ireland's finest ever back row in modern times with Willie Duggan and Slatts. He was at his best in the Lions' tour in South Africa in 1980. A very gentle and sensitive man he was just a bit different after a drink or two.

"The classic story to illustrate this is of the night he dangled Terry Kennedy by the legs as he held him outside the Elangheni Hotel window in Durban during Ireland's tour of South Africa in 1981. Kennedy was several storeys up and in O'Driscoll's condition he had reason to pray harder than he had ever prayed before."

Ollie Campbell has one very clear memory of John O'Driscoll:

"In 1981 after Tony was brought back onto the Irish team and I was at the centre John went out with me for a walk just before the game. I was never really comfortable playing in the centre. Suddenly John told me that he was delighted I was playing in the centre. My morale lifted straightaway and I inquired why. He said: 'Now at least we will have somebody at out-half who can make a tackle!' Thanks very much John! He really sucked me in for the killer punch and I never saw it coming."

Ward went on to consider one of his former Munster colleagues:

"Colm Tucker was unusual insofar as he won more Lions caps than Irish caps, three Lions and two Irish as far as I can remember. He was a great servant of Shannon and Munster. I played against him often. Many times he would come charging at me with the ball tucked under his arms and the crowd loved it. Although he was not the most mobile ever he was a good ball handler and had great upper body strength.

"Philip Matthews just fails to make my team by a whisker. In my opinion he almost had the lot. He was our one truly world class player before his illness. He had a great head for the game and was a great reader of it. He was one of the few players in Irish rugby who could drive players back in a tackle which is a real art in itself. I can think of very few players who can do that. He had great upper body strength like Shay Deering. He was unique insofar as he was one of the few Irish forwards who could actually sidestep. So many are content when they get the ball just to drive into their opponent.

"But for me the best by far in this position was Shay Deering. He was the ultimate personification of bravery. His biggest problem was his lack of fear. He would stick his head in where few would stick their boot. Fergus Slattery would be the first to admit that the way he and Shay complimented each other for UCD and Leinster was a significant factor in Slatts progression to the top.

"His caps were a paltry return relative to his ability and commitment. He was one of those players who oozed, and I mean oozed, physical presence and charisma. He was the original gentleman off the pitch but boy was he a hard man on it. He particularly loved showing a gap to an outside half or scrum-half and then when the player took the bait he pounced on him. My favourite rugby player of all time is Gerald Davies, but my all time hero is Shay Deering."

The Pluck Of The Irish

It is inconceivable that a discussion on great Irish second rows could begin without a reference to Willie John. The fact that it is unnecessary to use his surname says it all. Gareth Edwards has gone on record to say that Willie John was his sort of captain because of his creed of total commitment and he would have followed him anywhere. Willie John was wont to say: 'I hate small men.' Each match was rugby's high noon for him. He believed in all or nothing – 'lay down your life or don't come with me.'

Another story told about that 1974 Lions' tour shows a different side to Willie John's personality. One night a group of players were disturbed in their hotel in the middle of the night. An undiplomatic war broke out. The tiny hotel manager tried to keep the peace. Two scantily clad players were parading around the corridors and he roared at them to get back into their rooms. Not liking his attitude they told him with all due lack of politeness what to do with himself. The manager's threat to ring the police met with no reaction. At this point along came Willie John. The manager thought his problems were solved when the captain arrived. When McBride seemed to be ignoring the matter the manager repeated his threat to call the police. McBride called him forward with a tilt of his head. The manager breathed a sigh of relief. His threat had worked. He was in for a big disappointment as Willie John bent down to him and whispered: 'How many are you going to get?'

When the Lions won the series a magnificent party was staged in the hotel. The festive spirit got a little out of hand and every fire extinguisher and water hose in the hotel was set off. The problem was that nobody thought to turn them off. The result was that the next morning the hotel could have done with the services of Noah's Ark. The touring manager was summoned the next morning to explain the actions of his team. He had gone to bed early and had no idea what had happened until he discovered himself thigh deep in water.

He half-walked, half-swam up to Willie John's room and prepared to knock on the door only to discover that the door had been a casualty of the flood. To his astonishment McBride was calmly sitting on his bed, puffing contentedly on his pipe, as it bobbed around on the water. The manager lost control and launched into a viscous tirade. Finally, Willie John replied:

"Alan, can I ask you one question?"

"What?"

"Is there anybody dead?"

Ward did not play with Willie John when he was at his peak and thus did not consider him for a place on his team. Some of the second rows he saw who caught his eye were Ballymena's Harry Steele, Shannon's Brendan Foley, Bective's Louis Magee, Wesley's George Wallace and the Connacht pair of Joe Healy and Mick Molloy. However, he narrowed his choice down to five contenders beginning with a player who is still available for selection on the Irish team:

"Neil Francis was an extraordinary talent as a schoolboy. He didn't make it as quickly as expected in the senior ranks. Perhaps he was pushed too quickly by Blackrock. He won two caps in the '87 World Cup but in Auch in 1988 he gave a display the like of which I have never seen from a second row. He was unbelievable in the lineout and his driving was phenomenal. What we had that night was a committed Neil Francis and when Neil is turned on there's nobody better. Sadly, he has often failed to deliver his potential in the Irish jersey.

"The other extreme was Jim Glennon. What he lacked in talent he made up for with sheer commitment. He was a great character with a wonderful sense of humour, from something of a Cinderella club. What he has done for Skerries in terms of keeping them on the map, only they can appreciate themselves. He always gave 150% and was as honest as the day is long. He was never a great lineout winner but very hard to get a line-out ball from and as he said to me many times: 'Nobody uses his bum better in the lineout than Jim Glennon does'."

A very strong candidate for a position on this 'ideal' team was Willie Anderson – one of the more colourful characters in Irish rugby. He was on a tour of Argentina with the Penguins in the late '70s and took a shine to the Argentinian flag. He decided to climb up a flagpole and claim it as his own. Unfortunately he was caught in the act by the Argentinian police who promptly threw him in jail. The affair provoked a diplomatic incident and Anderson spent months in jail. All rugby players in Ireland were asked to contribute via the clubs to a fund to pay for the legal expenses in the attempt to have him released.

"Willie is one of the greatest characters in the game. I have a lot of fond memories of him. I played with him the first time he played in the second row. For most of his career he had been a number eight. It was Garryowen's centenary match against Cardiff in 1984 and he and I were Garryowen's two guest players that day. Within months he had his first cap for Ireland in the second row against Australia. I remember we had a great night in the clubhouse until the small hours. The next morning Willie was up at 6.30 to travel to attend a training session with Jimmy Davidson in Ulster. That was so typical of Willie. I doubt if any player has played in more exhibition matches to open club pitches etc., than he. I know it's a cliché but his enthusiasm is infectious. He is now development officer to the IRFU and he really is to the manor born for that position.

"One of his many party pieces is playing the bagpipes. I remember after we lost to Wales in the World Cup in '87 we went to the Welsh team hotel for the official dinner, Willie pulled out a plastic bag from under the table and took out his pipes. Needless to say a good night was had by all.

"I find it very hard to leave him off my team. I will never forget that night in Auch when both of us were crying tears of joy. He would be my reserve utility forward. He never had the bulk of Moss but boy did he make up for it in terms of attitude.

"My two choices are Donal (Mannix) Lenihan and Moss. Donal was a great player, a leader who led by example. He struggled a bit as Irish captain the first time but once he settled into the job he did well the second time. He was a great ball winner who learned a lot from playing with Mossy. He had great confidence and was a great servant of Irish rugby.

"Mossy was one of the greatest characters of Irish rugby. On the pitch he was a tiger but off the field a pussycat. My earliest memory of him goes back to 1975 when he was a big name and I was just a rookie and we were playing against each other in an exhibition match in Thurles. He came over after the game and asked me about a match I had played for Shamrock Rovers the previous weekend. I couldn't believe he knew who I was.

"I remember playing against England in '79 and he took off on a run. The crowd were chanting: 'Mossy, Mossy'. He was one of those larger than life characters who lifts the whole crowd and that in turn lifts the team.

"Mossy came down to Greystones to play in a match to mark our jubilee season between Greystones and Fitzy's '82 Triple Crown winning side. Former Manchester United European Cup winning full-back, Shay Brennan, was also down for the game. In Greystones they are well used to big names in the rugby world visiting but not famous soccer stars like Shay. Mossy was with him in the bar, having consumed quite a few drinks. He was a little cheesed off that Shay was getting all the attention, and everyone was asking him questions but nobody was passing any remarks on him. Eventually Moss threw in a question – a real show stopper: 'Who played soccer for Scotland and cricket for England?' There was total silence. Needless to say everyone in the bar was a sports fan and scratching their heads trying to figure out this riddle. Finally we were all forced to concede defeat. Moss walked out and as he left he told us the answer: 'Denis Law and Ian Botham'!"

Stories about Moss abound. On Test duty in New Zealand Moss predicted the outcome of a particular match in the best tradition of Kerry talkers: "The first half will be even. The second half will be even worse."

Another story told about Mossy dates from the same tour. After their Second Test victory the Lions threw the party to beat all parties in the team hotel. It was soon discovered that one of their players was missing. When everyone else expressed concern about him Moss said he knew where the missing person was – next door with his girlfriend. Moss was dispatched to bring the guilty party back – though given strict instructions not to break down any doors. (His nickname on that tour was 'Rent-a-Storm' so the decree seemed more than justified.) The rest of the squad listened to a slight flurry next door and moments later Moss came in the door with the missing player under one arm, completely naked and squirming like a fish on a hook. Under the other arm he held the player's girlfriend in a similar state of undress and embarrassment. Moss in his best Kerry accent boomed out: "To be sure, did you be wanting the two of them?"

Another classic story about Moss goes back to one of his tours with the Barbarians in Wales. At one stage his team went to the bar after a game of golf. Although everybody else was drinking beer, Moss, with commendable patriotism, was drinking Guinness and was knocking back two pints to everyone else's one. As dinner time approached it was decided it was time to return to the team hotel. As people prepared to leave somebody shouted, 'One for the road'. Ten pints later for the team at large and twenty pints later for Moss, the team was again summoned to the team bus. Moss was asked if the team should stay for one more drink. He shook his head. When questioned why he was opposed to the idea Moss replied: "No, I don't. To be sure, I don't want to be making a pig of myself."

Moss paid an interesting tribute to Ollie Campbell after the 1980 final trial. The probables beat the possibles 28-12 with Campbell giving a virtuoso performance, scoring 24 points, including three tries. Moss scored the other try to complete the team's scoring. In the dressing-room Moss turned around to Campbell and said: "Wasn't it great that it was only me and you who got our scores all the same."

One of Ward's most vivid memories of Moss goes back to Munster's match with the All-Blacks in 1978:

"We were leading 12-0 with only minutes left and there was a scrum close to the sideline. Our lads wheeled the scrum and drove the Blacks over the sideline right up against the wall. The All-Blacks were not very pleased about this and a scuffle broke out. One of their players, Andy Hayden, swung out his arm to have a swipe at Brendan Foley and Moss grabbed him by the arm and said: 'Don't. You'll lose that battle as well.' Hayden turned, smiled and accepted it. The meaning was clear."

The Boring Forward

Again there was no shortage of characters for the prop positions though Ward cheated slightly when making his decision about his two final choices, picking two loose heads and playing one at tight head. At loose head prop he first thought of Dolphin's Phil O'Callaghan:

"Like Moss Keane he was one of the great characters of the game and like Moss it was a real honour and pleasure to have been involved with Philo over the years. He is a very caring and compassionate man off the pitch which goes against the image many people have of him as a dirty player. He had a very quick wit. The most oft quoted story about him is the day a referee penalised him and said: 'You're boring!' (The term used to describe the way a prop-forward drives in at an illegal angle into an opposing prop-forward). Philo's retort, straightaway and without thinking, was: 'Well, you're not so entertaining yourself ref'. The ref penalised him a further 10 yards.

"Jim McCoy, 'Big Jimmy', was an incredible mobile part of Mick Doyle's 1985 side. He was a great tourist and had a great sense of humour. He competed very much with Dessie Fitzgerald for the number three shirt on the Irish side. Jimmy was better in the loose with Dessie the better scrumager.

"Ginger McLoughlin was a legend in his own lifetime. He gave up his teaching job to go to South Africa in 1981. He came back to open his own bar but it didn't really work out and now he is running a wine bar in Wales. He will always be remembered for his famous try against England in 1982. Ginger epitomises the spirit of Munster rugby.

"My choices for the prop positions are Phil Orr and Nick Popplewell and there are many comparisons between the two. Phil's career speaks for itself and now as a Test player with the Lions the same can be said of Nick, who I have seen develop from a raw recruit to the giant he is now. It is hard to separate the two but as I played most of my representative career with Philly I am picking him at loose head with Poppy in the unaccustomed tight-head position."

A Breed Apart

Ward considers that Ireland has been particularly blessed with hookers down through the years:

"The hooker in the modern game has to be a third prop forward – with a very strong upper body. The French started this trend. Into this category, straightaway was Ballymena's Steve Smith, a very quiet guy, who was marvellous in terms of throwing in to the lineout. He was also very hard to dispossess. The same could be said of Spud Murphy, whom I believe to be, pound for pound, the outstanding forward in Irish rugby at present. He is a great competitor. His commitment is in the Shay Deering category. If only his throw-in was up to Steve Smith's standard there would not be a hooker on the scene fit to lace his boots. Harry Harbison was a great hooker – very much in the Steve Smith mould.

"John Cantrell was technically the best striker of the ball Ireland has ever had. He lacked the ruggedness of the others and was unlucky to be around the same time as Fitzy and Pa Whelan. He was a lovely thrower of the ball.

"I find it very hard to divide between Fitzy and Pat Whelan. It's amazing that Pa never captained Ireland because he had an incredible will to win. Pat, like most hookers, was not afraid to get physically involved. It's a horrible saying, but 'You live by the sword' was Pat's motto and he was even more ruthless than Fitzy.

"Hookers are a breed apart. They are not so much interested in the final score as in their own personal battles in the scrum, particularly who gets the most heels against the head. Battles between Fitzy and Pa were always very intense.

"Ciaran is intense by personality. He always involved everybody in the Irish squad when we came together for weekends. When he spoke it always came from the heart and I can say that about very few people. He asked for nothing that he wasn't prepared to give of himself. For me he was far and away, and I mean far and way, the best captain I ever saw or played under. He was the biggest single influence in Ireland's Triple Crown wins in '82 and '85 and I say that despite the powerful presences of Tom Kiernan and Mick Doyle in their outstanding achievements. Nobody but nobody can ever take that from him despite his rough ride as coach."

Captain Fantastic

With the increasing importance of the coach and the manager in top class rugby the captain's role may have decreased as others have increased, but rugby matches can never be controlled from the bench. Someone has to take responsibility on the field.

The beauty of television coverage of sport is that it can occasionally capture an image which offers a telling insight into a sporting hero. No TV viewer will ever forget the glare on Packie Bonner's face as he prepared to boot the ball up the field just before Kevin Sheedy's goal in Ireland's match against England in the 1990

World Cup. The defiant glare spoke volumes about the heart of the Irish team.

For the Irish rugby fan a comparable image will always be Ciaran Fitzgerald's efforts to rally the Irish team as they appeared to be letting the Triple Crown slip from their fingers in 1985 against England. Even those who had no experience of lip-reading could clearly make out his plea from the heart: "Where's your pride? Where's your ******* pride?"

"In rugby, more than in any other team game, the captain has a vital role to play. In other codes the captain can be a figurehead and get away with it but in rugby he has a key job to do. Off the field he must work on the psychological preparation of the team and then on the field he must be a superb motivator to get the best out of his players.

"I have no hesitation in saying that Ciaran Fitzgerald was the best captain I had the good fortune to play under during my career. In fact I saw him as a man apart.

"What marked him out from everyone else was his ability to work so well with the different personalities in the team, handle their idiosyncrasies as individuals and collectively fire them with a burning will to win when they stepped on the field of play. Never was the dictum "All for one and one for all" better displayed, as far as the Irish team was concerned, than when Ciaran was captain.

"He was a great man for the big occasion, who revelled in the atmosphere when the Championship or Triple Crown was at stake. I believe that leaders are born not made. Of course you can develop your leadership qualities but, to be a great captain, you must be born with innate qualities and Fitzgerald had them in abundance.

"His record speaks for itself – Triple Crown and Championship in 1982, a share of the Championship in '83 and the triple Crown again in 1985. He was often criticised for his throwing-in at the lineout. My answer to his detractors who were so vociferous on that point is just one word – rubbish. Okay, so it was not his strongest point, but no one could ever say it was the cause of losing vital games. If it had been how could Ireland, under Fitzgerald's leadership, have achieved so much?

"Personally, I suspect that there was a hidden agenda in the approach of some sections of the British media to Ciaran. They could never accept him being named captain of the Lions for New Zealand in 1983, so they sought to attack him as a player. It is to his eternal credit that he did not allow the constant harping to diminish his self-confidence. He came up with the perfect reply by leading Ireland to famous victories, and some of his harshest critics were forced to eat their words after that second Triple Crown in '85.

"The only men who came close to Ciaran in displaying the qualities of leadership that I admire in a captain were Pat Whelan and Willie Anderson. How is it that so many of the great captains in the history of the game have been hookers?"

The Boss

The great Gareth Edwards once claimed: "Rugby football is really a simple game; it's only the coaches who make it complicated." This remark should be treated with caution because such was Edwards talent that he could make things look easy which other mortals would have found impossible. Although it may have more than a grain of truth the reality is that coaches exert a huge influence in the modern game. Ward played under six coaches for Ireland – Roly Meates, Noel Murphy, Tom Kiernan, Willie John McBride, Mick Doyle and Jimmy Davidson. In his eyes, representative coaches ought to be judged on three main characteristics – organisational ability, motivational qualities and, communicative skills:

"It's not the coach's job to get the players fit. Players have the responsibility of arriving at the sessions in as close to peak condition as is possible. The coach's organisational qualities come to the fore in

The Lions tame the Barbarians (1980)

This Caps It All "Down Under" (1980)
Tony Ward on a visit to a diamond mine
in Kimberly

Rugby Union International, 1981
Tony Ward passes the ball to Ollie Campbell

The graduates!
Dave Mahedy and Tony Ward qualify as teachers, Limerick,
October 1978

The family man
Tony with his wife, Louise and children

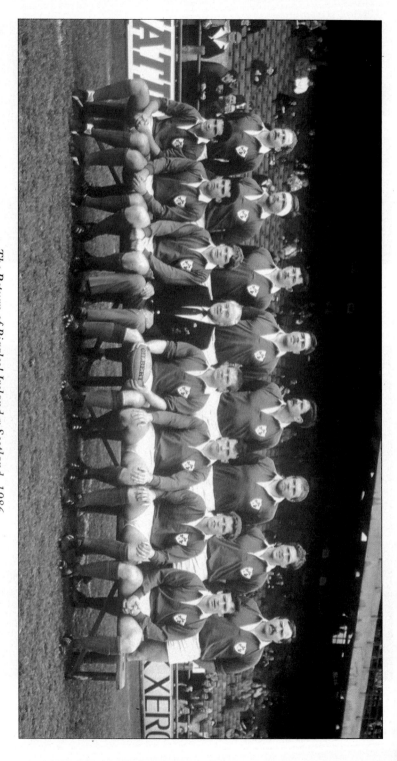

The Return of Biggles! Ireland v Scotland, 1986
Back (l – r): Nigel Carr, Des Fitzgerald, Brian McCall, Donal Lenehan, Willie Anderson,
Dave Morrow, Hugo MacNeill, Phil Orr.
Front (l – r): Michael Bradley, Tony Ward, Trevor Ringland, Des McKibbin (president of IRFU), Ciaran Fitzgerald, Michael
Kiernan, Brendan Mullin, Keith Crossan.

Flipper (Tony Ward) and the Commanchero (Jim Renwick)

With Kevin Keegan's jersey
Limerick v Southampton
1981 UEFA Cup

Dublin Schoolboy Under 15's v Northern Ireland Schoolboys at Portadown, March 1970
Back: (l – r): Eamon Gilroy, Noel Wynn, John O'Rourke, Mick Fogarty, Vivian Giles, John Courtney, Mick O'Toole, Larry Hackett, Donal Murphy, Dave Ramsey, Tony O'Connell (Manager)
Front: (l – r): Tony Ward, Shay Smyth, Liam Brady, Maurice Sheehan, Tommy Maguire, Mick Browne

Garryowen Cup Winning Team v Cork Constitution, Musgrave Park 1975
Back: (l – r) Liam Hall, Frank Hogan, Pat Whelan, Eugene O'Dwyer, Rusty Keane, Larry Moloney, Tom Carroll
Front: (l – r) Shay Deering, Pat Pratt, Mervyn O'Connor, Tony Ward, Des Quaid (captain), John McDonnell,
Micky Martin, Seamus Dennison

The Irish Rugby Football Union Tour of Australia 1979

Back (L to R): A.J.P. Ward, C.S. Patterson, A.C. McLennan, L.A. Moloney, S.O. Campbell, G.A.J. McLoughlin,
F.N. Ennis, C.F. Fitzgerald, T.J. Kennedy

Middle (L to R): D.E. Spring, P.A.J. Andreucetti, C.D. Cantillon, E.M.J. Byrne, T.C.J. O'Connell M.D. (Hon. Medical Officer),
B.O. Foley, B.P. McNaughton, A.J. McLean, M.E. Gibson

Front (L To R): P.C. Whelan, J.J. Moloney, C.M.H. Gibson, J.F. Coffey (Hon. Tour Manager) J.F. Slattery (Captain), N.A.
Murphy (Hon. Assistant Manager) M.I. Keane, H. W. Steele, P.A. Orr

the way he deals with the individual units, the collective units and the way he marries the whole thing together. That's why it's so important that if it is a forward that is the main coach that he has a back assisting him and vice versa. Ireland have generally utilised such a combination.

"In terms of the Irish rugby animal, motivation is very important. A good coach needs the sensitivity to know how to handle and get the best out of individual players and at the same time to be able to press the collective button to get the best out of the team as a unit.

"It almost goes without saying that good communication skills are an essential prerequisite for a coach at the highest level. However, it is a much more expansive notion of communication than people might expect. Obviously a coach has to be able to handle the media and encourage a good two-way communication between himself and his players. A really talented communicator though, is one who encourages interaction between players and a cross-fertilisation of ideas so that it all comes together at team meetings.

"Roly Meates was coach when I played my first B game for Ireland. He had an extraordinary rugby brain. In many respects he was similar to Jimmy Davidson. One of his greatest strengths was his attention to detail. I remember the night before one international in the '80s, he played us a video he had compiled of the referee for the following day's match, showing four or five incidents which showed the facets of the rules that the ref was particularly keen to enforce. After seeing that video we were all more aware in the match of what we shouldn't do if we wanted to avoid conceding penalties.

"One of Noel Murphy's greatest strengths was his ability to motivate. To our great surprise and disappointment the same could not be said of Willie John MacBride as a coach. After all the stories we heard about him from the Lions' tour in 1974 we expected so much from him but our great expectations were not realised. If Irish rugby is to succeed it needs the fire to burn inside. We lost that for a while as was evident in the dismal performance against Scotland in 1993 but recaptured it later thanks largely to the influence of Willie Anderson. No matter how advanced coaching techniques may become, it is the heart that matters most. We do not have the depth of players and skill to ape New Zealand. The traditional strength of Irish rugby is boot, bite and bollock. Our future is in our past.

"Tom Kiernan was a superb coach. He had the ideal combination of playing experience, coaching experience and great motivational qualities. What he demanded of you came naturally from within. When he was speaking you could see it came from deep down. There was always great passion in his voice. The memory I will always have of him is before our victory over the All-Blacks with his foot on the chair, as he bent over exhorting us to victory. In recent years I think he has become too much of an administrator. From personal experience I can't speak too highly of TJ though.

"He is a man of great integrity. Recently I heard a verbatim account of an incident during an IRFU meeting in the 1980s. Not for the first time my name was on the agenda. This was not an unusual occurrence because there were many queries addressed to me by the Union in connection with a whole series of episodes. They were concerned that I might have compromised my amateur status. At one stage a prominent personality and employee of the Union was introducing the next item on the agenda – namely me – and sarcastically said: 'Tony who?' Quick as a flash TJ intervened forcefully saying how dare any one be so disrespectful – to a player who has represented his country at the highest level. No one, least of all a leading light in the IRFU, was entitled to turn any international player into a figure of ridicule.

"If I was to select the best man-manager of them all it would have to be Mick Doyle. He was a great motivator and had the ability to cut the cloth to suit his measure. The memory I will always have of him goes back to 1986 when I came in for Ireland's final match of the season against Scotland. What line does a coach take at that stage when his side has lost their first three games and is facing a whitewash and missing key players through injury? What Mick did was to get John D. O'Brien of RTE to compile a 20- 25 minute video of the best moments of Ireland's Triple Crown winning side the previous season, to the music of the Queen classic: 'We Are The Champions'. Essentially his message was: That's 12 months ago, that's what you were capable of then – now go out and give it a lash tomorrow.'

"One criticism I have of him is that he used too many expletives. They began to lose their impact after a while. This macho exterior hides a soft centre, even more so than Mossy. He has a great mind as I have discovered through working with him for television. He took all the media pressure in '85, and wallowed in it because he is a real media man, which allowed the players to concentrate solely on rugby. The manner in which we won that Triple Crown is something we can all be proud of. It was arguably the greatest short spell in Irish rugby.

"There are so many stories about Doyler. Before he was coach to the Irish side he was a very successful coach with Leinster. The night before one of their matches Terry Kennedy, Ronan Kearney and Mike Gibson came in at an ungodly hour after a night on the town. Doyler decided to crack the whip. The next morning the three players were summoned to attend Doyler's room at 11 a. m. Doyle was sharing with Ken Ging. The problem was that the selectors had had a right old party themselves the previous night and the place was covered with empty bottles. Ken was told to tidy up and he hid them under a chair in the corner.

"The three lads arrived at the appointed hour and Ollie Campbell, who was captain that year, was asked to attend. Doyler proceeded to tear into the three lads using every cliché in the book about how they were a disgrace to Leinster and how they had let themselves down. Ollie was very uncomfortable to have to witness this tirade. He pulled out the chair from the corner to sit down and all the bottles went spinning all over the floor. Terry Kennedy burst out laughing and said: "**** off Doyler."

"Jimmy Davidson is a university lecturer and a brilliant performer. However, to my way of thinking he did go a bit over the top with the technical side – at times blinding us with science as it were.

"His fitness assistant, Colin Boreham, told me once that when they were driving down from Belfast to Dublin for a training session in the pouring rain they almost crashed a hundred times. Even though the wipers were going full blast, condensation was forming on the windows and even though he was driving, Jimmy kept drawing diagrams on the windscreen to highlight different possibilities on the field of play.

"After the match he would analyse games at the dinner. He was so intense that he'd have the sugar bowl as the goalposts, the salt-cellar for the out-half and the fork for the lineout. Certain guys would like that, for example Ollie would love it, but most players just want to switch off. There's nothing Irish rugby players like more than listening to Willie Anderson playing his bagpipes, having a few pints and the craic and by all means having an analysis of the game a few days later. Although as I have said, Roly Meates' approach was similar to Jimmy's, the difference was that Roly knew when to let his hair down.

"You are only as good as the players you have to work with. I think Jimmy got a very poor return for the amount of work and effort he put into that team. He deserved so much more than he actually achieved.

"I must also mention at this point, Syd Millar who was manager of the Lions' side in 1980 and the Irish side for the inaugural World Cup. My respect and admiration for him knows no bounds. The one trait I appreciate more than any other is honesty and Syd has that in abundance."

Ward also has enormous respect for the coaching talents of Pat Whelan, the Greystones triumvirate, Ken Ging, and Terry Diaper and Willo Murray amongst others.

Ward's final team then is:

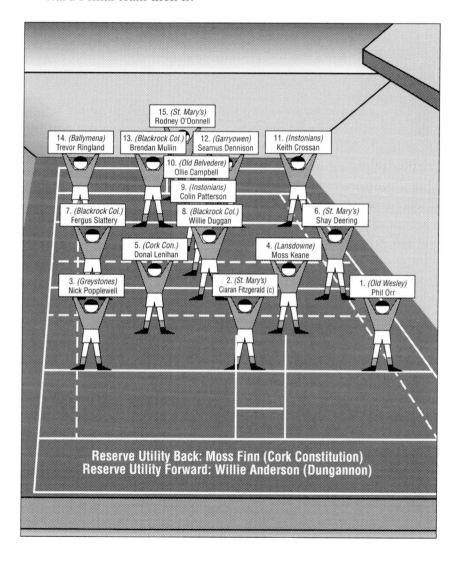

Reserve Utility Back: Moss Finn (Cork Constitution)
Reserve Utility Forward: Willie Anderson (Dungannon)

10. The Dream Team

Doing easily what others find is difficult is talent; doing what is impossible for talent is genius.

Henri Frédéric Amiel

Ward is as happy as a glutton at a banquet as he goes about the task of selecting his dream international team. Again the criterion for inclusion is that Ward must have either played with or against a particular player, a criterion which obviously prevents him from choosing many of rugby's greats. As was the case with his greatest Irish team he is spoilt for choice in a number of positions, coincidentally in almost the exact same positions, chiefly full-back, out-half, scrum-half, number eight and hooker, the positions he calls "the spine of the team". He began his analysis of his contenders for the full-back position with one of Scotland's most exciting players of all time, Andy Irvine:

"Andy came on the scene at a time when the role of the full-back was changing. He is no longer the traditional, Tom Kiernan type full-back, concentrating primarily on defensive duties like catching and kicking. As the modern game has changed the full-back has evolved into much more of an attacking force, particularly with the changes in the rules, a lot of which I don't agree with because they clutter up midfield. I would argue that the full-back has never been more important than now.

"Andy had blisteringly fast pace. He had excellent hands, a lovely swerve rather than a side-step, though he could side-step very effectively off his right foot and often played on the right wing for Scotland and occasionally for the Lions in 1980. He was a very talented player.

"Jean Michel Aguirre was a player I played against in 1978 and '79. He was very good on the counter-attack, strong under the high ball, extremely reliable, all the best traits of a good full-back plus the obvious one – we don't know why it exists – the "French flair".

"Many people would say that the finest full-back of them all was JPR Williams. In my very first season John Comyn wrote an article about the pretentiousness that goes on in rugby where suddenly I was no longer plain 'Wardy' but AJP Ward. There was also, for example, AJF O'Reilly or CMH Henderson. If anyone in rugby mentions the initials JPR people know immediately who you are speaking about.

"He was a great athlete and a former junior Wimbledon champion. What he had above all else was an incredible ability to mix the physical with the skilful, in some respects two diametrically opposing facets of the game. He loved physical contact but also had great skills, particularly his swerve, and side-step. He played one Test game against Australia when his team were stuck because of injuries as a wing-forward and this says much about his style of play. He was a great counter-attacker and deceptively fast, though not in the Andy Irvine mould as a runner.

"Another very talented full-back was Australia's Roger Gould. He was a very big man and I remember playing against him in '81 when he hit me with a tackle which was the hardest I ever received. The biggest single difference between interprovincial and international rugby, apart from the fact that the pace is obviously faster, is the intensity of the physical contest and there were few who could match Roger in that respect.

"South Africa's Gysie Pienaar was the man of the series in the 1980 Lions' tour. He had a dream game in each of the four Tests but sadly the masses never really saw his talent because of South Africa's isolation in the rugby world. Everything we kicked at him he coped with and just gobbled it up. He was an immense talent.

"My choice for full-back though would have to be Serge Blanco because of the breathtaking beauty of his game. He had almost everything although he was not as good defensively as JPR. He was the old cliché: 'poetry in motion'. He played in my last game for Ireland against the French Barbarians in La Rochelle and on that night he was magic, gliding through us like a knife through butter. He was one of those players who had a fifth gear, as soon as you got close to him he just took off and left you for dead. He was a tremendously talented player.

"With the retirement of Blanco the outstanding full-back in the game without question is Gavin Hastings. Hastings is a big man physically, extremely strong under a high ball, he just gobbles everything up and is very reliable – all the essential traits of a good full-back. Like Andy Irvine he has a remarkable capacity to kick goals. He is also very strong in the tackle and reads the game particularly well. I felt he was an inspired choice to captain the Lions."

Happy Days

Ward limited his choice for the position of right-wing to just four contenders. He began with a name that will be forever immortalised in the folklore of Munster rugby:

"Stu Wilson was a big strong winger, similar to John Kirwan, whom I never played against, and was extremely strong with the ball in his hands. He was very difficult to tackle though the memory that Irish people have of him is of Seamus Dennison's marvellous tackle of him. Wilson was a great player and one of the many, many great All-Black wingers.

"Keith Robertson played at both right-wing and centre for Scotland. He was brilliantly talented when it came to natural pace and side-step. He was like England's Clive Woodward in that respect. Those skills are sadly lacking in the modern game but Robertson was very skilful and talented all round player.

"Another very talented, though different type of player from Keith was John Carleton of England or JC. I became very friendly with him during the Lions' tour of '80. He was deceptively fast, but it was his great physique and his strength which were his greatest assets. When he got the ball on the right wing he was totally reliable in terms of retaining possession. He was so strong and very good with the timing of his intrusions into the line.

"However, in the end it was an easy decision for me. While soccer was my big love when I was growing up and my heroes were John Giles and Billy Bremner, the magic of Gerald Davies was something else. I remember watching a *Rugby Special* on television where his club, Cardiff, played against Pontypool, who were a very forward oriented side, in the Welsh Cup. Pontypool kicked five penalties but Cardiff got four unconverted tries with Gerald scoring them all. He was magic. He had a great side-step off either foot and could drift outside players. Everything he did was at maximum pace. There were very few players who would excite me sufficiently that I would be prepared to travel great distances to see them. I would have gone great distances to see Glen Hoddle playing soccer and Gerald playing rugby. Gerald was rugby's George Best in terms of charisma.

"I remember playing for the Wolfhounds against Cardiff in that match in 1975, where Ray Finn kicked that ball torpedo style. I came on as a sub early in that game when Conor Agnew got injured and Mick Quinn moved from out-half to full-back. I remember late in the game I got a pass and had the line in my sight and I had glory on my mind because I was going to score a try on my representative debut. I made about four yards when I was brought down by a crashing tackle from behind. I fell awkwardly because I hadn't seen the tackle coming. I was in agony after the game, but it was all worth it when I discovered that it was Gerald who tackled me. Then I was in heaven!"

Hi Ho

Another memory from Munster's victory over the All-Blacks was on Ward's mind when he began sorting out his candidates for the position of left-winger:

"Brian Williams, 'BG', was a very powerful player who was very hard to take down. A great servant of New Zealand rugby and now of Western Samoa where he is director of coaching. My clearest memory of him goes back to when we beat the All-Blacks in '78. We had heard a lot about New Zealand dourness and they can be, because they take winning so seriously. The dinner that night was in the Limerick Inn and we were all there in our dinner jackets waiting for them to arrive. They had been on what touring sides call their 'happy hour', when they have a few drinks on their own in their hotel, away from the supporters, and people they don't want to see for a while. Eventually they got to the hotel and I remember BG getting off the bus and leading the entire team in, everyone's arm on the person's in front of them's shoulder, singing: 'Hi ho, hi ho. It's off to work we go'. His attitude and theirs on the night was we've lost but what the hell let's enjoy ourselves, because they always enjoyed the Irish, especially down round Limerick and Munster. Needless to say we had a great night.

"Another possibility for this position would have to be Rory Underwood who is a very gifted player and a particularly fast runner. He has a very strong build and is hard to take down. It's great to know that when you give him the ball when he has space he is gone and it is game, set and match. The problem of course is finding that space.

"Whenever I'm picking a schools team I always look for two wingers who can primarily attack. One of the all-time great attacking wingers was Philippe Lagisquet, 'the Bayonne Express' an incredibly fast winger. Sadly the way the game has evolved wingers no longer get the space and time they need, so skilful wingers are giving way to big block-buster types and the finesse of the side-step is sadly being lost. Under normal circumstances he would have made my team but not with David Campese around.

"I love Campo's attitude and I don't care how outspoken he is. I don't care what his motivation is for making those outlandish statements. He loves Ireland. He may come out with comments suggesting our attitude to rugby is that we enjoy ourselves and our beer too much. I don't know if he actually believes that. Perhaps he only says it to motivate himself and the opposition.

"There is a very fine line to be struck between taking too casual an approach and too 'professional'. I have a very clear memory of captaining Ireland, managed by Fergus Slattery, for the World Sevens in 1986 as part of Sport-Aid and Bob Geldof's effort to raise money for the starving in Ethiopia. I found it ironic that he should be involved in it as he apparently hates rugby so much since his days in Blackrock College.

"All the teams were staying in the same hotel in Cardiff for the tournament. There was a lovely relaxed atmosphere for those four days and great mixing between the teams but the one thing that was noticeable was that the Kiwis kept totally to themselves. I found this type of attitude unusual and indeed unhealthy – where nothing is allowed to jeopardise the task of winning. Whatever fun aspect there is in the game is lost with that kind of approach. The Wallabies are perhaps the nearest to getting that balance right, they really know how to enjoy themselves but when they have to be serious they are very serious, none more so than Campo himself.

"In the semi-final of the last World Cup before the match, when the New Zealanders were doing the haka, he was at the other end of the pitch juggling the ball. His attitude was 'what do I care?'. He is so laid-back but what marks him out is his outstanding talent. He has all the ingredients to make a great player but the one thing above all else he had was blistering pace, though we've seen recently that he is losing a bit of it. Time stands still for no one – not even Campo.

"I remember playing against him in Cardiff in the World Sevens a few years ago, thinking I had him and like Blanco he found a fifth gear and left me for dead. They go on about his goosestep but it's not that. It's just great acceleration and drifting around players. The other thing I love about him is that he just wants to run the ball from anywhere. He is happiest when the ball is being moved, and taking risks. Of course, sometimes mistakes happen like the one which let in the Lions for the try which decided the series in '89. For every one he gives away he creates another nine and that's some ratio. He is unquestionably one of the all-time greats of rugby."

Flipper And The Commanchero

Ward unashamedly began his search for two centres for his dream team by considering the claims of one of his best friends in international rugby, Scotland's Jim Renwick:

"I became great mates with Jim and John Carleton on the Lions' tour in South Africa. Jim was a smashing character. He looked a lot older than he was because he was balding prematurely. He was the original dancer and was almost impossible to pin down. He didn't have the physique of the modern crash-tackling centre, but when it came to pure skill and creating space for others nobody could touch him. He had a great attitude and enjoyed the game. He was one of my favourite people in rugby.

"It was Jim who christened me 'Flipper' after I nearly drowned in Durban in South Africa. His nickname was the 'Commanchero' after the song of the same name. We were to play against each other in Murrayfield in 1981 in the Ireland-Scotland match. I arranged to have a message sent to him in the hotel on the day before which read: 'Commanchero beware. Flipper's in town.' About an hour before the kick off we went out to inspect the pitch. Part of the psychological warfare that goes on beforehand is that you seldom make eye contact with the opposition. You keep your head down and count the daisies rather than look at an opposing player in the face. We were coming out of the tunnel with the Scottish players already out on the pitch but neither Jim nor I could stop ourselves from looking at one another out of the corner of our eye. I smiled feeling I had one up on him because of the telegram. When we went back inside after the pitch inspection the Secretary of the Scottish Rugby Football Union came into our dressing-room saying: 'Telegram for Mr Ward'. It read simply: 'Flipper shut your zipper. The Commanchero!'

"Another great centre from the Lions' tour in '80s was England's Clive Woodward. He could play centre or wing and scored some memorable tries on that Lions' tour. He didn't like the physical contact too much. He just wasn't made that way, but he had immense natural talent.

"I would also have to consider the claims of Woody's teammate on the English side, Paul Dodge. They made a very good centre pairing. Paul was a powerful player and had a very good left foot. He was great to play with for a right-footed fly-half because of the options he offered on the right hand side of the pitch to place a long diagonal kick into the opposite corner.

"Ray Gravell too was a great player and your original Welsh nationalist. He adores everything that is Welsh. He has got a marvellous patriotism and would die literally for his country and in fact now presents Welsh speaking programmes at home. He is a great, great character. An out-half's nightmare is when there's a big number eight or second row forward coming charging at him from a peel at the lineout and of course he has to tackle him. Grav would always be on hand to do the donkey work for Phil Bennett. Grav was Benny's minder but was a marvellous talent in his own right though a very under-rated player with an amazing lack of self-confidence.

"I had heard all the stories about how he used to sing before big games to help the adrenaline and also to get rid of the butterflies. I learned in South Africa what he was really like. Before games he would sit in the loo and sing all the great Welsh anthems.

"The Lions' anthem by tradition is 'Flower of Scotland' which is a very uplifting song. I remember on that tour as we would arrive at the ground when all the Springbok supporters would be alongside the bus, shouting at us and giving us the thumbs down. Suddenly he would start singing 'Flower of Scotland' and that would simply lift everybody's spirits. Ray would always lead us and even though he was a Welsh man singing a Scottish song, it was the passion he put into it, the passion he puts into everything, that stood out. That's the memory we all have of him.

"Like Grav, another very under-rated player was Australia's Andy Slack. I would consider him and Scott Hastings to be the two most under-rated centres in the game. Andy played a season here with Wanderers. He did incredible work off the ball. He was one of those unsung heroes of the game. He was a terrific tackler although he didn't have particularly outstanding pace. People remember the great players he captained to win the Grand Slam – Mark Ella, David Campese, Michael Lynagh but Slackie will most probably be forgotten. To me he was the key piece of that particular jigsaw and came very close to making my dream team.

"Scott Hastings is a very brave player, one of the best tacklers in the game and also came very close to making my dream team. I remember one game I played for a Scottish touring side, the Saltires, and Gavin was to play full-back for us. He had to cry off and Scott took his place. I remember coming away that night thinking, and I have thought about it many times since, that had Scott not had Gavin for a brother playing for his club and country he would have been a devastating full-back himself because he is so immensely talented. That night we had two centres from New Zealand and they created so much space for Scott to hit the line.

"However, my choices for the two positions in the centre are Philippe Sella of France and Danny Gerber of South Africa. I would argue Sella as the greatest centre of all time. He had absolutely everything, side-stepping off either foot at pace. In addition, he had an extraordinary ability for physical contact. He had the ability to compete for the high ball which was comparable to a Gaelic footballer. Sella relished taking on the opposition either with the ball in his hand or getting physically involved. He stands head and shoulders above all the rest.

"The Springboks had an outstanding centre in 1980 Willie du Plessis. He was lightning fast and a great ball winner. Yet again the problem was that he didn't have the world stage for long enough. On the other hand Danny Gerber played against us for the Junior Springboks in 1980 and at the ripe old age of 34 he was back on the world stage for the Boks in their games against Australia, New Zealand and England in 1992.

"He is a huge man with a massive physique. Unfortunately, Rodney O'Donnell could not have chosen a more powerful centre the time he sustained his serious injury when he brought down Gerber with a cover tackle. He enjoyed physical contact yet for one so big he had remarkably fine skills.

"This is one of the big dangers of rugby in school where far too much role-typing takes place. People with very little knowledge of the game see a big guy like Gerber and say : 'Ah ha. He must be a second row forward.' The beauty of rugby is that it caters for all body types from the fat pudgy boy to the skinny beanpole. Gerber had the physique of a forward but the skill of a back. Both he and Sella are my centres because they had that indefinable quality – class."

The Princes Of Wales

Almost inevitably Ward's search for an out-half began with the Welsh out-half factory which appears to have gone into temporary liquidation in recent years:

"I was brought up on the magical Welsh sides of the '70s though sadly my representative career came too late to coincide with Barry John because he retired so prematurely. Phil Bennett was one of the best. He had a great side-step and I'll never forget his side-stepping run that set up *the* try for the Babas against the All-Blacks in 1973. I mean if you want to sell the game of rugby you just show it again and again. I loved the way Benny danced with the ball. He was so nimble-footed.

"I played against him many times and the most recent humble memory I have of him was when I played against him after taking a year off when I retired from rugby. We played in a golden oldies match in Anglesea Road. Whereas before I had always been able to read his game and nab him when he side-stepped, the lack of exercise took its toll and he just accelerated past me. He has kept himself in very good physical condition all this time.

"One of the least known facets of Bennett's rugby personna was his motivational style. He once psyched up his team against England with a history lesson, albeit a slightly one-sided one: 'Look what these b******s have done to Wales. They've taken our coal, our water, our steel, they buy our houses and they only live in them a fortnight every 12 months. What have they given us – absolutely nothing. We've been exploited, raped, controlled and punished by the English – and that's who you are playing this afternoon.'"

Ward gushes with admiration as he presents the case for Gareth Davies:

"Gareth followed Benny onto the Welsh side. I would argue that he was the most natural punter of the ball from his hands. He could just stroke the ball nonchalantly on the pitch whenever and wherever he wanted to, à la Barry McGann. He had many many great games for Wales and goes very close overall to making my all time side. I know that will surprise some people. Phil was at the end of his career when I played against them but Gareth was in his prime.

"I am a huge fan. He was a lovely balanced runner when he had the ball in his hand. I think perhaps Gareth suffered because of the expectations of the time and because he followed so soon after Phil and Barry John whereas if he arrived in Welsh rugby today he would be king. He was a real class act and is one of my favourite out-halves of all time.

"Another natural Welsh out-half talent was Jonathan Davies. Before he turned to League pro he was a great player. In my opinion he has been the biggest single loss to Welsh rugby in recent years. He had oodles of talent but what singled him out from other out-halves was his blistering pace. Neither Ollie, I, or indeed most other out-halves would have had anything like it – that ability to accelerate with the maximum amount of pace in the minimum amount of space. Jonathan could do that. He had that incredible cockiness which bordered on arrogance, though he's not an arrogant person by nature. The one thing I am sure he will regret at the end of his career is that he never played for the Lions but that was a decision he had to make to turn pro. He was one of the few to make a success of it and I for one am not surprised."

Like Ward himself, Jonathan Davies is remembered in certain quarters as much for activities off the field as his majestic performances on it. When he first wore the Welsh jersey, just three years after making his club debut for Neath, the once awesome conveyor belt of great Welsh out-halves seemed to have turned up another of its jewels. His pedigree was right – having attended Gwendraeth Grammar School, the launching-pad for Carwyn James and Barry John and where he was brought up on a great creed – run the ball at every opportunity. He made his mark immediately scoring a try and a drop goal on his debut. He was the undisputed star of Wales' achievement of third place in the inaugural World Cup in 1987 and their Triple Crown win the following year.

When he turned his back on Rugby Union, having won 27 Welsh caps, to join Widnes on 5 January, 1989 the Welsh rugby fraternity went into national mourning. The legacy of that move was a chain of prejudice and suspicion which has followed in his wake ever since. Davies was by no means the first Welsh rugby union international to join the professional ranks but no defection had quite the reverberations as his did.

Not only did Davies defect, he did not have the grace to go quietly – speaking out against the sham amateurism of rugby union. Such was the media circus at the time that he shed 11 lbs through stress. A number of doubters questioned his ability to survive in Rugby League and rubbed their hands in glee at the prospect of him falling flat on his face – but not only did he survive, he prospered and was eventually chosen at stand-off for Great Britain. Davies' had the worst of both worlds – antagonising both the Union and League worlds simultaneously. To a small minority of League aficionados he remains just a Union outsider. Ward saw some of the hostility to Davies at first hand:

"I met him in Cardiff Arms Park in 1991 for the Ireland-Wales match. He had had great difficulty getting a ticket for that game. There were a lot of people in Welsh rugby who didn't want him there so he literally had to sneak into the ground. In 1993 I met him in the Press box. I think this shows two interesting facts. Firstly, the changes that have taken place in Union's attitude to League. Secondly, the respect which Davies enjoys in the game.

An out-half whose career dovetailed closely with Ward's was John Rutherford:

"Himself and Roy Laidlaw had a great partnership for Scotland. Rud was very talented. He made the Lions in '83 and even though Ollie was first choice he got in for one test in the centre and everyone was delighted for him. He was a great servant of Scottish rugby.

"Likewise, Australia's Mark Ella was a very talented natural footballer, one of the Ella aboriginal brothers. Mark had beautiful quick hands and they would grab anything in sight, literally like a claw. He loved the running game. His attitude to the game probably reflects his origins. It was a lovely, free style of expression and that's the way he played rugby. He was a great friend of David Campese and it is highly significant that he is now coach of Rugby Milano, which is Campo's club in Italy.

"When it comes to drop goaling and massive punting of the ball and indeed place-kicking for that matter, Naas Botha had to be up there at the top, though a lot of his kicking was done in the high Veldt of South Africa where the ball travels further. He is very under-rated as an out-half and is actually a good distributor of the ball and a good reader of the game. Campese has given him a rough time in recent years about his lack of tackling, but few out-halves, myself included are renowned for their defensive qualities – the exception of course is Ollie.

"Although he played for something of a Cinderella country in rugby terms, Hugo Porta is recognised everywhere as a world class player. He was a very well-built player and a lovely all-round footballer. He is not the bravest of players. Not many out-halves are. But he did a great job carrying the flag for Argentinean rugby. I only played against him once when he lined out for the South African Barbarians in 1980. It was an honour and a privilege to play against him. One of my memories of him is of the function afterwards when Ollie and I had a great in-depth discussion on out-half play with him.

"One interesting thing about all those greats I mentioned is that none of them were as good at distributing the ball as Paul Dean.

"However I make no apologies for choosing Ollie Campbell at out-half. I know few people in the game will disagree with me. I've spoken about Gareth Davies' ability to punt and Jonathan Davies' acceleration etc., but if you were to take a bit of all those great players and put them into one player the outcome would be Ollie. He had all the little bits you would want. His greatest asset was his ability to read the game. His mind was like a computer. He always had a series of options. I have no hesitation about picking him in my dream team."

Gareth The Great

When it comes to talking about the greatest scrum-half of them all the obvious starting point is Gareth Edwards. However, Ward, despite his inclination to the contrary, did not consider him for selection for the same reason as he did not consider Mike Gibson, in that he did not play with or against him in his prime. Nonetheless he remains a huge fan of Gareth the Great:

"One of my happiest memories of my first season was going over to London to receive the Golden Boot Award as Ireland's player for the year. I shared a taxi to the restaurant where the reception was taking place, in the Sportsman Club on Tottenham Court Road, with Gareth Edwards. Here I was, a novice to international rugby sharing a taxi and going to receive the same type of award as Gareth Edwards. It was a real fairytale.

"That evening had an interesting ending for me. I was getting the underground back to Heathrow when there, standing beside me, was Duncan McKenzie. When I played for Rangers I used to pal around in Wyckham Park with Robbie O'Shea. Robbie's brother Dermot was an apprentice at Nottingham Forest and became friendly with Duncan when he was there and Duncan used to come over on holidays to Dundrum where I got to know him through Robbie. This was before Duncan went on to become one of the biggest stars in the first division in the mid '70s. I hadn't seen him for years and he didn't recognise me at first but once he did we had a great old chin wag.

"Gareth's successor at scrum-half, Terry Holmes, looked anything but a scrum-half. Like Danny Gerber he would be probably picked as a forward in schools rugby today because he had such great upper body strength and like Johnny Moloney and Donal Canniffe was perhaps a little too tall for scrum-half. He was unlucky to have to live in Gareth's shadow and what an act to follow but Terry was a marvellous passer of the ball and it was great to play outside him.

"I played against some great scrum-halfs who would not be so well-known in Ireland. South Africa's Divian Serofentein was absolutely brilliant in the four tests in 1980 but here again because of the lack of exposure of South African players I find it hard to include him in my side. He was the prototype of quality scrum-halfs – small, chirpy, bubbly and a great footballer.

"The only Romanian I have considered for my team is Mircea Paraschiv, although they produced some outstanding forwards. He was to Romanian rugby what Hugo Porta was to Argentina – a great all round player who just ran the show for Romania for so long. He ran the team in a manner of a Berbizier or Fouroux and comes very close to making my dream team.

"Of course I would have to consider Berbizier. He followed on from Fouroux, who had a great influence on him. Fouroux was a great organiser. His nickname was 'le petit général' and the same could have applied to Berbizier. Yet another French scrum-half I admired a lot was Jerome Gallion. He was a similar type of player and a similar personality to Colin Patterson. He had a great season in 1978 and he scored a brilliant try against us that year when he made a scampering run after he saw a gap on the short side of the scrum.

"Scotland's Roy Laidlaw was also a scampering player – very similar to Gary Armstrong the current Scottish scrum-half. I remember the game where they annihilated us in Dublin in '84 when they went on to win the Triple Crown. I got injured in attempting a break and the giant Scottish forward, Alan, 'Toomba' Tomes, came along and squashed me into the ground, like a whale squashing a herring. I was in agony afterwards, having cracked two ribs. I had to go to St Vincent's Hospital and was lying on the bed injured. Later in the game Roy had got a knock on the head and ended up beside me in the casualty ward. I felt sorry for him because he missed out on all the celebrations. Himself and John Rutherford were a deadly combination.

"Mind you in recalling that incident with 'Toomba' I would have to correct the balance by telling of a happier memory I have of him. The after-match dinners vary greatly from country to country but the Scottish dinners were always the best. The players sat in prominent positions at the tables and mingled together. In England you have only four players at each table and the other places are reserved for officials etc. The Welsh and Irish dinners are much the same – a kind of middle ground between the Scottish, where the players have pride of place and the English where that position is reserved for the 'hob-nobs'. The French affair is even worse where the teams are on opposite ends of the room and there is the obvious difficulty in communication anyway.

"The Scottish is easily the most egalitarian of the lot. Before the game the haggis is marched in, complete with pipers, and lit like a Christmas pudding with the Drambuie. After one dinner I mentioned to Toomba that the haggis had been particularly nice. The next day as we were leaving the hotel the receptionist told me that there was a message waiting for me in the kitchen. I was very puzzled that there should be a message for me there. When I went in I discovered that Toomba had arranged for me to bring a massive chunk of haggis home. Since then every time I go to Scotland I call into the butcher for some haggis.

"However, although it was a difficult decision my choice for scrum-half is Nick Farr-Jones. He is tall and not the classic type of scrum-half but I go for him because of his ability to read a game. He is the master tactician. You could almost see his mind working. He's the clichéd third wing forward and, incredibly, he is also the leader of the pack. He is a remarkable passer of the ball and possesses great ability to break and take the pressure off Michael Lynagh. His linking is great and his use of the ball at all times is incredible. I think he and Ollie would have been an outstanding combination at half-back.

"He would also be captain of my side. I have never understood why a full-back, winger, centre or front row forward is chosen as captain, because they are cut off from so much of the play, mind you, Ciaran Fitzgerald was an exception to this insofar as captaincy ideally suited his personality and style of play because he always led from the front.

I feel, however, that ideally the captain should be either a half-back or back row forward, i.e., the middle five, because they can link up much better with all the players on the team. Farr-Jones was the ideal candidate in the ideal position."

Donkeys And Fairies

Ward prefaced his selection of the forwards with a plea for understanding:

"Backs refer to the forwards as 'donkeys', affectionately of course! The donkeys refer to the backs as 'fairies'. As a 'fairy' picking my 'donkeys' I will own up to not having the in-depth knowledge of the intricacies of forward play that some people have. I have tended to go for mobility. The connoisseurs of the game will say that the best forwards are technically good scrummagers. I think that the game has changed so much that the onus is now on the forwards to get around the field, with less scrums than in the past and more lineouts.

"My first candidate for loose-head prop is Gerard Cholley of France. When I started off he was playing in a massive, awesome French pack. For a big man he was very mobile, a very good technical scrummager, with all the basics. The French turn out front row prop forwards with amazing regularity. While Wales, New Zealand and Limerick are regarded, and rightly so, as the three democratic centres of world rugby, so too is the south of France, where it is a bit like Gaelic games in this country with teams representing villages and many of the prop forwards are particularly tough, hard men. I remember our French tour in 1988 when we were out for a walk on the waterfront in Biarritz and there we saw the then prop forward on the French international side, Pascal Ondarts, come up from literally a hole in the ground where he had been working in the sewer. This typifies the working class aspect of French rugby which is marvellous.

"It also reinforced for me the camaraderie that this peculiar oval-shaped ball creates. The second Jimmy McCoy saw him he was over like a shot and although Jimmy had hardly any French and Pascal hardly any English they were totally at ease with each other despite the communication problems and somehow they had a great chat.

"I would have to consider two Irish players for this position Phil Orr and Nick Popplewell. Phil is one of the few front row forwards I have ever seen who would be out challenging the out-half. Poppy has achieved a lot already with Ireland and the Lions but, having played with him at Greystones, I know he hasn't fulfilled all his potential yet and in a few years time could be spoken of as one of the all time greats.

"When you talk of front rows you have to feature the famous Pontypool front row of Charlie Faulkner, Bobby Windsor and Graham Price, celebrated in song and folk-lore by Max Boyce. The camaraderie between front row players is amazing, especially between the Pontypool gang. It's a strange fact of rugby life that people in the same positions on the field tend to pal around together, e.g., on the Irish side in the '80s Keith Crossan and Trevor Ringland were inseparable. Charlie was a great prop forward and a great servant to Wales.

"Likewise Ian McLaughlin, 'Mighty Mouse', was one of the most famous Scottish players of all time. The only reason he doesn't make my dream team is that he was at the end of his career when I played against him. He was a very mobile player and a great thinker on the game.

"My choice for the team is another Scottish forward, David Sole. This is perhaps an example of the way forwards and backs look at things differently. Originally the word was that David was much criticised for his scrummaging. It's the age old story when a forward is seen chasing all over the pitch it's assumed that he is not putting it in at the scrum but Sole more than held his own regardless. He had a huge influence on the Scottish team as captain and I think he retired prematurely though he had a very fulfilling career."

Price Is Right

Ward restricted his choice for tight head prop to just three players beginning with England's Fran Cotton:

"Fran was a big man in every sense of the word and a great player into the bargain. One sad, outstanding memory of him will always be from my first game in the Lions' tour in 1980 in Stellenbosch when he got a mild heart-attack. It gave us all a scare to hear that his condition was so serious afterwards, needless to say.

"Robert Paparemboarde, 'Papa', was a huge prop forward for France. When he had the ball in his hands he was an awesome sight coming at you. I remember having to face him once in Lansdowne Road but in that highly charged atmosphere when the adrenaline is pumping, you are prepared to metaphorically die for your country, but the fear factor is absent and you'll take anything on. There was no prop forward more intimidating than Papa.

"However, my selection is the Welsh number three, Graham Price. He was not the most mobile forward ever but he could get around the field. Anyone I've ever spoken to in the game who has experienced his scrummaging ability at first hand supports my view that he was one of the greatest forwards of all time."

The Model

Ward began his deliberations about the hooker position with the final member of the Pontypool three, Bobby Windsor, 'the Duke', one of the most celebrated individuals of them all in rugby folklore. On the flight to South Africa with the Lions' tour in '74, Windsor was taken ill with food-poisoning. He was so ill that he was taken to the back of the plane and told to suck ice-cubes to help him cool down. The team doctor, Ken Kennedy, came to take his temperature without knowing about the ice-cubes. When he looked at the thermometer he shouted out: "Jaysus, Bobby you died 24 hours ago!"

Windsor was one of the game's great raconteurs. One of his favourite stories was about a Welsh Valleys' rugby club on tour in America. On coming back from a night on the town, two of the players could not find their rooms. They decided to check for their teammates by looking through the keyholes. At one stage they came on an astonishing sight. There in her birthday suit was a Marilyn Monroe lookalike. Close by was a man who was chanting out with great conviction: "Your face is so beautiful that I will have it painted in gold. Your breasts are so magnificent that I will have them painted in silver. Your legs are so shapely that I will have them painted in platinum." Outside the two Welsh men were getting very aroused and began jostling each other for the right of the keyhole. The man inside hearing the racket shouted out: "Who the hell is out there?" The two Welsh men replied: "We're two painters from Pontypool."

Wheelbrace

Apart from the Duke, Ward's other possible selections were Wheelbrace, England's Peter Wheeler, Andy Dalton of New Zealand, Philippe Dintrans and Daniel Dubroca of France, Willie Kahts of South Africa, Tommy Lawton of Australia and Scotland's Colin Deans:

"Deans was a very mobile player and as his autobiography shows, a great believer in his own ability. He was, from what I am told, part of the 'conspiracy' to undermine Ciaran Fitzgerald's position as captain on the Lions' tour in 1983. The English media tried to manipulate him into expressing the belief he should be hooker in preference to Fitzy. Of course everybody on the tour has to believe in their own ability, I felt though that some of the comments he made were unhelpful. That kind of thing undermines morale in the camp but Deans was a great hooker and captain in his own right.

"All the hookers I thought about have essentially the same qualities so I won't dwell on them individually. Again the way rugby has evolved, the Sean Fitzpatrick or Philip Kearns type of hooker is becoming increasingly prominent. They are mobile, third prop forwards and also have 'fine skills' by which I mean that they throw the ball into the lineout accurately, strike the ball cleanly. Although they are big men they have fine motor skills. While I find it very difficult to leave out Dintrans, who I played with and against, out of the side because he was a very under-rated player and an outstanding hooker, my choice is Australia's Tommy Lawton. He was a huge man who was extremely mobile around the field with his own unique style. He was in so many ways in the vangard of the changing role of the hooker."

Skylab

In selecting his two second rows, Ward began with a player who played a large part in the best exhibition of rugby he has ever seen:

"The most awesome display of complete and total rugby that I have ever seen was Australia's demolition of Ireland in the first half of the World Cup in 1987 when the Aussies just played text book rugby with Lynagh playing at out-half kicking huge touch-finders. Every time the ball went into the lineout, whether it was ours or theirs, Australia's giant second row Steve Cutler, nicknamed 'Skylab' for obvious reasons, won the ball back with ease. It was an awesome performance. They peaked in that game and lost an outstanding semi-final after that. It was the most complete 15 man rugby I have ever seen. The closest thing I have seen to it was Australia's form when they defeated New Zealand in the World Cup semi-final in 1991. In '87 Cutler was absolutely brilliant.

"New Zealand had a tremendous second row pairing in 1978, Frank Oliver and Andy Hayden and Hayden comes very close to making my team as does Wales' Alan Martin, 'the Panther'. He is one of the few forwards I have seen taking place-kicks. Most forwards have enough to be doing without becoming great kickers of the ball. He was a great tourist on the 1980 Lions' side.

"Another great Welsh second row was Robert Norster, a brilliant lineout exponent, now manager of Wales. He always gave Donal Lenihan a hard time. While Donal is an excellent lineout player by any standards, he always got a hard time from him because his timing was so good. He is a good example of a recently retired player who is made manager of an international side. This is the road we need to go down in Ireland. A recently retired player is ideal as team manager because he is closely in touch with the game at grassroot level. He understands what the players are going through, their gripes and pains. Another good example of the Welsh approach is the appointment of the recently retired David 'Dai' Richards, who is now a selector of Wales and the Lions.

"We are so far behind in this regard in Ireland. For example, an ideal candidate for Irish team manager at the moment in my opinion would in fact be Donal Lenihan, a former Irish captain and a man who knows exactly what the players are going through. He would relate to them so well and has plenty of experience of handling post-match press conferences etc.

"Strangely you did get an example of a recently retired player being made coach of the Irish side, Ciaran Fitzgerald. I learned a lot from that episode because I had not adequately appreciated the gap between coaching and captaining at representative level. Now I know that you must serve an apprenticeship as a coach at representative level. However, I don't believe the same applies in the case of a manager and I would love to see the IRFU move in this area.

"Another great forward was Wade Dooley who made an immense contribution to English rugby. I believe the action of the Four Home Unions Management Committee in not bringing him back to the '93 Lions' tour after his father died is scandalous but sadly so typical of the rugby administration and administrators in general. Mind you, I believe that Neil Francis has at least as much natural ability as any of those second row forwards I mentioned but unfortunately is not exactly a player I would be rushing to bring to the trenches with me.

"However, my two choices are South Africa's Louis Moolman and England's Bill Beaumount. Moolman was as wide as he was tall and had a big, ugly beard which made him look awesome. He would remind you of a big grizzly bear. Before the first Lions' test in 1980 Ollie and I went kicking before the game and in the process I tore muscle fibres in my thigh. It was really bad and looked as if I couldn't play but there was nobody else. I went into the Western Provinces impressive medical unit in Newlands just before the test match to have a cortisone injection. I remember being put lying on the bed waiting for the doctor to give me the jab. It was like a hospital with the curtains draped around me. I was really nervous because 20 minutes later I was about to play in the biggest game of my life and I was lying there petrified waiting for the doctor. Suddenly, through a tiny gap in the curtains, I saw this huge bulk of a man in a Springboks' jersey. It was Moolman. He didn't see me but when I saw this curly haired, bearded monster – bad and all as I felt beforehand I was really terrified after this apparition! It was a frightening sensation and I'll never forget it. On that tour he was absolutely brilliant. He had a great ability to win the ball at two in the lineout.

"Bill Beaumount was not the most mobile forward but he still managed to get around; not the greatest lineout jumper yet he still managed to win ball à la Jim Glennon. He was not an awesome forward in the Wade Dooley sense. Second row forwards today seem to be like basketballers, in some cases just short of seven foot tall, almost freakish. Billy though had tremendous ability to use his own physique. He was always a great scrummager. He was nicknamed 'Sun Bum' on that tour because he had plenty of padding in those places which made him ideal for scrummaging. He was christened that by Peter Wheeler. Sunday was always our day off training and Wheelbrace arranged tee-shirts for us which read: 'Sun Bum's Sunday Sessions Side.' The one thing that really struck me about him on the Lions' tour in 1980, apart from the fact that he was an excellent captain, was that he was the one forward who, every time he went into a ruck the ball, came back on our side."

Bending The Rules

In selecting his two wing forwards, Ward was faced with an agonising choice for the open-side position which he resolved by cheating slightly and picking two open-side players – thereby going against one of his most deeply held convictions about forward play, the importance of balance in the back row. His starting point was Graham Mourie:

"Graham was not just a great forward but a great leader as well. His influence on the '78 Kiwi touring side was extraordinary. He was a great reader of the game. His angles were so good, like Fergus Slattery, that he always managed to put the opposition under pressure, forcing either the centre or out-half to release the ball. The significance of this is that when this happens it is the wing forward who is dictating the game and not the out-half. Mourie was a brilliant forward.

"Peter Winterbottom was in my view the crucial piece of the jigsaw in England's Grand Slam winning sides, in the same way that Nigel Carr was on Ireland's Triple Crown side in 1985. Like Fergus Slattery he had an extraordinary ability to put his body through great pain. I would have to mention two other great players in this position, Scotland's John Jeffrey and South Africa's Rob Lowe, two outstanding players.

"However, I was faced with a virtually impossible task of deciding between two truly marvellous players, Jean Pierre Rives and Fergus Slattery. Although Slatts played his best rugby on the Lions' tour of 1974, as he got older he read the game so well. He lived his life in the fast lane and enjoyed it to the full and always had a few 'scoops' after a game. I went over with him at the end of 1980 to Cardiff to play in the special Ireland-Scotland match against Wales-England to mark their centenary. There was a lovely relaxed atmosphere. Terry Holmes, Gareth Davies, John Carleton, Jim Renwick and I stayed up until all hours playing cards but Slatts and Peter Wheeler and a few others went on an almighty razz in the Angel Hotel. Despite that, the next day Slatts went out and played an absolute blinder. That was something I couldn't do in a million years. Slatts was a brilliant player.

"The same could be said of Rives. He was and is a national hero in France, and rightly so. For a small man he was a great forward, with the blonde hair and sometimes blood streaming down his face he was one of the most extraordinary players ever. You were always aware of his presence on the field. He was a scavenger par excellence. Anything on the deck and he was first to it. He was at the bottom of a ruck one minute and then he suddenly cropped up on the other side of the field.

"On the blind side I came across some great wing forwards like Jean Claude Skrela of France. When I came onto the Irish side the French back row was Rives, Bastiat and Skrela – what a back row! I don't think there's been a finer back row than that. Then, when Skrela left the scene he was replaced by Jean Luc Joinel and what a great forward he was. The French strength in depth is frightening.

"I have a very vivid memory of playing against the great Welsh flanker, Terry Cobner, in my first season especially the chat I had with him and Phil Bennett after the game. In their preparation for the game they saw that I favoured the inside break. In that game Benny stood deliberately wide and left a gap for me. In my innocent ignorance I charged through it only for Cobner to pounce on me. There is no substitute for an old head. I remember Shay Deering doing likewise. I particularly recall a game between Mary's and Bective in the Leinster Cup at Lansdowne Road. They had a most promising young player in Kevin O'Farrell, who was making a break. The Deero left a tempting gap, O'Farrell went for it and Shay lifted him out of it.

"I know Irish people will best remember Findlay Calder for his terrible tackle on Jim Staples but that should not take away from his great contribution. He was a very strong player and very physically mobile around the pitch. I find it hard to pick a best side without him.

"The modern flanker seems to be about 6' 3" with big powerful hands, yet Simon Poidevan was not like that, but a tough hard man nonetheless and one of the reasons why Australia became one of the superpowers of world rugby. On the other hand, Theuns Stofberg was a typical Springboks' forward, big and powerful and virtually impossible to get the ball from. He complimented Rob Lowe so well. Unfortunately, it is not often we have such a brace of wing forwards who compliment each other on the Irish side – the exceptions being the pairings of John O'Driscoll and Fergus Slattery, and Nigel Carr and Philip Matthews. I find it hard to leave Stofberg out of the side. The way the game has evolved wing forwards have to be a massive height to win extra lineout ball. Lineouts have become increasingly important so wing forwards have to become bigger and stronger although I'm not sure it's for the better of the game.

"There is now an over emphasis on physical fitness in rugby and the game is none the better as a result. The International Rugby Board have understandably tried to curtail the amount of time the ball is out of the spectators' sight trying to eradicate, for example, the New Zealand tactic of rolling the maul ad infinitum. The problem is that the 'use it or lose it' rule has created more problems than it has solved because it has cluttered up the midfield area so much. The International Board has got to get its act together and try and bring the high skill level back to the game, particularly as regards three-quarter play.

"However, to return to the task on hand. It was a very difficult choice but I go for Slattery and Rives as my two wing forwards even though I am contradicting myself somewhat in terms of the importance of balance in the back row but it is a liberty I am allowing myself because they were such great players. I don't think too many in the game would quibble with the two Irish players I have selected in my team."

The Law Of The Jungle

Jean Pierre Bastiat was a number eight Ward has particular reason to remember:

"Bastiat is a huge man. I had forgotten how big he was until last year when I met him before the French match in Paris. I was going up to the commentary box, which is an awful place, way up in the clouds almost and is a horrible viewing position. There's a tiny lift to the TV position and I got into it with him, only then did I remember how big he was.

"The first time I played against him was in Paris in 1978. Willie Duggan told me before the game that very early on, either from a 22 drop-out or a kick-off I was to kick the ball as hard and as high as I could close to the touchline. The risk though was that the margin for error was so great. The ball could cross the line and you would end up with a scrum in front of the posts and on the 22, which is defensively the worst place you could be, but Duggan guaranteed me that if I got the ball high enough he would at least get his fingertips to the ball. This was something I tended to do regularly with Mary's. Declan Fanning always stood on the touchline, which means you could get an extra bit of height which gave the forwards time to get under the ball. Duggan had noticed that Bastiat tended to stand on the touchline. Sure enough we had a 22 after about 15 minutes. I put the ball up high in the air and while everyone was watching the ball Duggan hit him such an almighty belt that he went off injured and although he came back for a short while he was eventually forced to leave the field. It was, perhaps, within the rules but more importantly, it was a real lesson for me as regards the law of the jungle in international rugby. Bastiat was a great exponent of number eight play."

Another player Ward had to think seriously about for this position is DQ, or Derek Quinnell of the famous Llanelli club in Wales, where he played with Phil Bennett, Ray Gravell and JJ Williams etc. Ward retains fond memories of DQ from his Lions' tour:

"The most controversial incident in the First Test occurred at the back of the lineout when Quinnell hit his opposite number Morné du Plessis an almighty thump and gave him a huge black eye which of course the South African media highlighted and broke down frame by frame on the following day. Some time afterwards we went to Morné's factory, where he was branch manager for Adidas in Capetown, and he dished out freebies naturally in the hope that we would wear them around South Africa and get good publicity for his sports company. All the workers on the machines in the factory were blacks or coloured and when we came in there was a nice, friendly ripple of applause. A few minutes later DQ came in and Morné was there at the time, modelling his black eye, the cheer that went up was incredible because here was the guy who had clocked their boss! It was all very light-hearted, with no real racist undertones.

"Scotland's John Beattie, or Jock, was a tremendous number eight but because of his laid-back attitude he did not always get the attention he deserved. He loved strumming away at the guitar but was as tough as teak on the field.

"One player who came very, very close to making my side was Roger Uttley. He went on to coach England and is one of my favourite people in the game. I got to know him particularly well through competing in Superstars and Superteam competitions with him over the years. He's a deep thinker on the game and was a great forward. He too was as tough as teak though a scrupulously clean player and a gentleman in every respect.

"I never played against Wayne Shelford. In fact I think the biggest mistake New Zealand made in recent years was to leave him out. However, my choice in this position is another New Zealand player,

Murray Mexted. He had many of the traditional strengths of an All-Black number eight but was not your typical dour New Zealand forward. In fact he's quite the opposite – a very colourful personality and talented player. He was very slim with a big knee lift, like Mike Gibson the younger in many ways, and very hard to knock off the ball. Whenever tackled, he always made the ball available to his flankers or half-backs. He could play the game wide or mix it up front.

"Looking then at the side I have picked it is primarily an attacking side with a lot of mobility. Looking at the pack, they are all technically good players and would guarantee a good supply of the ball. It is ideally suited to the demands of the modern game. Although I never enjoyed the privilege of playing with him as coach, what about Ian McGeehan to take charge?"

Ward's dream team in full then is:

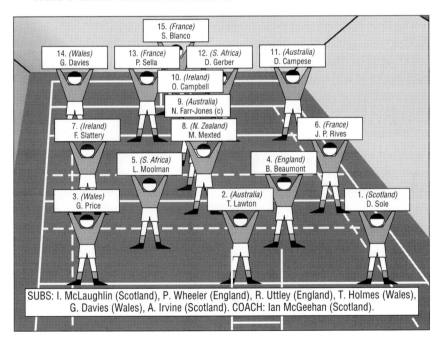

15. *(France)* S. Blanco

14. *(Wales)* G. Davies

13. *(France)* P. Sella

12. *(S. Africa)* D. Gerber

11. *(Australia)* D. Campese

10. *(Ireland)* O. Campbell

9. *(Australia)* N. Farr-Jones (c)

7. *(Ireland)* F. Slattery

8. *(N. Zealand)* M. Mexted

6. *(France)* J. P. Rives

5. *(S. Africa)* L. Moolman

4. *(England)* B. Beaumont

3. *(Wales)* G. Price

2. *(Australia)* T. Lawton

1. *(Scotland)* D. Sole

SUBS: I. McLaughlin (Scotland), P. Wheeler (England), R. Uttley (England), T. Holmes (Wales), G. Davies (Wales), A. Irvine (Scotland). COACH: Ian McGeehan (Scotland).

"The long arm of the Lawless"
Limerick UTD v Bohemians, 1982 F.A.I. Cup Final.
Gino Lawless and Tony Ward

11. Limerick My Lady!

What is the city but the people?

Shakespeare, *Coriolanus*

Rugby is a somewhat unique sport in Irish social life. Most of the year it acts as a poor relation to the fanaticism evoked by Jack's Army since that glorious Sunday afternoon in Stuttgart in June, 1988 when Ray Houghton's header propelled Irish soccer to a new status in World football. Rugby has never brought the whole country to a standstill like Ireland's World Cup exploits did in 1990 when not a car seemed to move on an Irish road while the famous penalty shoot-out was taking place against Romania and when the entire population appeared to embark on a communal celebration when the clash was resolved in Ireland's favour.

Moreover, there is the class factor. Rugby is and always has been a middle class, if not upper-class, pursuit, in Ireland. The vast majority of the rugby playing population began their careers in the most prestigious fee-paying schools in Ireland like Clongowes and Blackrock College. Hence it cannot compete in terms of popularity with the GAA where banker, priest and small farmer come together to celebrate the magic of a Munster hurling final between Cork and Tipperary or an All-Ireland football final between Dublin and Kerry.

This point is reflected in Brendan Behan's observation:

"I never heard rugby was a proper game for anyone except bank clerks. It was a game for the Protestant and the shop-keeping Catholic and I never thought it had anything to do with me."

All this changes though on the days of international matches when Ireland becomes a rugby nation and each pass and kick is not just passively observed but lived like a heartbeat. This applies particularly to matches against England in Lansdowne Road, which are matters of national pride – bearing in mind that unlike the soccer team, the team is an All-Ireland side. Victory, when it comes is a huge bonus. There is always a generous allowance for honourable failure as in the case of the day when we almost beat Australia in the last World Cup.

The exception to this tepid enthusiasm is Limerick, where rugby is like a religion, touching a deep nerve in the psyche of the people of the city. It is recognised worldwide as one of the great cathedrals of rugby. The lifting of the infamous GAA ban only served to legitimise players who played rugby on Saturdays and Gaelic games on Sunday.

One of the stories often told to demonstrate the love of rugby goes back to 1960. When a fishing boat was devoured in the flames of one of the multitude of bonfires that heralded Shannon's first Munster Senior Cup success that year, a sympathiser who offered his condolences to the owner met with an unexpected reply: "You can buy a boat at any time, but not the Munster Cup."

With his dark good looks, Ward would be loved by the popular press but from the start rugby followers on the terraces in Limerick took to him with extraordinary warmth because of the subtlety, invention and spirit of adventure that enabled him to terrorise opposing defenders.

Allied to that was his creativity on the ball, his genius for penetration and his killing finish with his place-kicking that commanded their respect. The fusion of great commitment and dazzling skills would be the stuff of cult status and sporting legend.

In Limerick they appreciate style – but equally they are quick to see through a veneer if there is no substance to match. From his earliest games, as he lengthened his stride towards maturity, the gossip in Limerick was about how good a player Ward would become. Nobody had any doubt he had enough class to go all the way. Reared on a diet good players they responded to somebody with something extra.

Sport, like entertainment, is in the business of fantasy. The celebrated English actor, Ralph Richardson summed up acting in the phrase: "At three minutes past eight you must dream." In Limerick Ward would be the conduit for many dreams. Few dreams come true. Rugby dreamers tend to see a terrific rainbow every time it rains so when a new sensation's limitations are exposed it is a crushing letdown. Dreamers are forever assuring themselves that the truly great player is on the horizon but like the skyline he never comes any closer. It is always just out of reach. The problem is easily identified – much more difficult to remedy. Ward was to change all that.

Such adulation brings its own problems. From the young player's point of view it could delude them into fostering unrealistic delusions about their own importance – encouraged to imagine they are better than they are, only to become embittered when their careers failed to deliver what they appeared to promise. Far more damaging than anything opponents can do to them is the burden of unrealistic expectations.

Ward could not have chosen a better or more nurturing environment to begin his career. Over the next decade he would both feed off and fuel the fires of passion in one of rugby's greatest shrines. The passion created in Limerick is the envy of nearly every touring side in the world and Ward is quick to acknowledge the debt of gratitude owed to the most benevolent of patrons. He was, to rugby aficionados, what Nureyev was to the ballet enthusiast. He received their highest accolade when he was finally accepted by the Limerick population at large as "one of our own".

It is alleged that Ireland's favourite spectator sport is politics. In Limerick politics is their favourite blood sport but is a mere trifle when compared with the major sports like rugby, hurling and soccer. In the Shannonside city, sport is a communal obsession as is evident in the astonishing breadth and depth of knowledge on all major sports and the highly polished and refined sense of the sporting aesthetic. Popular interest feeds on success such as a National League title, in hurling or rugby, which in turn creates a demand for more.

Woolly Horses And Cave Men

To listen to the affection in Ward's voice as he talks about Limerick is akin to listening to Packie Bonner talking about Donegal or Alice Taylor talking about Cork. Yet Ward's first impressions of the city were anything but favourable:

"When I was a child I went with my mother on holidays to Tralee. We were driving through Limerick when we got a puncture. We found ourselves stranded, as we came up Patrick Street, onto O'Connell Street and ended up sheltering under Cannocks' clock. I remember it was lashing rain. It was my only memory, a horrific one at that, of Limerick for years.

"My next memory is more pleasant when I played for the Dublin under-18 soccer side against Limerick and we won 4-3 after extra-time in 1973. However, we travelled down by train, went down the steps from the station and almost immediately were on the pitch at Priory Park so I didn't really see anything of the city. It was only when I went to live there and started college that I got to know and love the people so much."

However, a typically impulsive decision of the young soccer player meant that Ward almost turned his back on the city after just one week!

"After a year out of school the academic aspect of college life was a big culture shock for me. I found the lectures pretty tough going. I remember one in particular, it was a lecture in Education given by T.V. Power, or 'the man from the year 2000' as we nicknamed him because his lectures were so 'highbrow'. The lecture was entitled: 'Woolly Horses and Cave Men'. Suffice it to say it was way, way over my head. I thought it was me and me alone who was feeling so out of my depth, not realising at the time that everybody else in the class was in the same boat. I went home after my first week and that Sunday played for Rovers against Athlone Town in St Mel's Park. Two of my new classmates from college were at the match and offered me a lift down. I declined, because I wanted to go home and think about it, as I was having serious doubts about going back at all. That was one of my big failings when I was young, I was prone to making blind impulsive decisions. Thankfully I have put that tendency behind me in recent years.

"I applied for a job, I think it was as a sales representative, that Sunday. The interview was held the following Tuesday. I got some shock when I went for interview to see the number of graduates who were there. This really frightened me and brought home the reality of life in the big, bad world and how important it was for me to achieve my dreams, particularly having worked so hard academically to get the results and the financial resources I required to get into college in the first place. Common sense prevailed and I went back to further my studies."

One of Ward's earliest Limerick residences was in Elm Park, close to Terry Wogan's original home. In his third year he lived in a rugby household – with his friend and mentor P.J. Smyth, his classmate Dave Mahedy, who coached the Limerick soccer team in Eoin Hand's reign before going on to become their manager and, in more recent years, train the Limerick hurling team, and Mick Sherry who played wing forward for Ireland. While Mickey McEligott, who played scrum-half for Garryowen, and Cormac O'Carroll, who played for Bective Rangers and Ireland B, were also part-time residents. For the two students it was bliss to live with so many wage earners because the fridge was always full! One memory from that year sums up the egalitarianism of rugby in Limerick for Ward:

"I was travelling with Mick Sherry to play in the Blake Sevens, which is an annual event on Easter Monday run by Galwegians' rugby club. We stopped for petrol in Martin Bradshaw's service station on the Ennis Road. The pump attendant was John 'Fox' O'Halloran, the former president of Shannon rugby club – a great rugby gentleman. That epitomises Limerick rugby. You would never get anything like that in Dublin. Can you imagine driving into a petrol station in Dublin and being served by the president of Lansdowne or Wanderers? 'Fox' was one of the many great characters of Shannon with people like Michael Noel Ryan, Micky Yelverton, the late Enda McNamara, Gus O'Driscoll (a former Mayor of Limerick), Thady Coughlan (the youngest ever Mayor of Limerick), the late Willie 'Whack' Gleeson the renowned Limerick historian, Bob McConkey, Frankie Flynn and Tommy Creamer.

"Whenever Shannon won the Munster Cup final Frankie and Tommy would take turns to sing 'The Isle' which is the traditional Limerick ballad and rugby song, particularly of the Shannon rugby club. One of my own saddest memories is of sitting in the dressing-room in both 1977 and '78 when Shannon defeated us in the Cup finals in Thomond, because, believe me, there is nothing worse than losing a Munster final, particularly to another Limerick team, and then having to listen to the Shannon fans singing 'their' song and virtually lifting the roof off the stand. I can still hear it to this day. It was an eerie sound. Nonetheless I could still appreciate their passion for all the despair and self-pity I was feeling. 1977 was the start of Shannon's glory years and nobody did more to bring them to their current high status in the Irish game than their then coach, Brian O'Brien, their first Irish international and a former Ireland and Lions selector.

The big song at the time was 'Don't Cry For Me Argentina' but they adapted it and came up with 'Don't Cry for Us Garryowen'. Of course their other great club song is 'Roll Along Shannon Forwards. Roll Along'. Forward play has been the traditional strength of both Shannon and Young Munster. Nowhere do they know their forward play better than in Limerick.

"Another example which always encapsulated the spirit of Limerick rugby for me was when I would visit the AIB branch in 106 O'Connell Street. The first person I would meet was the porter, Seamie Kiely, God rest him, the former president of Thomond Rugby Club – indeed many would say 'Mr Thomond'. Then as I got to the counter the branch manager, Paddy O'Callaghan, former president of Bohemians and former chairman of the Irish selectors, would come out for a chat. I can't think of any other place on this island – where two men who had such contrasting positions of responsibility in the one financial institution would be president of two such famous rugby clubs."

Chalk And Talk

During his years in Thomond College, Ward's career snowballed to the point that he became a full international in his final year yet he was still expected to maintain the same academic standards as everybody else. He could have done with a 34 hour day, particularly when he had to complete his thesis whilst attending lectures, doing teaching practice, preparing for his final exams and training and playing for Ireland. Things came to a head when he was chosen to play for the Barbarians on their Easter tour in 1978:

"I was due to hand in my thesis on the Wednesday after Easter. My personal tutor was Dave Weldrick. That year Dave had been up to his eyes training the college football team and steering them to All-Ireland glory. He was a great coach even though he was essentially a soccer man who played for Pike Rovers, one of the top junior sides in Limerick. He applied the principles of soccer to Gaelic football. The lads on the team like Pat Spillane or Fran Ryder who played on the great Kerry or Dublin teams will tell you that Dave was every bit as professional in his approach as Mick O'Dwyer or Kevin Heffernan. He is a larger than life character and an institution at the college.

"Because Dave was so caught up with the football team and I was so immersed in my rugby career we didn't meet as often as we should have during the year. My thesis deadline was looming. It was a serious business because if I didn't hand it in on time I didn't qualify. It was as simple as that.

"I was picked for the Barbarians' Easter tour and I badly wanted to play in it because every player wants to be a Ba-ba for the first time. I had to play for Garryowen on the Saturday and the plan was for me to fly out on Sunday to play in the Barbarian game against Swansea on the Monday. My mentor, P.J. Smyth did not want me to miss my thesis deadline but equally he wanted me to play for the Ba-bas. He was coaching the backs in Garryowen at the time and after the match on the Saturday he came up with me on the train from Limerick to Dublin and we worked the whole journey up on my thesis. When we got off the train we went to the Abbey Mooney pub, as it was at the time, and worked the rest of the night until closing time on the thesis sipping minerals as everyone else in the place was on the razz to celebrate Easter. I flew back to Dublin on the Tuesday, went straight down to Limerick, finished it off that night and got it in on time the next day.

"Even if you were a 'name' you still had to meet the same academic standards as everybody else, which is proper order. At the time the college had a plethora of sporting stars, but that seems to be no longer the case because the academic requirements are now so high. The ideal PE teacher need not be a superstar in any one sport but, ideally, proficient in all sports. I would like to see a return to the middle ground between academic attainment and achievement in sport.

"While, as I say, I had to knuckle down the same as everybody else to the academic aspect of college life, being a rugby and soccer player did bring its own advantages which made life as a student a little more pleasant. Initially I played soccer for Pike Rovers, while my best friend in college, the brother I never had, Dave Mahedy played for one of the top junior sides, Wembley Rovers. This meant that we were well in with the chef in the college canteen, who was a big soccer buff and a Wembley Rovers man to the core, Seanie Shinnors. Accordingly our helpings at dinner-time were the envy of every other student in the canteen. When you are a student, and that is your main meal of the day, those helpings meant an awful lot.

"Another Pike Rovers man who was an invaluable help to me at the time was my great friend, Brian O'Brien. Whenever I mention Brian's name in Limerick people always assume I am talking about Shannon's Brian O, so I have to constantly explain it's the Pike Rovers' Brian O.

"At one stage *The Sunday People* did a feature article on me. My thesis was on the development of soccer in Ireland and the article's angle was of a rugby star doing a thesis on soccer. I also got great help from Jimmy Magee and Philip Greene preparing my thesis. Brian is the soccer buff par excellence, he saw this and shortly after a big box of books arrived for me in college full of details on soccer even though he didn't know me from Adam then. I went to meet him and we became very good friends. He is nature's original gentleman.

"To this day Brian still keeps me informed about every detail of life in Limerick. It's an old cliché now about me being a naturalised Limerick man but I still love to hear all the news because I loved my years in Limerick so much.

"Another great friend to this day is John Fahey, manager of the Limerick Inn, which has been Garryowen's and Munster's base for many a long day. At the end of my first year he arranged a part-time summer job for me with his building firm at the time on a building site in Tallaght. I wasn't really cut out for it and moved on to painting and decorating instead but it was nice to be able to go back to college and say I had been a labourer like so many of my classmates. It sounded good at any rate!

"Since I was paying my own way through college it was important that not only did I get a summer job but that I took part-time work also. Frank Hogan arranged work as a petrol pump attendant in his garage for me – with Dave Mahedy and I alternating evenings from 5 to 9. That way we had the best of both worlds – we got paid and we'd like to think our college work didn't suffer too badly in the process.

"If Frank was a father figure to me then his wife, Fran, certainly had a comparable influence. Now she spends much of her free time visiting underprivileged families on behalf of the St Vincent de Paul, identifying what their needs are and answering them. So many people talk about doing this type of voluntary work, but I admire her particularly because she goes out there and makes things happen.

"When you are a student one of the biggest problems is always accommodation. I was lucky insofar as I played with Pat Chessor for Garryowen. He was in the auctioneering business and always ensured Dave and I had somewhere to stay. All in all my sporting contacts made student life much easier for me and this continued when I started in business, for example, a very influential figure in Garryowen, whom I first met on our preseason tour to Holland in 1975, was Hans Droog and he became not only our company accountant, but much more importantly, a true and valued friend."

Strangers On A Train

College life initially only provided Ward with a taste of what life was like in Limerick because the Plassey campus is somewhat physically isolated from the city. Everything changed though when he started his career in club rugby:

"When I accepted that invitation to play for Garryowen it was to change my life. I knew that rugby meant a lot to the people of Limerick, but it was not until I had direct involvement that I realised just how much that was. The game is quite literally a way of life in Limerick. After I had played just one match for Garryowen I was walking through what one might call Young Munster territory a few days later and a stranger approached me and said: 'Well, Wardy boy, you did alright on Saturday.' You can't walk 20 paces in Limerick without being stopped for a rugby discussion. If you are interested in sport, Limerick is where it's at. It's sporting Utopia.

"If you walk through the city when two Limerick clubs are meeting in a Munster Cup final it's like walking through Dublin on St Patrick's Day. Every shop has a display featuring the appropriate team colours. You simply don't get that anywhere else.

"Let no one be in any doubt Limerick is absolutely and utterly the home of rugby in Ireland. I believe that people in Dublin pay lip-service to that but they have no conception of what it *really* means. Unless you actually live, play, and experience the passion of real competitive rugby you can never fully understand it.

"Each club has its own watering hole. You know a person's rugby affiliation by the pub he or she drinks in, for example Angela Conways (or The Mall Bar) is a famous Shannon pub as are Gus O'Driscolls, The Triple Crown Bar and The Office. Souths and The Locke Bar (owned by Richard Costello) are Garryowen pubs while Willie Sexton's attracts many of the younger Garryowen fans. Bobby Byrnes is unique in that it draws on both Garryowen and Young Munster supporters. Charlie St George's is a true Young Munster pub as is Austin Quinlivans (which is located at the entrance to the Yellow Road and proudly displays the club's crest in black and amber), Kevin Frosts and Eddie Tuites. It's hard to associate a particular pub with Old Crescent because they made a decision once they sold Rathbane to concentrate on their new clubhouse in Rosbrien. All the junior clubs too are associated with particular pubs; Thomond with the North Star and Hogan's which are both located in Thomond Gate; Richmond with the A1 Bar; St Mary's with Clohessy's and Presentation with Flannery's. Myles Breens is probably the most famous and most cosmopolitan of them all, although it is fair to say that it is primarily a Bohemians' watering hole. It's a hot bed of, to use Limerick parlance 'ballhopping', i.e., swopping stories and gossip. If you want to know what's going on in Limerick rugby all you need do is go to Myles Breens – and meet up with the likes of Garryowen's Morgan Costello, Young Munster's Clem Casey or Bohemians' Frank Malone."

As Ward gets swept away on a tide of reminiscing about his adopted home one character in particular has a very special place in his reflections. His tone changes when he speaks about him – a fascinating mixture of deep affection and reverence – of the type normally reserved for a close blood relative:

"One of my fondest memories of my first season in Limerick was while travelling down by train to Cork from Dublin for my first Munster Cup final. The train stopped at Limerick Junction and this gentleman came on. He immediately caught my eye and to my astonishment asked: 'Oh, Mr Ward, can I sit down beside you?' I couldn't believe this especially considering that I had only played three senior club games up to that point. He told me his name was Paddy Walsh. We became friends straightaway and to this day we have a very close relationship and are regularly in touch with each other.

"Paddy is now in his late eighties and a fanatical Garryowen supporter. He lives in Janesboro in Young Munster territory. His wife Mary is a staunch Young Munster supporter. People in Dublin cannot appreciate the way families split down the middle in Limerick over allegiance to rugby clubs and the passion that it generates.

"Paddy ('Sef') never missed a rugby international until very recent times when his arthritis started to slow him down. He was a well-known figure at all the big matches because he would arrive two hours before the game with his flask of tea and sandwiches. To this day whenever I go to Lansdowne Road for big games the ground staff ask me: 'How's your friend, Mr Walsh?' I have always found people in Limerick nice beyond belief but Paddy in particular is such a lovely,

lovely gentleman and his whole life is Garryowen. He is their number one supporter.

"Paddy has also been my number one fan throughout my trials and tribulations. He has gone on local radio many times to defend me and has written countless letters to the national newspapers to defend my cause but more importantly he has always encouraged me when I needed a boost.

"I cannot adequately convey how much I have valued Paddy's friendship down through all these years or how much he means to me."

Blessed Art Thou Amongst Women

It is only with the benefit of hindsight that Ward has fully appreciated just how special Garryowen is. Initially he imagined that all clubs were more or less run the same in terms of the way they were organised off the field. As he tasted life in other clubs he realised that this was not in fact the case:

"One of the things I remember especially is the ladies' dinner. It was something I took for granted, but even now I'm not aware of any club that has anything like it. There are some marvellous ladies associated with the club – very special people like Rita Dolan, Cecil Reid, Marjorie O'Sullivan, Peggy Mayne, June O'Grady, Rose Keane, Rose Pratt, Ann Hall and Margaret Griffin to name but a few. They served up smashing dinners for us after matches. Rita Dolan would always bring boxes of fruit to our training sessions especially before Cup matches, which I as a student, particularly appreciated – it saved me going home to have a half tin of beans! This extra attention highlighted the importance of the Cup to Garryowen and because you were treated so well as a player you felt that you had to go out there and try that bit harder.

"In May when the season was over the roles were reversed. The players had to, and still have to dress up, for one night and serve the ladies, who are wined and dined for the evening at the club's expense. It is a wonderful touch and a nice way of saying thank you.

"Each of these ladies is a character in her own right. One of the main reasons why Garryowen will always have a special place in my heart is that the club has so many great characters. I'll never forget the late Dom O'Brien on his crutches booming out in a deep Limerick accent: 'Come on the boys in b-b-b-lue'. There are so many more like Dessie Quaid, Frankie Prendergast, Leo Colgan, Gerry O'Mahony, Martin O'Shea, Jimmy Harris, Steve and Paul McDonagh, Derry O'Donovan (Sr and Jr), Gerry Mayne, Davy Keane, Mick Lucey, Joe Mulqueen, Michael Murnane, Danno Hayes, Noel Earlie, Johnny McCrory, Gerry Locke, John Noonan and Paddy Reid et al. The list is endless. Paddy played on Ireland's 1949 Triple Crown winning team. He turned to league afterwards and was only officially allowed to get involved in the game about three years ago. He had a 'discreet association' with Garryowen under age teams when I was there. I learned a lot from him. He had a rule with all his teams that they could never, ever kick the ball during a match. Now I have the same rule with my under-13s except that they cannot kick the ball outside their own 22. We may lose games because of it but it's amazing to see how their skills develop as a result.

"Paddy is Pa Whelan's father-in-law. One of the reasons why Garryowen have made such a big impact on the All-Ireland League is that they have had far thinking people like Pa involved. As soon as the All-Ireland League was announced Pat and Frank Hogan moved swiftly and secured the services of the former Scottish international, Nairn McEwan as coach. There was a lot of opposition to it initially from the traditionalists, including his own father-in-law, Paddy Reid. They argued that the club had managed on its own for a hundred years and didn't need any blow-ins – but Nairn came and succeeded. He was followed by Murray Kidd – an unqualified success – for three years and now Andy Leslie has taken the reins. Frank and Pa's vision and foresight has paid handsome dividends in terms of Garryowen's recent success."

Those Magnificent Men In Their Flying Machines

When Ward got involved with the commercial aspect of Limerick life through his sports shop his bond with the city deepened. Such were the demands on his time that he could have done with the gift of being bi-locational:

"Ken Goodall had asked me to play in a game in Derry one day to mark the opening of City of Derry RFC's new clubhouse. The problem was that John 'Batsy' Harnett's paper, *The Limerick Weekly Echo's* Sportstar of the Year awards were on that same night. It was the social and sporting event of the year and I was due to receive one of the awards so there was no question of me missing it. Ken arranged a small plane to fly me from Galway to Derry that day, play the match and return to Limerick for the awards ceremony. There was no airport in Derry at the time so we landed in a big corn field and drove the plane into an old shed and locked it inside. It was like something from Green Acres.

"When I think of entertainment in Limerick my mind goes back to the night Max Boyce came to perform in the city. I had met him a few times at international matches. He called to the shop before he was due to go on stage in the Savoy and asked me to collect him after the show. Needless to say he put on a great show in front of a packed house and had everyone eating out of his hand but he came back with us to Garryowen clubhouse afterwards and was a hundred times better because this was not just performance, this was straight from the heart. He said afterwards that he felt as at home as if he had been in the valleys in Wales. He went on until 6 a.m. He told me that he had been asked to record Denis Allen's hit of the time 'Limerick You're a Lady' but to substitute Swansea for Limerick. He refused because he thought it would have been a sacrilege. I must say I agree with him because it is *the* Limerick anthem. Another aspect of my time in Limerick which I particularly enjoyed was getting to know some of the great entertainers, people like Denis Allen, Shaun O'Dowd, Ger Cusack and two regular visitors to the shop – Tom and Pascal.

"When I worked in the shop in Thomas Street I had my own daily rituals which were sheer bliss. I loved going across to Finns' coffee shop for tea and pineapple cakes (Harry Gibson Steele's favourites). On a recent visit to the city I was very sad to see that it is no more. When Dave and I were training with Limerick we would lock the shop in the evening and go across to 'The Olde Tom' pub to Ray and Ena Herrity for a cup of tea and a game of Space Invaders. Both of us became very proficient at it. It's great to have so many happy memories about that time.

"Another great memory I have is of the local pirate radio stations which were a huge novelty in Limerick at the time. The great Limerick institution then was the late John 'The Man' Frawley – star of Radio Luimní. He was one of the great pioneers of local radio and everyone was glued in when he read out the local obituaries. He would read out Mass times and also times of the Novena when it was on which was and is always a big thing in Limerick. He had his own pet names for the weather like 'Billy Breeze' and 'Sammy Sunshine'. Everyone knew his old Volkswagen car which he called 'The Galloping Maggot'. All he had in front of him was a copy of *The Cork Examiner*. He worked in the most primitive conditions but he was way ahead of his time.

"The big station in Limerick, however, was Big L which was also way ahead of its time. It was run by Mike Richardson and was extremely professional. He had a most controversial sports programme on Saturday mornings which was compulsive listening with Sean Murphy covering GAA, Tony McMahon soccer, Jim Upton tennis, Ronnie Long, athletics and Len Dineen, the rugby angle.

"Len is the voice of Limerick rugby, the local Bill McLaren. He is one of the great characters of the Old Crescent club in addition to people like Cyril Downes, Paddy Lane MEP, Tom Barry, Seamus Gubbins, Don, Mick and Pat Reddan and of course Johnny 'Touchjudge' Downes.

"The junior clubs too have all their own great characters. You can't talk of Presentation club without referring to Gary Lawlor, for example. Thomond is an unbelievable rugby club and a man who has done so much to bring them to their extraordinarily high ranking in junior rugby is Sean McNamara – a legendary coach in Limerick who was so far ahead in junior rugby in his knowledge of forward play. Another great Thomond man is Liam Fitzgerald. Then of course there's Dick Smyth and Declan Cusack – great 'Soda cakes' of the club.

"St Mary's too have wonderful personalities like Joe 'the Dane' Hayes, Tony Colbert and Johnny Barry. Richmond have Gerry and Donal Moore, Tom Cusack, Joe Markham, Dermot Waters, Mick Faul and Donal Brock. One of their great mentors was Milo McInerney. He died tragically whilst refereeing a match I was playing in for Garryowen – the annual fixture against Bective Rangers for the Hyland trophy.

"He was part of a long tradition of great Limerick referees which included people like Shannon's Johnny Cole, Bohemians' Tony O'Sullivan, Paddy D'Arcy, Eoin McCann and of course the incomparable Martin Walsh."

When Silence Is Not Golden

What appeals most to Ward about Limerick people however is their passion:

"One of the biggest differences, of course, between club rugby and international rugby is the attendance. And that's an advantage Wales have over everybody. Have you ever been to a top club game in Wales? It's like premier league soccer even down to the souvenir sellers.

"The top Welsh players in front of crowds of up to 10,000 every week and when they step up to international rugby it's no great problem for them when suddenly they're out in front of 60,000 belting forth a cacophony of quadraphonic sound! You may think it's noisy being on the terraces but just imagine what it's like when you're out in the middle with the noise coming from all sides.

"In Ireland we have nothing exactly comparable – except that is the Limerick fans! What soccer is to Dublin, rugby is to Limerick – everybody plays it. They love the game. For atmosphere, Thomond Park is out on its own next to Lansdowne Road on international day. Somebody once said that rugby is only played democratically in three places – New Zealand, Wales and Limerick – and he's probably right."

John B. Keane tells a story which typifies the fanaticism of Limerick supporters. He recalls meeting a supporter in Thomond who was full of the spirit, in more senses than one, after Munster's defeat of the All-Blacks. His friend greeted him with a quotation from Shakespeare's *Henry V:*

And gentlemen in England now abed
Shall think themselves accursed they were not here
And hold their manhoods cheap while any speaks
They fought with us upon St Crispin's Day.

He then went on to inform John B. that: "This will be worse than the Black-and-Tan war one day" – explaining that by the end of the twentieth century every man, woman and child in Limerick would have been at the match.

The wit of the Shannonsiders is typified by a letter written to Mick English, one of the great out-halves, by the late Mai Purcell of *The Limerick Leader,* when English won his first cap. The letter read:

Mick. I should like to impress on you that I'm spending a whole week's wages visiting Dublin just to see you play and I beseech you not to make an idiot of yourself on this occasion.

I furthermore request that on this auspicious occasion mindful of your duties and responsibilities not only to your club and the people of Limerick but to your country as a whole, that you keep your bloody eye on the ball. Good luck and God Bless.

The great Earl Kirton, the former All-Blacks out-half, remarked about playing in Thomond: "When you play Munster in Thomond Park you can appreciate how the early Christians felt in the Colosseum."

Thomond Park is also famous for the 20 foot wall which was insufficient to prevent the ball from leaving the ground from time to time. When balls were lost the crowd were wont to shout: "Never mind the ball get on with the game." Mick English was fond of deliberately kicking the ball over the wall when his side was defending a narrow lead near the end of a game.

A story told in New Zealand is that if the Prime Minister died and if he had played for the All-Blacks the headline in the paper's would be "All-Black dies." Limerick people are every bit as fanatical in their worship of their sporting heroes.

Them And Us

Ward has an apparently inexhaustible supply of stories about Limerick rugby:

"Another thing about Limerick clubs, and Munster clubs generally, is that they regard beating Leinster clubs not as the be all and end all but pretty close to it because they perceive Leinster clubs to be arrogant. This is why Munster teams raise their game so much against Leinster sides and why a team from Munster has won the All-Ireland League every year so far and will win many more in the future.

"I remember this being brought home to me forcibly in my first full season with Munster when we prepared to play Leinster. They were hot favourites having had a great win in Llanelli. Kevin Flynn was coaching them at the time and he was asked for a prediction of the result. He said that if they played as well as they had against Llanelli they could win by up to 30 points. Of course, that was like a red rag to a bull. To say they would win by even one point would have been an insult to Munster's pride but to suggest that there might be 30 in it was an unbearable outrage. We had a meeting in the Metropole Hotel before the game and I remember our captain that day was Pat Whelan, he held up the paper with Flynn's comments and said: 'That's what those **** think of you.' We went out and demolished them after that. It was a really big game for me and one that in many ways launched my career.

"A comparable incident occurred a few years ago when Babs Keating made a derogatory comment about Cork hurlers and of course, in their Championship match, Cork beat Tipperary."

A classic story about the passion of Limerick teams' intense desire to beat Dublin teams goes back to a visit of Lansdowne to the Shannonside city to play Shannon. The dressing-room was being renovated at the time and there was a six inch gap in the wall which allowed the visiting side to listen in to the Shannon team talk. Their captain was exhorting the team to beat these 'pansies from Dublin'. His concluding remark, much to the mirth of the Dublin players, was: "I'll finish with just two words for you – (there was a pregnant pause) – A Tack"!

Ward's friend, Ken Ging has a very special memory of travelling down to play Shannon in Ward's first match with the Wicklow club. He was coach at the time and had to suffer the frustration of seeing his side annihilated. After the game he got a bit worried when he saw a man, no more than five feet tall but seemingly the same width, wearing a black beret approaching him with a menacing look. The stranger barked out at him: "Are you that team's coach?" Ging knew instinctively that it was not one of the times when honesty was the best policy and said: "No. I'm their coach driver!"

Ward attributes the success of Limerick clubs to three main characteristics: their passion for the game, their competitive spirit and their great personalities on and off the field:

"When you think about it it's extraordinary that a city with a relatively small population has five senior clubs, including four in the top two divisions of the AIL, not to mention a wealth of top class junior sides. When we would play Dublin clubs in friendly games, for example, it was approached almost like a Cup tie. It's going to take a huge effort for either Dublin or Ulster teams to win the AIL because of this attitude in Limerick and Munster in general – mind you the others are beginning to learn how to adapt and cope with it better.

"Each club has so many wonderful characters who play such a key role in building up spirit. Take a club like Bohemians for example and you think straight away of people like Benny O'Dowd, Alan Condell, Corrie Ward, Frank Malone (Limerick's equivalent of Max Boyce), Eamon Tobin and the late Pat Lawler who died tragically but who has the distinction of having the trophy for unarguably the greatest mini-rugby under-13 tournament in Ireland named after him. With people like that involved they can't go wrong."

Jurassic Park

One of the personalities Ward admires most in Limerick today is the Young Munster coach Tony Grant:

"The biff-bang-wallop approach to motivating teams before games is almost dead everywhere but to stand outside a dressing-room in Limerick, especially outside Young Munster or Shannon and listen to their warm-ups is frightening, and I mean frightening. That is why Young Munster's ground is variously known as 'The Killing Fields' or 'The Garden Of Get Somebody' and most recently 'Jurassic Park'!

"I would be less than honest if I said matches against Young Munster were ones I particularly looked forward to. Pa Whelan would talk about going to war and that's what it was like – a form of tribal warfare. There's no comparison between the passion in the rest of the country and in Limerick. It really is dog eat dog.

"Young Munster's achievement in winning the All-Ireland League was extraordinary considering they have such a small geographical base and no old boys network to feed them new talent. In Dublin, clubs depend on schools but in Limerick they get boys from the age of under-10 and work with them all the way up. Young Munster have such an incredible community spirit. It would be like having a club rugby side in the Liberties in Dublin. Remember how St Francis got to the FAI Cup final a few years ago and the community following they generated – well Young Munster is that multiplied by 20 because they have gone on to claim the biggest domestic prize in Irish rugby.

"A lot of the credit for their achievement must go to their coach, Tony Grant. I can't understand why he has never been involved in coaching Munster at representative level. His genius is his ability to cut his cloth to suit his measure. The best Munster final I have ever seen was Young Munster's defeat of Bohemians in 1980. At that time Young Munster had great backs so they selected a mobile pack. Now they have gone back to their traditional strength – forward play, and because of that are almost impossible to break down.

"I have had many great friends in Young Munster over the years especially people like Clem Casey, Charlie St George, Tom Clifford, Joe Kennedy, Mick Sheehan and Johnny Brennan. Johnny took me to his house one evening to show me his rugby museum which needless to say has a black and amber tint to put it mildly! I remember one time when we played Young Munster and Johnny, as ever, was touchjudge. At one stage Deero got pushed over the sideline and Johnny hit him on the head with his flag! That is typical of the passion which the game generates on Shannonside.

I have many fond memories of Charlie St George – a grand old gentleman of Limerick rugby. He was on the Bateman Cup winning team in 1928 which is part of Limerick folklore. Many's the letter of encouragement I received from him down through the years.

"When we had the shop I would often meet Tom Clifford and Clem Casey in Jack Burkes for morning coffee or lunch. Tom would leave his bike outside unlocked but no one would ever touch it because everybody knew whose it was and treated it with such reverence. "

An occupational hazard for big match analysts is to bend over backwards and to call it as they see it. A classic example of this was the way RTE was flooded with phonecalls complaining about Johnny Giles' comments and accusing him of sour grapes after Ireland's win over England in the European Championships in 1988. Although Giles is a close friend of Jack Charlton he feels obliged because of the nature of the job he has been given to compliment and to criticise when and where it is appropriate. Ward found himself in a similar position in 1993:

"It goes without saying that my love-affair with Limerick will be eternal. But one thing that disappointed me greatly was when I was accused of bias when Young Munster beat St Mary's in the decisive match of the AIL and of not giving the Munsters a fair crack of the whip, as it were, in my analysis. Because of Fred Cogley's connections and indeed mine with St Mary's he was considered, most unfairly, to be 'less than totally objective' in some of his comments. In my case it was guilt by association. I attribute the slur on me to a few local media people trying to stir things up in Limerick. (They know themselves who they are.) I was there at that match to do a job which I did as honestly and objectively as possible. Those who said I was biased that day could not have been more wrong and I was hurt by some of the comments and innuendoes. The irony is that on my Christmas mailing list for clubs St Mary's would be a very, very long way from the top – and quite a way behind Young Munster at that."

A Reunion Of The Heart

As Ward's rugby star ascended in Limerick he decided to make a return to soccer.

"Up to joining Garryowen I had been playing nothing only soccer with Rovers and nothing else. The travelling though was killing me and that was why I had to leave Milltown. I had spent two years at Glenmalure Park and it was a troubled period for Rovers. The slump was beginning to bite and after my first season, the man who signed me, Liam Tuohy resigned. That's when everything went really downhill. We had a number of managers then including Shay Noonan, Dickie Giles (Johnny's Dad), Mick Meegan and Sean Thomas. Sean asked me back in '77 when I played about half-a-dozen matches for them.

"John Herrick, the then Limerick manager, had come to me on a few occasions after that but I was solely concentrating on rugby then. When Eoin Hand and Dave Mahedy came along they got me at the right time."

On 10 August 1981 Ward played his first soccer game for Limerick – a friendly against Spurs with Glen Hoddle putting on an exhibition of football at its very best. A few weeks later he played against Southampton in the UEFA Cup. Thrown in at the deep end Ward did more than just play, he set the soccer public agog with his performance. Although Limerick lost 3-0 Ward's display caught the eye of Kevin Keegan who was sufficiently impressed to remark:

"Some players have the ability to generate excitement merely by running onto the pitch. Tony Ward would appear to be one of them. It was a fine performance from a man who could have made a name for himself in top class soccer. He could probably make a lot of money for himself. . . Money is not everything but it makes life a lot easier."

Lawrie McMenemey was generous in his praise for Limerick: "They certainly hit us with everything in the first half and Tony Ward buzzed around like he was at Twickenham. For a while I was half expecting Terry Wogan to come on!"

He was also impressed by Ward's tremendous display of wing play and expressed the view that Ward had what it takes to make it in the big time: "With fulltime coaching it would not take much to play him in higher company."

For his part Ward was very impressed by Keegan:

"Soccer and rugby have at least one thing in common – the higher you go in class, the easier it is to play. Sharing the same pitch with Kevin Keegan, Mike Channon, Dave Watson and Alan Ball, was a marvellous experience. And of these Keegan was easily the greatest.

"Soccer has always meant a lot to me, but when it came to priorities, it was no contest – it has got to be rugby. When it comes to playing nothing could compare to the involvement of rugby. And to me, sport is all about enjoyment.

"Young people, who work hard all week, crave the satisfaction of playing at the weekend. In that I was no different from anybody else. Put another way, representative honours came low down the list, when I was asked to explain my motivation in sport."

Ward became particularly close to Eoin Hand in those years:

"Eoin was brought to Limerick by my dear old friend, the late, great Harry Gibson Steele, a great character, friend and indeed Peter Clohessy's father-in-law. Eoin was far and away the best soccer manager I ever played under. He was a brilliant organiser, as honest as the day is long and he played with total commitment. His success in Limerick is unparalleled. In his three years there they qualified for Europe each season and they won both the League and Cup. To be a successful manager you must have a ruthless streak. Perhaps that was Eoin's weakness but there was nothing he liked better than a night with the lads. Eoin was a great singer and he became very close friends with Frank Hogan. They were inseparable during Eoin's time in Limerick.

"I was a bit annoyed to see the way Eoin was portrayed in the media towards the end of his reign with the Irish team. Perhaps he did allow himself to be excessively influenced by the star players on the team like Liam Brady and Frank Stapleton but one thing he brought to every job in which he was involved was total professionalism down to the smallest of details. He was a very good manager and Limerick will never forget him.

"One thing about playing for Limerick, which I always had some misgivings about, was that I only played at the start of the season, usually in the glamour friendlies against teams like Tottenham and Manchester United and at the end of the season in Cup matches. The result was that I missed much of the hard toil in the winter months on muddy pitches in dreadful weather. I feared some people might resent that I was only around for the big games because I missed so many 'bread and butter' matches during the rugby season but Eoin was happy, Limerick were happy and so was I. We had great players and marvellous characters in the squad like 'Muckles' O'Donnell, Kevin Fitzpatrick, Johnny Walsh, Al Finnucane, Joe O'Mahony, Pat Nolan, Des Kennedy and Tony Meaney to name but a few and great supporters in people like Michael Crowe, Mick Webb and Willie Flaherty."

Sunday, 2 May saw Ward play for Limerick in the FAI Cup final at Dalymount Park against Bohemians before a crowd of 12,000 people who paid £25,000 to watch a memorable match. He had a significant impact on the match by being involved in a move with Gary Hulmes and man-of-the-match Johnny Walsh to force a corner in the 33rd minute. Ward took a low corner for Brendan Storan to get a touch and stroke the ball home through a tangle of legs for the only goal of the game. In the second half Ward tortured the Bohs' defence with a dazzling display of old-fashioned wing play. It's a game he remembers with understandable affection:

"You can't compare the two sports. As regards rugby internationals there is nothing on the domestic football scene to compare with them. Naturally, I was more nervous before such occasions but I admit I was edgy before playing in the FAI Cup final. It's good to have butterflies and I always liked to get them. I was always a worrier anyway.

"After we won the Cup in '82 we had a fabulous session in the Burlington arranged by Eoin Hand. Shaun Connors was MC and Luke Kelly, the Dublin City Ramblers and the Wolfe Tones performed for us.

"I played for Limerick because I enjoyed it. The Cup medal was a bonus. I'll never forget though the reception we got when we arrived home to Limerick the Monday after the final and parading through the city on an open-deck bus. It was a really special occasion and memory.

"My one regret was that I was forced to miss the celebratory dinner to mark Garryowen's first Munster league win since 1954 which was on the night before we played Bohs. My cup final appearance deprived me of opportunity to play for a team I had selected myself, to play against Thomond rugby club, arguably the best junior club in the country, at the request of Seamus Kiely and Declan Cusack to celebrate the opening of their new pitch in Woodview. I had organised my back row to be Shay, David and Kevin Deering. It was one thing both Kevin and David thanked me for subsequently – for giving them their only opportunity to play with their brother Shay.

"A few months later on 12 August 1982 I played my last competitive game of 11-a-side soccer in a friendly match between Limerick and Manchester United. It was a lovely way to finish though it was not planned that way. It was the day that the Leaving Cert Results came out. Kevin Moran, Bryan Robson, Ray Wilkins, who is one of the most charming people I've met in any sport, and I ended up in the Parkway Hotel. There was a marvellous atmosphere because of the exam elation.

"I never accepted a penny for playing for Limerick, even when we won the Cup, despite the fact that they were one of the wealthiest clubs in the country at the time. Pat Grace was at the helm and he put a lot of money into Limerick soccer and to the League of Ireland in general. I suppose you could say more fool me! The reason for that was because I was being so careful in avoiding anything which would antagonise the IRFU, particularly in relation to my amateur status, even though they were two totally separate sports!"

Rugby's Aristocrats

Having played with and against so many great Limerick players and having watched so many classic games between Limerick sides like the Bohemians versus Young Munster final in 1980 and the decisive clash in the All-Ireland League in 1992 between Shannon and Garryowen, Ward decided to pay his tribute to them by selecting his greatest Limerick team.

There were two possible choices for the full-back position, his former Garryowen clubmate Larry Moloney and Shannon's Terry Fitzgerald:

"Terry was a great player having joined Shannon from one of the top junior clubs in Limerick, St Mary's. Down through the years St Mary's has been a great nursery for Shannon, though it has also provided Garryowen with a great many players. Junior rugby in Limerick is unique with a huge participation. There are so many top junior sides in the city; St Mary's, Thomond, Richmond, Presentation, each having very rich traditions – not to mention the great country sides like Abbeyfeale, Bruff, Galbaly, Newcastle West, Newport etc.

Terry put over many crucial kicks for Shannon, particularly in their Cup winning campaigns in 1977 and '78. He had a great big match temperament. However, I think that few people in Limerick will disagree with my final choice, the 'Prince', Larry Moloney."

For the right wing position Ward's candidates were the former technical officer of the IRFU and erstwhile Garryowen and Munster player, Eddie O'Sullivan, Old Crescent's Ken Lyons, now one of the top rally drivers in the country, and his eventual choice, Garryowen's Richard Wallace.

Ward bent his own rules slightly when selecting the other three-quarters on his team in the interests of attaining the best balance in the side. In the centre he considered the claims of the Shannon pair Eric McNamara and Denis O'Sullivan, Young Munster's Frank Brosnihan and Pat Cross and Bohemians' Peter Rolls and Rory Moroney. However, his final choice was an all Garryowen pairing Johnny McDonnell and Philip Danaher.

On the left wing, despite the rival claims of Garryowen's Eugene Griffin and the fighting and scavanging qualities of Bohemians' Micky Bromell, Ward went for Seamus Dennison:

"I know it may seem a contradiction to select Seamus on the wing for my Limerick team having chosen him in the centre on my Irish team. There is no doubt in my mind that he was *the* outstanding centre in Limerick rugby. Himself and Philip Danaher would have made an excellent combination. Had they played together they would have been a tremendous force. Coincidentally, both were from Abbeyfeale in Co. Limerick. One observation I would have to make is that although Philip has captained Ireland I don't think he has yet played to his true potential in an Irish shirt. To give a balance to my side though I would play Seamus on the wing and bring in Garryowen's Johnny McDonnell. Johnny was an excellent player and selected for Ireland B before sustaining a bad injury which prevented him from ever making it on to the international side. His great strength was his cutting break."

Out-half is a position which has posed a problem for many Limerick clubs down through the years as is evident in the high turnover of players in this position in most of the clubs. Out-halves who caught Ward's eye were Old Crescent's Denis 'Tricksy' Twomey and James Rael, Shannon's Johnny Ryan and Mick Wilson. Ward preferred not to consider himself for any team. He laughs at the memory of a bit of advice he got in that respect:

"I recently went down to Limerick for a few days with Louise. It's always great to go back to my home from home and especially to meet up again with so many old friends. I had a great chat with Dave McMahon, author for so long of the much loved, though hard-hitting when the occasion demanded, 'O'Grady Says' column in *The Limerick Weekly Echo*. Like his brother Tony, Dave is a sporting connoisseur and we were reflecting on the relative dearth in out-half talent in Limerick when compared with the phenomenal flair in many other positions. I was explaining the difficulty I had in making this selection when Dave said the obvious solution was to pick myself, the way John Robbie did when he picked his teams in his own book. I refused to do that. He paused for a minute and then in a very matter-of-fact voice said: 'Yeah, I suppose you're right considering everybody else has dropped you. You might as well drop yourself!'"

In the end he chose Young Munster's Gerry Casey:

"Gerry tells a great story against himself. It goes back to his selection at full-back on the Munster team against Romania in 1980. His father, Clem, was mayor of Limerick at the time and gave a civic reception for the Romanians. In the match Gerry's cover was not all that it might have been. The story around Limerick was that in the morning Clem gave the Romanians the freedom of the city and in the afternoon his son gave them the freedom of Thomond Park. Gerry had very good hands; a massive punt of the ball and was deceptively quick. In addition he was a prolific points scorer and put over many pressure kicks for the Wasps. He retired last year and his loss to the game is great."

A popular choice at scrum-half would have been Garryowen's Liam Hall but Ward only played with him in his final season before he retired from the game. He makes the point forcibly that if his team stretched back five years before his own career started Hall would have been an automatic choice. Other possibilities were Shannon's Paul O'Shea, Young Munster's Eddie Costello and his final choice, Oliver 'Sonny' Kiley, who has formed such an effective partnership with number eight, Niall O'Donovan, over such a long period of time.

As was the case with his Irish team Ward cheated slightly when selecting his two prop forwards. He was a keen admirer of a Young Munster player, whose career was tragically cut short by injury, Brendan O'Connor, also Shannon's Noel Ryan and Garryowen's Mervyn O'Connor not to mention Tom Carroll, Young Munster's Jim Brislane and Bohemians' Ted Mulcahy. In the end there were three outstanding candidates for two positions – Ginger McLoughlin, John 'Packo' Fitzgerald and Peter Clohessy.

"My biggest headache in selecting this team was which of the three to leave out? Ginger had the advantage of playing on both sides so I picked him in preference to Packo at loose-head prop with Peter at tight-head. I must say, like so many others, I believe the Lions blundered badly in not selecting Peter for the '93 tour."

Despite his great respect for Shannon's Noel Glynn it comes as no surprise that Ward's choice as hooker and captain is Pat Whelan.

"Pat's competitive instinct is very strong. He's a born winner and ruthless in every respect. I see him as a possible future Irish coach. What's particularly good about him is that he seeks out and listens to advice, particularly about back play where obviously he has not the same level of expertise as he has about forward play."

Somewhat surprisingly, Ward began his reminiscences about great Limerick second row forwards by considering the strengths of a player from a junior club:

"One of the real characters, and a great player into the bargain, was Dick Smyth of Thomond. Thomond rugby club is his life. At one stage he was president and player at the same time. Every senior club in the city sought his skills but he would not budge."

Others to impress were Garryowen's Eddie Molloy, Shannon's Mick Moylett, Bohemians' John Madigan and Ken Rennison ("Ken played once for Munster – against Cardiff – and although Munster players were not allowed swop jerseys at the time, he did. He was a taxi-driver and for weeks afterwards he drove around Limerick in his Cardiff jersey"), and Young Munster's Peter Meehan. In the end Ward opted for an all Shannon pairing of Brendan Foley and Michael Galwey.

In selecting the wing forwards Ward was spoilt for choice. He smiles at the memory of the candidates, his former Garryowen team-mate, Micky Martin:

"Micky 'Squash' was and is rugby's Cliff Richard – the Peter Pan of Limerick rugby. He still looks like a spring chicken even though he patently is not. Whenever we went on tour he guarded his passport like the crown jewels because he simply didn't want anyone to know his age.

"One of the myths that built up in Limerick rugby was that whenever I lined out against Shannon I feared their flanker, Johnny Barry. While blind courage may not have been my middle name I never feared any flanker and Johnny's onfield presence never caused me undue concern. So unfortunately perhaps for some Shannon supporters that is one myth that I must lay to rest. Johnny was like Fergus Slattery in the sense that you were always aware of his proximity. He was however, an outstanding forward and a great player. He had a reputation for putting people away, a bit like Paul Ringer if you like, but he was certainly not that type of player. He had many opportunities to 'take me out' but never did. To sum him up he was one of the hardest but fair flankers I ever played against.

"Like Young Munster, Shannon have had so many great forwards down through the years and another wing forward I have tremendous respect for is Mick Fitzgibbon. He hit me with some of the hardest tackles I have ever received. I can pay him no higher compliment than to say he was in the Shay Deering class when it came to tackling."

Other players who created a favourable impression in this position included Garryowen's Willie Sexton and Mick Sherry, Shannon's Gerry McMahon and Young Munster's John Hayes, Ger Earles and Gerry Quaid. In the end though he had no difficulty making his final selections, Shay Deering and Shannon's Colm Tucker:

"Colm was such a strong player. The crowd loved it when he had the ball tucked in under his arm and was running at me or indeed at any of the midfield backs. In picking greatest teams there are always differing opinions but everyone who has been involved in Limerick rugby will agree with the choice of Shay Deering. The attitude in Limerick, when forwards came down from Leinster was one of: 'Here's another pussycat'. Accordingly, they get 'the treatment', a real roasting from the forwards on Shannonside. When Shay first came down he got that treatment at first but earned their respect by giving twice as good as he got."

Again Ward was spoilt for choice in the number eight position ranging from one of the heroes of the 1985 Triple Crown team, Brian Spillane to his great friend, Frank Hogan and another former Garryowen player, Billy Cronin, Shannon's Eddie Price, Young Munster's Mick Sheehan, Bohemians' Ger Madigan but in the end he picked Shannon's Niall O'Donovan because of his tremendous strength and timing but above all for his telepathic understanding with Sonny Kiely.

As a utility reserve player Ward opted for Bobby Roche who has played in so many different positions for Old Crescent, both in the backs and forwards before moving on to Shannon.

The Limerick Team Of All The Talents

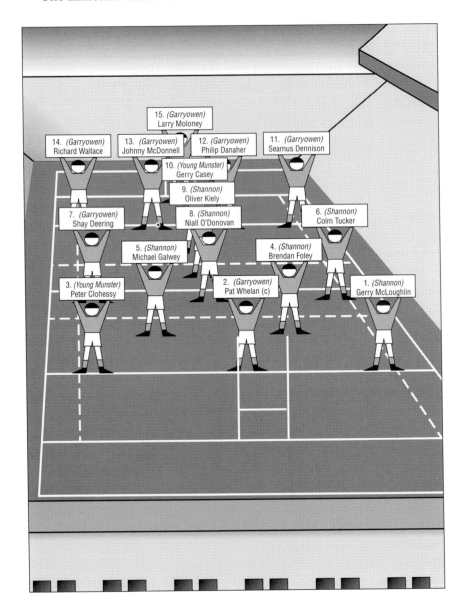

15. *(Garryowen)* Larry Moloney

14. *(Garryowen)* Richard Wallace

13. *(Garryowen)* Johnny McDonnell

12. *(Garryowen)* Philip Danaher

11. *(Garryowen)* Seamus Dennison

10. *(Young Munster)* Gerry Casey

9. *(Shannon)* Oliver Kiely

7. *(Garryowen)* Shay Deering

8. *(Shannon)* Niall O'Donovan

6. *(Shannon)* Colm Tucker

5. *(Shannon)* Michael Galwey

4. *(Shannon)* Brendan Foley

3. *(Young Munster)* Peter Clohessy

2. *(Garryowen)* Pat Whelan (c)

1. *(Shannon)* Gerry McLoughlin

For Whom The Bell Tolls

Limerick folklore abounds with rugby stories – real and apocryphal. Ward was the unnamed culprit in a story that did the rounds just as he broke onto the Irish team. The story involved two conversations between a Young Munster supporter and his parish priest.

Priest: "Tis a long time since your face has been seen in this sacred house my son. Anyway we cater for all types here. Can I be of any assistance to you at all?"

Fan: "I don't know if you can, Father. You see this could be a job for the bishop. I am in an awful way. My state of mind is such that all communications with the wife, both verbal and otherwise, have temporarily ceased."

Priest: "My son confession is good for the soul. What is the terrible secret that you bear?"

Fan: "Father, the truth is . . . I . . . . I . . . am in danger of becoming a supporter of the Garryowen team."

Priest: "I see. That's bad, in fact, it's very bad."

Fan: "I knew you would understand, Father. All my life I thought that rugby consisted of rucks, scrums and lineouts with a few fights thrown in for good measure. Where I come from, shouts of 'ahead, ahead' have a different meaning than that employed elsewhere. To be candid, Father, I was happy in my ignorance, but now 'tis all jinking and running, reverse-passing and blind-side moves. And to make matters worse, Father, I am being entertained by it all. Tell me . . . Do you think I could be losing the faith?"

Priest: "My son, the ordinary, everyday problems of life – wife-swopping, divorce, drinking – are but minor problems compared to your dilemma. Come back to me tomorrow, I shall have spoken with a higher authority by then."

The next day –

Priest: "My son, you can put your mind to rest. A solution to your problem exists and where else was it to be found but in . . . religion. Within a year or two the blackguard most responsible for Garryowen's madness and for your unhappy state of mind will be plucked from our midst and transported away. Normality will return."

Fan: "But how can I be sure of this?"

Priest: "My son, the bells of St Mary's will ring out for him . . . and he will answer their call."

An Everlasting Love

Clearly Limerick and its people retain a special place in Ward's heart.

In the four or five days before he left Limerick to open a shop in Dublin in 1982 (when Ollie Campbell performed the ritual cutting of the ribbon) a stream of people came up to him to express sorrow at his departure. Some even sympathised with him:

"It was almost as if I was going before a firing squad or as if I was just disappearing off the face of the earth! And the number of Mass bouquets!

"I loved that shop in Limerick. The beauty of it was that from nine o'clock in the morning until we left in the evening, it was just sport all day long, talking sport and all the time learning from the public. That was the great thing. It was a two-way process the whole time. You met such fantastic people. It was really a great time.

"Now Brian O'Brien sends me the Limerick papers each week so that I can still keep in touch with affairs on Shannonside. It is extraordinary the number of people to this very day who think I was born in Limerick. This happens to me regularly and I consider it to be the supreme compliment. What's also very nice is the number of Limerick people who ask me with total sincerity if I'm settling in Dublin!

"I wish I had a musical talent and could write a song about my feelings for Limerick as Denis Allen did. My opening would be along the lines of:

Give Limerick my love,
I will always remember her
My Lady."

12. Home and Away

The supreme happiness in life is the conviction that we are loved.

Victor Hugo

To write about Ward the rugby player is relatively easy. To attempt to write about Ward the family man is an absolute nightmare – for a long time producing nothing but a severely chewed biro and an acute anxiety attack. The problem is that to tell the truth, the whole truth and nothing but the truth is to leave oneself wide open to the accusation of being mawkishly sentimental – that the description of life in the Ward household is too good to be true. While no marriage or family unit is perfect, the Wards make a valiant attempt to reach the pinnacle of domestic bliss. If it sounds almost idyllic then the portrait fairly represents the reality. However, Ward's family life was not always so bountifully happy.

Look Before You Leap

Since Ward was dropped on the Australian tour in 1979, much of his life in rugby and outside sport was shaped, and to some extent, remains defined by that experience. Fourteen years on from those heady days Ward is still to a certain degree, despite his best efforts to the contrary, wearing the invisible scars from that experience.

We all live with deep frustrations and broken dreams. Rather than face the incompleteness of our lives and our feelings of loneliness and inner emptiness, we often desperately search for companionship in order to feel a sense of belonging. At the root of much of our restlessness is an impatient yearning for something to fulfill our lives – a marriage partner, power, fame etc. We stand before life with unrealistic expectations. We all seek intimacy and healing in our lives. We seek intimacy because we cannot live without love and affection. We seek healing because we experience sickness and pain.

Ward's story is at once universal and particular. The shattering damage to his self-confidence because of his fall from grace in rugby terms cried out for intimacy and healing. He wanted someone to eradicate his sense of brokenness. The opening line of Sylvia Kantris' *Lad's Love* sums up Ward's emotional condition at the time: "I bruise more easily than in my youth."

To some of his closest friends the immediate chain of events, which followed his experience in Australia 1979, offered conclusive proof that he had lost his reason – only they used more colourful language to describe his behaviour at the time. As a young man Ward had always been prone to impulsive actions. However, he normally was prevented from doing anything which would damage either himself or anybody else because of the intervention of good friends, particularly "the father he never had", Frank Hogan, who always took him aside and had words of rock solid advice to put him back on the right track. What was different about the summer of 1979 was that Ward was too wounded to heed advice he didn't want to hear at the time. Oscar Wilde certainly had a point in Ward's case anyway, when he said that youth is wasted on the young.

Having had more than his fair share of heartbreak in rugby Ward was to experience even more intense pain in his private life. At the time though, it seemed the opposite was the case. In the months before the tour to Australia, Ward had been swept away on a whirlwind romance with a student from Thomond College, Maura O'Regan. He was twenty-four, and still in need of further emotional maturity. She was only nineteen. Although they became engaged the night before he left on tour, there was no ring nor any talk of setting a date. A little over a month after returning to Ireland they were married!

Emotionally or financially Ward was in no position to be even contemplating marriage in the immediate future. He was still living virtually a student existence, away from the shop, with little money and with no house. Frank Hogan's was the loudest of a number of voices which warned him that he was running before he could walk. Ward took exception to the suggestion that he did not know his fiancée well enough to know whether she was the right woman for him or not. He had nothing but contempt for the widely held opinion that he was going too far too quickly.

Whirlwind romances always produce a "happy-ever-after" ending in Mills and Boon novels and Hollywood blockbusters but real life is much different and almost invariably more brutal. Fourteen years on Ward looks on the marriage with a radically different perspective than he had at the time:

"It is easy to look back in hindsight and see your mistakes. We were both very young when we got married and while it may work out for some couples I've little doubt from my own experience that young marriages are not to be recommended. Most young people are just not prepared for the commitment needed in marriage.

"Being involved in sport at any level, but particularly at the highest level, does not help. It does put pressure on a marriage. It's not so much that you are selfish but the time and commitment required is enormous. And all the controversy surrounding my rugby career did not help the family situation.

"As our marriage was collapsing we were both obviously going through a really bad time. It was not a pleasant experience and it certainly affected my rugby very much. Everything just seemed to happen together. It's not a trauma I would wish on anyone.

"Although we both have gone our separate ways, the one thing we both agree now is that our marriage was a big mistake."

The Dark Night Of The Soul

Initially the marriage was a happy one but as the dust settled and the novelty wore off the cracks started to appear. The birth of a daughter, Lynn, on 31 July 1983 might have been expected to transform the tense situation that had developed, but eighteen months later, Ward suddenly found that he was a single parent. Irony has always appeared to have a peculiar attraction for Ward.

His pride was shattered because she had walked out. She had formed a new relationship. He felt a failure but the practicalities of the situation took precedence. He was left literally holding the baby and the priority was to safeguard Lynn's welfare.

"Lynn was the only apple of my eye at the time. I think all fathers are the same with their little girls but ours was a unique situation. She gave me strength when I was weakest. Her physical presence alone helped to lift the clouds of darkness around me. There was a special bond between us and there still is but now each of my three children are equally important to me. Everyone seems to go through a period of 'life in the fast lane' but my priorities changed with Lynn. I know the teaching profession is not the most lucrative but the hours meant I had more time for her.

"Even when I was teaching Lynn was never too far away. When she reached school-going age she began her education in the junior school at St Andrew's. We travelled to school and back home together, and knowing I was on hand, helped her adapt quickly."

Parenting is a complex business. The problems are exacerbated when one partner has to carry the responsibility without the support of the other. Ward was not left to flounder on his own. Not for the first time his mother made heroic sacrifices for his sake, but for him it was like landing on an alien planet to begin a new life.

The most difficult time for him was the night. For months he could not sleep properly as he fretted over the uncertainty of the future both for Lynn and himself:

"I dreaded the nights. The night seemed endless. To wake up at five or six in the morning to see the daylight coming through the curtains was a great relief because I had made it through the night. A major obstacle had been overcome."

The practical needs of Lynn's survival dictated that he could not wallow in a dull fog of self-pity. For her sake he kept his half-healed hurts as camouflaged as possible.

A Friend In Need . . .

Even more so than in the Australian experience, he learned quickly who his true friends were as invariably one does in the hour of crisis. As is so often the case in Ward's moments of need one person was there for him in his hour of greatest darkness like a lighthouse on a stormy sea – his mother, a well of bottomless generosity:

"When the chips were down my mother, as always, came up trumps. Words cannot adequately express how she helped me in that period. She made sacrifices, though, typical of many mums she would never think of it in those terms. Without her support I could never have come through that ordeal. As I mentioned earlier she had a night time job with Bord na gCon but she gave that up and came to live with Lynn and me to help both of us when we were both very vulnerable for different reasons. She helped me carry on regardless and, somehow, to get through those terrible months. I will always be eternally grateful to her for what she did even though I will never be able to thank her adequately. I can't overstate her importance in my 'rehabilitation'.

"As time went on, my mother became Lynn's new mum. Lynn called her 'Mum' at the time. The most normal relationship developed between them. To this day there is a very special bond between them.

"Another knight in shining armour, as it were, was my aunt René. While I was gone to work, either she came to my house or I left Lynn to her. Again I will always be in her debt for her unfailing kindness and practical assistance to Lynn and me during those difficult years.

"The support I received from my in-laws, the O'Regans, could not have been warmer or more sympathetic in very trying circumstances for them as well. From the outset I made a conscious decision that the normality of relations would remain between Lynn and her maternal grandparents and I make sure that they still see her every week. When Lynn was in play school I dropped her to the O'Regans on my way into work, they would bring her to the school, collect her when school was finished and mind her in their house for the afternoon until I collected her on my way home from school. This was of great practical help to me but it was also a great way for Lynn to get to know her grandparents better and vice versa. Maura has lived abroad now for some years but has regular contact with Lynn and has open access to her when she returns to Ireland which is only as it should be.

"At the time it was very important for me to have friends that I could talk to and share my problems with. In this respect no one was more important to me than my closest friend, Denis Hooper. He was my best friend in school and was best man at my wedding to Louise. He's a Benedictine brother and through religious life he has found an inner happiness that I just have no conception of. The day he came to tell me he was joining the order in 1981, I nearly passed away because I don't understand what a 'calling' is. He is now house master in Glenstal and is a very special friend to me and he is our youngest daughter, Nikki's godfather. Even though he was a hundred and twenty miles away, he was on the phone almost non-stop to me. We met for lengthy chats many times. He was a crutch in every sense of the word.

"Another huge help in that way was one of my business partners at the time, Gerry Smith. It was a tremendous help to be able to talk so openly and exhaustively with him about my emotions.

"Some of my rugby friends gave me a lot of support when I needed it most – none more so than Ned Van Esbeck. Ned was always there for me when I needed him.

"There were some lovely gestures from some of my former playing colleagues. Before Christmas 1984 I had been invited to attend the Bermuda festival the following Easter. When your marriage breaks up your entire social confidence is shattered and you don't really feel like going anywhere. I had decided not to travel to Bermuda but my mother talked me into going for two reasons. Firstly, the obvious one, for my own sanity – just to get out and do something different. Secondly, to play some rugby for a change as the Leinster Branch had deemed me an illegal player for Greystones and I had been unable to play any competitive rugby for the club that season.

"When I came home from the trip I discovered that Lynn was the proud owner of three Colly Dollies. Mick Quinn's family at the time ran the H. Williams chain of stores. They were about to start a Colly Dolly promotion based on the Cabbage Doll phenomenon which was huge in America just then. Mick had called to the house while I was away. It was very considerate of him and it captures the oft quoted camaraderie between the rugby community. At the end of it all when you put your caps away, the one thing you have is this incredibly close bond in relation to this funny shaped oval ball. Quinny's gesture typified the essence of what rugby is all about.

"You really appreciate your friends when your world is collapsing all around you. Shortly after my marriage break-up Ollie Campbell sent on a track-suit for Lynn. It was a few sizes too big for her but it was such a lovely gesture on his part. I could write a book of stories of Ollie's kindnesses and thoughtfulness, but that gesture, and the timing of it in particular, encapsulated the inherent and extraordinary goodness of the man."

Catastrophe

As the months passed Ward gradually adjusted to single parenthood though he was still a long way short of returning to equilibrium. That would have been like putting all the pieces back together after Humpty-Dumpty fell off the wall but he was coping better and returning to a semblance of his old self. Throughout all this time, up to the end of 1985 there was no contact with his ex-wife. Then, like a bolt from the blue, came the bombshell. She was seeking custody of Lynn through the courts.

The wounds from that nightmarish period are still incised in the body. Yet he is much too honest to shirk a difficult question and always gives a considered response regardless of the pain the memory of those months triggers off.

He had learnt to cope with the break-up but he knew that his life would be just an empty shell without Lynn. The thought of losing her reduced him to a state of virtual paralysis. Even more pain was to follow:

"Even though the hearing takes place *in camera*, it's terribly traumatic to have every detail of your private life revealed in court. I found it devastating. It was an emotionally crippling, acrimonious and traumatic ending to a chapter of my life which began with so much promise."

The humiliation he endured during the court proceedings was as nothing compared to the recurring nightmare that he would lose Lynn. His anxiety was accentuated by the fact that statistically the odds against the father winning custody of a child were extremely high. In his case though the court ruled in his favour. With that millstone off his neck and his future with Lynn secured he was at last free to try and pick up the threads of his life again.

Ward is visibly angry as he speaks of the continuing plight of the victims of marriage breakdown in Ireland today:

"I dislike the hypocritical attitudes which prevail in Ireland in relation to marriage break-up. We're a good Christian family and we attend Church regularly, but the position of the Catholic Church confuses us greatly. There is still no real compassion for or understanding of what it is like to have your marriage break down. Nobody wants a situation where divorce is freely available but surely there must be a way to allow for divorce in the case of irretrievable marriage breakdown. The reality is that you get one chance and if you blow it – tough. That's so wrong, I think. That's not what Christianity is about. To say it's not easy for people with a broken marriage in this country is one great understatement.

"I'm very fortunate in my own life, I have remarried. I've never been so happy in my own life as I have been in the last few years but the Church's attitude is that I should have been denied that happiness."

His great friend and former international teammate, Colin Patterson did all the legal work to arrange his marriage to Louise. However, Ward is sad that the issue of marital breakdown has not yet found either a constitutional or legislative solution. He finds the failure of the legislature to enact appropriate legislation inexcusable.

He becomes very animated as he recalls one prophecy from his darkest days: "Although I am the supreme pessimist I remember vividly going for a cup of coffee with Dave Mahedy just after my marriage breaking up and saying: 'Someday I know I'm going to meet somebody and I am going to fall madly in love with her and it's going to be so different next time round.' Little did I realise at the time that all my prayers would eventually be answered so bountifully. It's an old cliché but time heals. There is definitely someone up there who is watching over us all and things come right in the end."

There is awe in his voice at that recognition.

Up to this point of the story his eyes have been glazed with the pain of reliving the trauma of the break-up of his marriage and the custody battle for Lynn for the millionth time; when we reach the part about his second wife, Louise, he becomes animated:

"When Louise came into my life she completely bowled me over. I had no idea I could be consumed with so much love for someone. I had been involved in other relationships after the marriage break-up and neither Louise nor I were seeking permanent relationships at the time. When Louise and I met we knew, not straightaway but within a short time, that we were right for each other."

When Louise's name somehow crops into any rugby conversation his voice habitually softens as he speaks of her, assuming an air of deep affection. For all the gentleness there is a great passion and power in his testimony of love. Then the words flow like a tidal wave. There are no hang-ups about feeling the need to be macho. It seems as natural to him to sing his wife's praises as to talk about the weather.

Louise

The enduring memory of meeting Louise for the first time is of an incredibly energetic woman, with a radiant smile and a warm voice who is totally fulfilled in all aspects of her life. She transmits happiness and inner peace like electricity. She is the perfect tonic for drooping spirits. Her vitality is uplifting. Her world is amplified to the sounds of respect, integrity and decency.

Her career choice as mother and housewife would not be for every woman but there is something very endearing about her single-minded devotion to her family and the glow in her face as she goes about her tasks in the kitchen, still managing to answer a smooth stream of questions from their two eldest children, Richie and Lynn, about their hopes for the summer holidays. Patricia Scanlan would describe her as 'a very motherly, mother.'

Listening to the conviction in her voice and watching the intense expression as she talks about Tony, the inescapable conclusion is that they are made for each other.

She has made a new beginning possible for Tony – freeing him largely from his fears and healing his past hurts. She has penetrated to the centre of his being, enabling him to let go of his anxiety and restlessness and to live again.

Greystones' Rugby Club – Where Love Stories Begin

Greystones rugby club will always have Ward's eternal gratitude. Not only was it the centre of his rehabilitation to the Irish team – which brought him back on to the Irish team in 1986 and on to the World Cup squad the following year but it was through Greystones that he met Louise. The occasion was a celebratory function by the club to mark their victory over Belvedere in the final game of division two of the Leinster Senior League and their consequent promotion to division one. Ward recognised the same face as he had seen eight months earlier at a "do" in Jim Doyle's for the two Greystones players who made the Irish touring party to the inaugural rugby World Cup – Tony Doyle and Ward, and he inquired discreetly as to who she was. He was told she was Eric Cole's daughter. He had known Eric and his wife Angela for many years, even before he joined Greystones. Eric was, and still is, a stalwart of the club, and is also one of its former presidents. As Louise points out: "Rugby is his life". Ironically Ward had left Eric home many times after matches or functions never knowing anything about the daughter inside or thinking that his friend would one day be his father-in-law.

Astonishingly, when Ward showed the first sign of interest in Louise, one of his friends warned him off her because she was a single parent with a young son. Ward was not to be put-off by this crass narrow-mindedness. Cupid's arrow was hard at work that Saturday night because they both ended up sitting beside each other. If Ward was going to have a relationship with this girl he would have to overcome the reservations which Louise freely admits to having about him initially:

"I have hardly any interest in rugby apart from watching the internationals. I suppose, like a lot of women, I always thought Tony was gorgeous. At the time though, I expected that because he was such a big name he would, accordingly, be really big-headed. Yet as soon as I got talking to him I saw that he was the complete opposite. We talked for hours and hours about absolutely everything and nothing."

A meeting was arranged for the following day though the setting could hardly have been less romantic. They met at a Greystones J3 match in Farrankelly on a winter's Sunday afternoon in muddy conditions. Their mutual friends, Michael and Paul O'Loughlin, were playing and that was 'the attraction' of the game. Ward brought company, his German Shepherd called Steffi with the intention of bringing her for a walk. Such was Steffi's strength that it was the dog who was bringing her owner for a walk as she almost dragged him through the mud.

Another lengthy conversation ensued with the honest toil of the players largely passing them by. Then it was off for a pizza. The portions of pizza were too large for both of them and they brought some out to Steffi. The plan was for Ward to simply drop Louise to her home but when they got to the house they became embroiled outside in yet another long chat which went on to the early hours of the morning – occasionally stopping to feed a piece of pizza to Steffi.

Within a very short time after meeting they were madly in love with each other. This time though Ward was not going to rush things. His mind is a theatre of happy memories of their "courting days". It helped a lot that Louise's son, Richie, was almost the same age as Lynn and the two children quickly became the best of friends:

"It's astonishing to this day the number of people who think they are sister and brother through blood because they are so close."

The romance between their parents grew ever more stronger. On 25 June 1989 Ward pulled a major surprise on his true love with his own and Louise's immediate family present. The occasion was a dinner party organised by Louise's parents to celebrate her birthday.

The setting was the Vale View Hotel in Avoca. As the conversation flowed in a very convivial ambience, Ward suddenly produced a ring. He had already sought and received permission from Eric and Angela Cole for their daughter's hand, without Louise's knowledge, and had told his mother of his intention to propose that evening. Louise was visibly overwhelmed. Although it is not every man's fantasy to have the love of his life burst into tears when he proposes marriage the memory is firmly and fondly lodged on Ward's brain:

"Louise is a very emotional person and she reacted accordingly. When she eventually recovered her composure, and believe me it took quite a while, she said yes. I have seldom known such happiness."

On 20 July 1990 they were married. It was not possible to have a wedding Mass but Fr Brian D'Arcy said a special Mass for the happy couple and their parents in Mount Argus the day before the wedding. Not surprisingly the wedding reception was held in the Vale View Hotel.

The newly weds thought they could never be happier but they discovered they were wrong. A year later they reached the new high of elation when their baby Nicola was born:

"When Nikki was born we were in heaven and our family unit was complete."

Although Ward enjoys a pint he is not a great party-goer. He derives as much, if not more, pleasure from the "ordinary world" of family life as he used to from the extraordinary world of rugby at the highest level. Happiness for him is pottering around in the garden or watching sport on the television. However, he has not let himself go to seed in physical terms:

"One of the maxims I always remember from college is the old Greek idea of the importance of the mutuality of a healthy mind and a healthy body.

Wardy

"I jog a lot but I am not a fanatic, far from it – that extreme where people become quite addicted to running. I play quite a bit of indoor football. It's exercise, but it's enjoyable as well. If you can come up with an activity that you find enjoyable, without the psychological barrier of drudgery, that should be enough.

"What I found most difficult when I retired from rugby was to impose a rigid discipline on myself to keep fit. It's so much easier in a team situation than for individuals. Nowadays, of course, it's easier for me with my job. Even with that, understandably I suppose, I'm not as fit as I used to be. I've the metabolism to put on weight, so I have to watch it.

"My motivation in keeping fit is different now than what it was. Originally, it was to help me to play to the best of my ability. Now, however, I'm more motivated by health, fitness and sheer enjoyment."

And I Will Always Love You

The French have a word which has no direct equivalent in the English language – *tendresse*. It describes a love which goes much deeper than physical attraction, something sweet and tender, where consideration is at a premium and when two hearts beat as one (Tony wouldn't even think of asking Louise a question when she is watching her favourite programme, *Knot's Landing*). That term could fairly be applied to describe the relationship between the Wards.

Many aspiring rugby players must have envied the God-given talents Ward was born with. Yet a visit to his home confirms that the blessings he was showered with in rugby terms are but a speck of dust when compared with the extraordinary good fortune that has been conferred on him in having such an absolute jewel for a wife and such a strong family unit.

He has never been happier – and it shows.

13. Wired For Sound

Critics are like eunuchs in a harem: they know how it's done. They've seen it done every day, but they're unable to do it themselves.

Brendan Behan

Congratulations

Given both Ward's popular appeal and his knowledge of the game, it is not surprising that approaches were made to him from the journalistic world after he announced his intention to retire. He celebrated his 34th birthday in an unusual way by becoming a sports broadcaster when he read the Sunday sports results on RTE 1 television, when he replaced Brendan O'Reilly and John Kirwan, who were taking a break after their exertions in the Seoul Olympics in 1988. Only 24 hours earlier Ward had played in the Greystones 19-12 win against Wanderers in the Leinster Senior League.

However, as Ward's broadcasting career developed over the following 12 months, the IRFU were concerned about this development. Accordingly, in 1989 he received 'two reminders' about his responsibilities in the media as an amateur.

The use of an impersonal introduction 'Dear Sir', to one of the letters rankled with the handful of former players who received such communication at the time, as they felt it all too typical of the Union.

Ward spent a year reading the Sports Results on Sunday evenings and later became co-presenter with Jerry Kelly on the Friday night sports programme on Network 2. Kelly and he never met while the series was being recorded. Both recorded their inserts for the programme at separate times. However, Ward was never really comfortable simply doing straight pieces to the camera, which calls for particular presentation skills. His forte was the interview medium and he later carved out a niche for himself as a big match analyst.

SECRETARY & TREASURER
O. P. MOSS

TELEPHONE DUBLIN 68460l
TELEGRAPHIC ADDRESS,
"FOOTBALL, DUBLIN"
TELEX 90528

IRISH RUGBY FOOTBALL UNION,
62, LANSDOWNE ROAD.

DUBLIN, 4

21st February 1989

Dear Sir

The Committee of the Irish Rugby Football Union is concerned that some prominent members of the rugby fraternity in Ireland may, perhaps unknowingly, be putting their amateur status at risk by writing or broadcasting about the game. I am therefore getting in touch with those known to be involved with the media so that the position can be clarified.

In general it is an infringement of the Regulations of the International Rugby Football Board relating to Amateurism to 'communicate for reward'. This term covers written, oral and visual communication and the Regulation applies not only to those actively involved in the game, such as players, referees, coaches, and persons concerned with organisation and administration, but also to all who remain members of clubs affiliated to the Irish Rugby Football Union.

There are ways in which persons can be exempted from this restriction, for example, if any payments are donated to the Union or to a club or to a charity. And there are circumstances in which the restriction does not apply, for example, if the communication is in connection with the person's bona fide and full time occupation.

I should be grateful if you would let me know if you have, during the current season 1988-89, received any payments for writing or broadcasting about rugby football, and, if so, how these have been disbursed.

Furthermore I should like to know if you intend to continue with these activities so that you may be advised how your amateur status would be affected.

Yours sincerely

Patrick Moss,

G P MOSS
Secretary

"SECRETARY & TREASURER
G. P. MOSS
TELEPHONE DUBLIN 68460I.
TELEGRAPHIC ADDRESS,
"FOOTBALL, DUBLIN"
TELEX 90528

IRISH RUGBY FOOTBALL UNION,

62, LANSDOWNE ROAD,

DUBLIN, 4

REF: GPM/mc

1st May 1989

Tony Ward Esq.,
St Andrew's College
Booterstown Avenue
Blackrock
Co Dublin

Dear Tony

I now enclose a copy of the revised Regulation 4. of the I.R.F.B.'s Regulations
relating to Amateurism.

If you wish to have clarification on any of the points, kindly contact
this office and I will assist you.

Yours sincerely

G.P. Moss
Secretary

REGULATION 4. COMMUNICATION FOR REWARD

4.1 No person shall, save only as provided for in Regulations 4.2 and 4.3, receive, either directly or indirectly, any payment, benefit or other material reward (including the promise of any future payment, benefit or other material reward) whether by instalments or otherwise (these matters being jointly and severally referred to as "the payment") for any form of communication which refers to the game and/or to related matters. Communication about the Game, both personally and in association with others, includes:

(a) advertisements;

(b) written communication, such as books and articles

(c) oral communication, such as broadcasting and speeches; and

(d) visual communication, such as television and films.

4.2 A Person may be exempted by his Union from the provisions of Regulations 4.1 when

(a) upon entering into a contract relating to communication he immediately furnishes his Union with a sworn statutory declaration of his intention (which must be expressed to be irrevocable) to donate the payment to his Union, or to a Club, or to a charity, and immediately upon receipt of the payment he donates it to his Union, or to a Club, or to a charity; or

(b) the communication is in connection with his bona fide and normal full-time occupation; or

(c) as the leader of a tour connected with the Game, he is only in receipt of free travel, free accommodation and subsistence expenses in relation to the tour.

4.3 A player and/or referee may be exempted by his Union from the provisions of Regulation 4.1 if during the season or at the end of the season when he has irrevocably ended his career as a player or referee he gives his Union a sworn statutory declaration that he will not in future participate in the Game as either a player or a referee.

4.4 Any Person in breach of Regulation 4.1 automatically forfeits his amateur status.

4.5 No Person shall disclose any privileged or confidential information obtained through his connection with the Game or communicate in such a way as to damage the Game or bring it into disrepute.

(Note 1. When the payment relating to an advertisement accrues to a Union, or to a charity, or to a Club, which has sought and obtained its Union's permission, Persons taking part in the Game are not debarred from appearing in the advertisement.

Note 2. Notwithstanding the generality of Regulation 4.1 a Person may use his name or any other means of personal identification in advertisements which are related to his full-time bona fide occupation or business provided it does not refer or relate to his activities or involvement with the Game)

An analyst offers a great service to the viewer, particularly in rugby because rugby codespeak lends itself to much confusion: "There's some discussion between Michael Bradley and the touchline" for instance does not actually mean what it suggests. There are some classic stories told about supporters mistaking messages given on the pitch: "Nineteen sixty two" was a coded signal before a throw-in from the line-out. "Jaysus, they are ordering the champagne already", shouted a supporter.

The print media too made approaches and Ward agreed to work for Independent Newspapers. As far as Ward is concerned it was a marriage made in heaven:

"I have been very lucky because I have been fortunate enough to work with so many good people in Independent Newspapers through my work for *The Sunday Independent* and *The Evening Herald* – people like Michael Denieffe, Aodhmain O'Sullivan, Aengus Fanning and Pat Courtney, who was a real hero of mine in his Shamrock Rovers days. I can honestly say though, that I have never worked with anyone better than the sports editor in *The Evening Herald*, P.J. Cunningham. He really showed me the ropes when I was starting off and has been a great mentor to me in my journalistic career as indeed he's also been to Mick Doyle."

As a regular columnist with *The Evening Herald*, Ward pulls no punches when it comes to dealing with the issues of the day. One of the areas where he nailed his colours to the mast most visibly was in relation to Brian Smith's brief 'flirtation' with the Irish rugby team. Ward denies that he went over the top about Smith:

"I must emphasise I was not begrudging in the least. It is just a point I feel very strongly about. Indeed whatever faults may lie with soccer's rules in relation to qualification to play for one country or another the situation in relation to Brian Smith on the Irish rugby team was indefensible. If a player has declared and played for his native place of birth, unless there are extraordinary circumstances, then that should be his lot. To think that Smith, having played for Australia against Ireland in the '87 World Cup could have ended up playing for Ireland against Australia in the World Cup in 1991 if he had hung around a bit longer, doesn't bear thinking about. The entire principle is wrong.

"It must be said that the fact that Smith did not exactly set the world of Irish rugby alight had nothing to do with my feelings. Whether it is Brian Smith or Grant Fox – the principle I emphasise again – was wrong. At least 'Sean' Aldridge, 'Antóin' Cascarino, 'Micheál' McCarthy have declared their hand and opted for Ireland not having represented their countries of birth."

When news broke of his defection to Rugby League in March 1991 Smith lashed out at both Ward and Mick Doyle: "Ward and Doyle did not want me in the first place. Their attack has been a personalised one."

Ward reacts angrily to the suggestion that his criticism of Smith was personalised:

"Why would it be? I didn't even know the chap. It was the principle of his selection I objected to. It was a mistake by the IRFU and I hope they learn from it. The whole idea of playing for your country is a matter of national pride. Brian Smith was opportunistic. He was just passing through. But I would like to stress that I criticised other players too. I was always careful to analyse him as a player. I had no axe to grind."

Play As You Earn?

Ward's entry into journalism coincided with a period of dramatic change in rugby in relation to amateurism.

Conflicts over sponsorship in sport date back to the 1930s in the case of Tolley versus Fry. The leading amateur golfer of his era, Cyril Tolley, went to the courts suing for defamation because of an advertisement in cartoon form which showed him hitting the ball with some Fry's chocolate sticking out of his pocket. Tolley claimed that the cartoon suggested that: "He had consented to the use of his portrait as an advertisement for reward and has prostituted his reputation as an amateur golfer."

The issue of sporting sponsorship came sharply into focus in Ireland in 1981 with a controversy over the Kerry football team's use of Adidas' products – track-suit tops and tee shirts boldly emblazoned with the word 'Adidas' were worn by members of the Kerry squad on the bench during the All-Ireland final against Offaly that year. A GAA directive insists on items of Irish manufacture being worn by Gaelic football and hurling teams. Subsequently the Kerry team were embroiled in another row over an association with a company promoting washing machines.

In 1981 Ward, too, found himself enmeshed in a sponsorship controversy when he was forced to decline participation in RTE's Superstars event, because, it was insisted, competitors wore sports gear from the German company Puma. This presented Ward with a problem. Because of his business he did not want to alienate one manufacturer by promoting the goods of another:

"I offered to wear gear without any commercial markings but this was unacceptable to the organisers."

Ironically Ward was to cross swords with the IRFU after he aligned himself to Cougar Sports Ltd in the mid '80s and started wearing Puma boots. This time he was told not to wear Puma gear:

"In the mid '80s the IRFU, like all the international unions, reached a contractual agreement with one of the main sportsgear companies, in our case Adidas, where Irish players would only wear Adidas gear. I had transferred to Puma and was very happy with their gear. I had always loved their boots because I remembered seeing Eusebio wearing them in the 1966 World Cup and the way he jumped up after scoring his goals. I was always taken by the white stripe on his footwear. While it makes very little difference to forwards what kind of boots they wear, it is of the utmost importance to place-kickers. The amount of times I changed boots in my career was minimal, even though I could have had any amount of them. You stick to the old ones for as long as you possibly can because, with me, there was a psychological advantage in wearing the same boots. It's the old story of the workman and his tools. I was damned if I was going to wear different boots when I came back into the side in 1986 so I painted over the logo which emphasised it all the more. The following year the IRFU put the boot in as it were and insisted we all wear Adidas. There were a few others like Paul Dean in the same boat so the compromise they arrived at was that no stripes were allowed at all."

Much has changed since the heady days of Ward's career, particularly in England and Wales. Commercial possibilities have opened up to the likes of England captain, Will Carling and fellow centre, Jeremy Guscott. Top players there can combine well-paid jobs with widespread perks such as club car, rent-free accommodation and generous travelling expenses. Welsh players now have a powerful material reason to avoid what they call *hiraeth* (the homesickness in changing from one code to another) and to stay with Rugby Union rather than defect to League.

In his glory days in 1979 Ward had approaches from four Rugby League clubs – Salford, Wakefield Trinity, New Hunslett and Blackpool to defect to Rugby League:

"At the time Rugby League had little appeal for me. I've got to know the game since from watching it on Sky Sports Channel and I think that rugby union can learn a lot from it in the way it is marketed and indeed introduce some rule changes to make for a more attractive game. In none of the above cases did I meet the League chairman involved. They were all serious offers. One came via Ronnie Teeman, one of the first football agents, who was a good friend of John Giles and wanted to sign me for New Hunslett. They rang up but I was not interested and saved them a trip. In 1981 whilst visiting London for the FA Cup final between Spurs and Man City, I met with Ernie Clay and Colin Welland who offered me terms with Fulham but again I was not interested."

Ward would like to see a more flexible approach pursued to give more freedom to players:

"The game is changing. Nobody ever wants to see the day when players are paid to play, but what they do in their own time is their own business. The reward the players get at present is the pride in playing for their country.

"After that if they give interviews or write books or make personal appearances in their free time they should be allowed to do so. I often felt that the attitude of administrators seemed to be that, what has worked for 100 years should not be changed, but that only applied to their treatment of players. They accepted many changes for the benefit of the Unions.

"It is a petty minded attitude off the field which prevails among some of our administrators that could affect our performances on it. No player wants direct payment, but the least they deserve is to be reasonably treated. The reason players in this hemisphere generally do nothing about it is fear. They know that if they don't accept it, the Unions will say off you go and pick someone else instead.

"Even in this country where we have a small pool of players they wouldn't hesitate to drop anyone who stepped out of line. What makes it so difficult for players to accept in this hemisphere is that the International Board seems to turn a blind eye to what goes on in the southern hemisphere where players openly appear in advertisements. What makes it frustrating is that change eventually comes, but it is disappointing that the pace of that change is so dreadfully slow. We have not moved with the times.

"Down through the years people on the IRFU committee have been successful businessmen, many of them retired. They meet on the first Friday evening of every month. Their love of rugby is immense, that cannot be questioned. Almost without exception, I have got on well with each of them on a one-to-one basis. However, problems arise when you put all of them in a room together and many of their attitudes change dramatically. Fortunately, down through the years I have always had a mole or two in the camp so I was never completely in the dark about their deliberations.

"Initially I found it difficult to understand why my name was surfacing at their meetings so often. But I got accustomed to hearing regular reports about various individuals who were airing their opinions on me (seldom flattering!). One prominent personality made a point of bringing up a copy of a free newsheet called *The Limerick Citizen* which I contributed an article to. My column was subjected to intense scrutiny and tested for 'orthodoxy'. If a fairy godmother was to grant me one wish, all I would ask for is a copy of the minutes of all the IRFU meetings in which I was discussed. But I'm not holding my breath!

"Quite frankly, I think the IRFU could have used their time much more productively to advance the game in Ireland and to create a more 'player-friendly' environment. For example, during my career I was an avid listener to the late night *Sports News* programme on radio to find out if I had been dropped/selected for the international side. Many, many times I was first informed of my selection or otherwise by Ned Van Esbeck. The failure of the IRFU to let the players know first says much about their attitude to those who wear the green jersey.

"Having said that, I'm a little disappointed about recent soundings from some players in this country which suggest that their motivation for playing the game is not purely a sporting one. There has to be a middle line."

The Shepherd's . . .

Although Ward has not always been happy with rugby administrators a recent development which has pleased him is the appointment of Mick Cuddy as president of the IRFU:

"Mick will be a very real players' president. 'The Cud' is a great character and a master of the art of the misnomer. One of his many classic comments is: 'There were so many people there they were coming out of the woodworm'!

"I have a fond memory of attending a schools' match in Donnybrook with him in 1985 after Ireland clinched the Triple Crown and before the fixture against France. A French camera crew had come over to Ireland to record that schools' game as part of a feature on Irish rugby for transmission the day of the match. They saw me in the crowd and asked me for my opinion of Ireland's chances. Not surprisingly they asked if I was disappointed not to be part of Ireland's success. To ascertain the state of popular feeling in the country they decided to ask the person beside me if he thought that my exclusion was grossly unfair – not realising that he was the Chairman of the Irish selectors at the time. True to form the Cud agreed that the selectors treatment of me was outrageous!

"Another great character is Greystones' Ken Ging. He is also one of the games great raconteurs. One of my favourites of his is about Karl Mullen. Karl is a top gynaecologist and famous captain of Ireland in the 1950's; one day during a match was asked to attend a prop-forward who had put out his shoulder. Karl said: 'I'll put it back but I warn you it will be painful.' He did and it was. The prop forward, Phil O'Callaghan, it is said, was screaming his head off with the pain. Karl turned and said: 'You should be ashamed of yourself. I was with a 16-year-old girl this morning in the Rotunda as she gave birth and there was not even a word of complaint from her.' The player replied: 'I wonder what she bloody well would have said if you tried putting the ******* thing back in!'

"Possibly one of best known and most popular 'backroom' characters in Irish rugby is UCD and Leinster's Ned Thornton. One of the umpteen stories told about Ned is about the day that he went to General Costello's funeral. There was a huge crowd outside as well as inside the Church. The carriage came out with the coffin draped in the tricolour, with a hat and a stick on it. The troops sounded the death march and everybody was very solemn. Ned was standing beside Blackrock's Dan McCarthy at the time and turned around to him and said: 'I see he only got the one cap!'

"However, the all time classic goes back to the time he went with Leinster to Bath. Leinster lost the match and two of the Bath officials went over to console Ned and Ken Ging. They said all the right things like how unlucky Leinster were and asked what the Leinster contingent thought of the Bath players. The Leinster duo expressed their great admiration for John Hall, a great back row forward. One of the Bath officials said: 'He's a shepherd, you know." Quick as a flash Ned replied: 'And he's in the British army'. There followed a pantomine-like scene. 'Oh no, he is not.' 'Oh yes, he is.' Such was Ned's conviction that the Bath selectors became convinced that he was right. Then Ned said: 'He's an undercover agent in the British army – part of an elite squad – he's what's known as a shepherd's spy!'"

Little And Large

Ward's experience as a player at the highest level married to his intelligent comments makes him an ideal candidate as match analyst. A feature of RTE's coverage of the 1991 Rugby World Cup was the way Ward and Mick Doyle slotted smoothly into the roles filled by John Giles and Eamon Dunphy for soccer matches. Like their soccer friends, both men could graphically illustrate their points with the aid of diagrams and had the affable Bill O'Herlihy to spark them into new heights of animation.

The analysts mixed insight with comedy. At one stage guest analyst Mick Quinn joked: "Ah Wardy, there's a rumour going around that you'll be lining out for the Japanese today. You're the right height apparently." Not to be outdone at one stage Doyler observed: "The

Aussies didn't look in the same league as the All-Blacks. They were very busy without doing anything. A bit like election agents."

The humour of the RTE team contrasted sharply with the ITV equivalent. Their most memorable moment was unintentionally provided by Clive Woodward assisting on the commentary on the Australian-Western Samoa game. When the camera honed in on the Samoan hooker, Woodward remarked in a very earnest fashion: "That's the hooker. They call him Stan . . . that's his name."

Ward had additional duties as co-commentator for the big matches where he was able to draw on his vast reservoir of experience to shed new light on key moments of the match. During Ireland's "nearly game" against Australia, when silence fell in the most spine-chilling way as Ralph Keyes faced up to his kicks, Ward revealed the value of his own inside knowledge to the viewer when he remarked: "It is when there is complete silence that the kicker is conscious of the crowd, not when there's noise. It's easier when you have a din all around you."

One of the first lessons Ward learned about working in television is that things are seldom as simple as they seem from the comfort of an armchair.

A Day In The Life Of A TV Analyst: Saturday, 26 June, 1993

The alarm goes at 6.45 a.m. Ward closes his eyes "just for a second". The previous night he had been out in the Wicklow Arms with his wife, Louise, and some friends to celebrate her birthday. A very untypical "late night" for him had ended at 1.30 a.m. The next thing he knows it is 7.40 a.m. He is due in the RTE studios at 8.00 a.m. Panic. Time for just a quick shave. There is little or no traffic on a Saturday morning, so the short dash to Montrose brings him in with seconds to spare. He is casually dressed in jeans and a shirt. A jacket and tie is thrown on the chair. The task in hand is to watch a re-run of a recording of the second Lions' Test of the night before with producer John D. O'Brien. The object of the exercise is twofold: to enable Ward to give an analysis of the match in a segment which will be recorded before transmission time and to select three key moments in the match will be used to highlight particular points about the game.

By 10 a.m. the objective is achieved, John D. is off to the editing room and the three selected pieces are rolled together on the one tape. Meanwhile Ward heads down to the make-up room to prepare for his stint in front of the cameras. The jacket and tie is then retrieved and within seconds Ward is transformed into a picture of sartorial elegance – from the waist up.

Then it is up to the engine room to wait to record his piece with Ger Canning. The room is a real eye-opener – a feast of high-tech. Thirty-two monitors adorn the wall showing a proliferation of different images. Six people, three men and three women, equality of opportunity is taken seriously here, are beavering away on the feature for *Gaelic Stadium.*

Every year the winners of the Jacobs' Awards appear to trot out ritual clichés about their success being due to a real team effort. It often seems like false modesty but it is only when you go behind the scenes that this truth strikes home. It really is a team performance. Director, Maurice Reidy is calling the shots, like a conductor of a grand orchestra, calmly and gently calling the appropriate person, some in the room, others heard but not seen, into action at the appropriate moment. Ger Canning is interviewing Joe Lennon but it is Reidy, the face the public never sees, that is feeding him the carefully structured questions. The final product looks casual and spontaneous, the image belying the reality. The enduring impression is of amiable professionalism, encapsulated in Reidy's quietly effective stage direction.

There are light moments too. Smiles all round when a tray of paper cups of tea and coffee come around. A delightfully, good-humoured man enters offering photocopies of both *The Irish Times'* crosswords to anyone who can afford to take their eye off the screen for half a second. In a lull in the recording a cameraman, Joseph and the amazing technicolour shirt, takes centre stage on screen to a chorus of waspish comments on his dress sense. He takes the plethora of friendly insults in the best possible spirit.

Watching Ward observing the monitors evokes memories of Simon and Garfunkel's classic song, 'The Sound of Silence' and an appropriate paraphrase of the same: 'Watching without seeing/ hearing without listening.' Although his eyes are on the monitors his mind is still on the recording of the game. Occasionally he scribbles down a note.

The *Gaelic Stadium* feature complete, Maurice Reidy vacates the chair and heads to the editing room, passing the torch in the director's chair to John D. O'Brien. Canning takes a quick cup of tea as Ward takes his seat. A few complimentary words are exchanged between them about Nick Popplewell's performance. Ward is told not to lean forward too much on camera, and they are off.

Five minutes later they are finished. Ward heads down to make-up and removes the cream. He leaves the studios at 11.58 a.m. It has taken four hours to make a five minute insert. The piece is transmitted two hours later by which time Ward is at home watching South Africa draw with France in a Test match on another channel.

Despite the early rising Ward enjoys the activity with RTE:

"The nice thing about working with RTE is that the people are so easy-going and good to work with. The great thing about it for me is that it gives me a great outlet to still be involved in the game. When we are doing live pieces the adrenaline is really flowing and the heart beats a little faster, like it did before playing a big game. There was a huge gap, and I mean huge, in my life after I retired and broadcasting fills that void somewhat.

"I see soccer players like Kevin Moran, Ray Wilkins and David O'Leary continuing to play at the highest level and I have to take my hat off to them. I think you should go on as long as you possibly can. A huge void appears in your life after retirement. That is why so many players come back. I made a comeback for Greystones in the 1990-91 season. The difficulty I found was combining playing the game with my role as a rugby commentator in the media.

"The problem when you retire is that you lose all power to influence a game. When you are a player you can read reports in the paper about games and think that you can change things but once you stop that power is gone. As the years go by the mind stays the same but the body is very different."

The Right Of Reply

No rugby player in the history of Irish rugby generated as much column inches as Ward. Like Charles Haughey it was always a case of pro or anti. There was no half-way house. The print media rely as much on opinion as on fact as was cleverly exposed in a speech by Mick Doyle.

During his time as national coach Doyle was guest speaker at a luncheon of the Irish Business Association in the London Metropole Hotel and was quoted as attacking newspaper reporting of rugby as "insensitive", "wildly inaccurate" and "pseudo-aggressive". He made particular reference to the harsh treatment given by newspaper reporters to the Irish selectors because of their failure to pick Tony Ward. As an example of the distortions in the print media he told the "parable" of an Irishman who fell under a tube train in London and was killed. *The London Times* reported it straight, *The Sun* that an Irish terrorist had disrupted British Rail schedules, *The Irish Independent* that a Scotsman had been killed at Heathrow, *The Irish Press* that British Rail had murdered an innocent Irishman and *The Irish Times* that Tony Ward had his travel schedule disrupted because of a mishap on British Rail.

Having read many of the countless articles written about him throughout his career, Ward decided to reverse the equation and subject his critics to some of the scrutiny they put him under. He began with an assessment of the journalist he most admires and with whom he will always be most associated:

"Ned Van Esbeck is a very dear friend from early days and even more so during the dark times, particularly during my personal traumas. He really has been a marvellous ally and support. Our friendship goes way beyond the realms of rugby. I suppose it could have been said that our relationship alienated me from a section of the written media – that said, I would never change my friendship towards Ned; we were far too solid for that.

"Ned is the doyen of rugby writers in Ireland and if you ever want to know anything about a match Ned's column is the one to read. He has a great in-depth knowledge of the game and his familiarity with all the relevant statistical data is awesome. I am also very close with Mary, Geraldine and the rest of his family and Geraldine has been a true blue supporter in times good and bad."

Reading through Ward's vast correspondence from fans down through the years, one critic's name appears frequently. Ward is totally at a loss to understand this journalist's attitude towards him because never has a bad word passed between them:

"Karl Johnston of *The Irish Press* seemed obsessed about writing how obsessed everybody else was in writing about me. Consequently he wrote more about me than almost anybody else. He seemed particularly fond of using 'the folk hero' tag about me, but he used it in an ironic way and with a strong undercurrent of begrudgery in it.

"One incident I particularly remember, because of its unfortunate timing, goes back to 14 December, 1984 when he did yet another 'folk hero' piece about me and used the infamous *Daily Mirror* picture. The article was entitled: 'TONY WARD – THE MAKING OF A FOLK HERO'. It began:

'*Like the Blessed Virgin, the folk hero has been held in especial esteem in Ireland. Which is why we're inclined not to view those who shaped our history with warts and all, preferring instead to see them as the epitome of manliness and saintliness and all that is perfect ... The present loud and largely uniformed outcry about the alleged maltreatment of Tony Ward parallels this national characteristic.*'

"It was a particularly difficult time for me personally because my marriage was teetering on the brink (not that he was to know that) but when I was praying for something to still the troubled waters that was the last thing we needed at that precise moment I can assure you. I found it very hard to take the anti-Ward feeling he portrayed for so long.

"Another journalist who had a peculiar attitude to me was Jim Sherwin. Since I started working with RTE my relationship with him has been much improved but in my playing days I picked up hostile vibes from him all the time. One unpleasant incident in Lansdowne Road in 1982 comes to mind when I was asked to make a comment on radio before a home match on Ireland's prospects. His reaction to me was negative in the extreme. Shortly afterwards I got a letter from Maurice Quinn in RTE Sport apologising to me about the incident. Obviously some of the production staff in RTE noticed his reaction and brought this to Maurice's attention.

"A few years earlier in March '79 there was another incident. Nigel Starmer-Smith came down to Limerick to do a piece on me for the BBC's *Grandstand* programme. A week later I got a call from Sherwin to do the same but what struck me most was the way he said it: 'I'm under pressure here to do a piece as the BBC have done a feature on you.' Straightaway I should have told him where to get off. Anyway I naïvely welcomed him down with open arms which meant that we had to close the shop for the whole morning. A mistake was made with the editing of the film so he had to come down a week later and again we had to close the shop. On both days I could sense his antipathy towards me. I just could not understand his begrudging and dismissive attitude where I was concerned. I have never actually seen that interview but he seemingly followed it with an interview with Fergus Slattery about me. People who saw it told me afterwards that it was very revealing about both and their attitudes towards me. Just a few months later Slatts was involved in dropping me in Australia.

"Another journalist whose writing I've always admired but who was never a particular fan of mine was David Walsh. He is somebody I have got to know much better in recent years. The one thing about him was that he tried to be objective and analyse the match and the player rather than the man. However, he wrote a very begrudging piece about me in *The Sunday Tribune* after I retired. There was quite a response to the paper afterwards about it.

"One particular problem I had with him arose from the controversy about Brian Smith's position on the Irish team. He opened his article on the subject by saying how ironic it was that an Irish man dropped in Australia should be advocating the dropping of an Australian in Ireland. I saw red and for the first time ever I wrote to a journalist about something they had written about me. I viewed this not as a journalist commenting on my performance as a player but David Walsh having a swipe at Tony Ward the journalist. I pointed out to him that as a 'journalist' I was entitled to express my opinion as to who played out-half for Ireland or indeed who played left-corner forward for Carlow. At the end I wrote that this letter was not for public consumption because what I feared most was 'an open letter to Tony Ward' article in the paper subsequently.

"Three days later I received a very pleasant letter of apology. At the end of it all, he said he would love to meet me for a pint sometime. I rang him back and we met for a lengthy chat on a whole range of issues. It was an eye-opener for both of us and it goes back to what I said earlier about building bridges. I have learned that lesson so often in life even more so than in rugby – it's so important to communicate.

Although, in my playing days, David was no great fan of mine, what I liked most about him was that he was big enough to admit he was wrong on this occasion and anyone who does that stands very high in my book."

One journalist with whom Ward enjoyed a great relationship was *The Irish Independent's* Seán Diffley, although their relationship cooled for almost a year after Ward's retirement:

"I had agreed to write an account of my life to be serialised for a few weeks in *The Sunday Independent*. The paper announced it was coming the Sunday before the series was due to start. The next day I got a call from 'Diffo' in school. Normally Seán is very courteous but straightaway he went on the attack and asked whether I realised I might be breaching my amateur status by doing this. I said: 'Well, Seán I am deeply touched by your concern but frankly it's none of your business.' I may have expressed that sentiment a bit more colourfully at the time.

"The next day he wrote a story with a news journalist in the *Independent* which tried to scuttle the series by stating that I was in breach of my amateur status and suggesting that the IRFU would have to carpet me about it. I couldn't understand the logic of one paper threatening a story in a paper in their own group by trying to get the IRFU on my back.

"A few weeks later Diffo was involved in writing Ciaran Fitzgerald's story and he used the episode to have a go at me by implying that in 1979 Fitzy had seen my dropping in Australia coming. Ciaran told me after he had never said that and apologised to me for the way the article misrepresented him.

"I did not speak to Diffo for almost a year afterwards until one day I rang him up and said it was ridiculous and we met for a cup of coffee in the Montrose Hotel where both of us agreed we had been at fault. It was a minor blip in our relationship. I have tremendous respect for him. He has done so much for the game in Ireland. He would have been one of the people I admired most down the years in the journalistic world as well as Ned, Con Houlihan, Charlie Mulqueen, Fred Cogley, Tom Rooney, Dave Guiney and John Redmond.

"Charlie has a great in-depth knowledge of the game. He holds his own in the company of rugby's elite journalists. His loss to Limerick rugby was enormous when he moved from the *Limerick Leader* to the *Cork Examiner*. Although Connie too has a great knowledge of rugby, having played the game himself, what I love most about him is his romanticism. You have to go down about two-thirds of the way through his article to find out what he is writing about but his prose is always a treat. I also like the way he seldom if ever goes to the Press Box at a match. You will always find him on the terraces. Fred Cogley is one of my favourite people and I guarantee you will go a long way to find anybody who has a bad word to say about him. He is the milk of human kindness, great company and great to work with. I also have great admiration for Tom Rooney because he's such a professional journalist and has retained his boyhood fanaticism for all sports.

"One of the profession's great gentlemen is Dave Guiney. The earliest contact I had with Dave was in my first game in the green jersey when I played in a B international in Dijon back in 1976. I sat beside him on the plane back and we had an incredible discussion about sport. That was the beginning of a great friendship between us. Down through the years Dave has taken the credit for my career achievements because he claims that the main reason I made it on to the Irish side was that he plugged my case for selection so much after the game in Dijon!

"Another journalist I have particular affection and admiration for is John O'Shea and I really value his friendship. He has incredible neck and doesn't know the meaning of the word 'No'. I am one of the patrons of his organisation GOAL. This does marvellous work not just in terms of raising money for the Third World but in bringing people from different sports together in an atmosphere of fun.

"John has an uncanny ability to rub people up the wrong way with his outlandish statements. A very clear memory I have of him goes back to the Angel Hotel in Cardiff in 1979 during the post-match dinner for the Wales-Ireland game. I remember going into the toilets and seeing only two people there – John O'Shea and Pa Whelan. John had obviously said something because Pa had him up against the wall and was lacing into him with knuckles rather than words. I had to try and drag them apart.

"In the broadcasting world there is one rugby man that stands head and shoulders above the rest – Bill McLaren. Bill leaves nothing to chance because he attends to the most minute details. He always goes to see the two teams training before matches and watches players from every angle so that he will recognise them instantly on the pitch. Colin Patterson and I got on particularly well with him. Bill always carried a bag of sweets in his pocket and when he came to our training sessions Colin and I would run over for our sweet! Like myself, he combined a career as a PE teacher with rugby journalism until he retired from teaching a few years ago."

Putting Your Foot In It

Ward is the first to admit that he was the architect of his own misfortune when he found himself embroiled in a media controversy about the announcement of his retirement:

"After the French tour in 1988 I more or less made up my mind that I would retire from representative rugby at the start of the following season. I told Ned Van Esbeck and he 'sat on it'. Jimmy Davidson was pressing me to make a decision one way or another. I understood his reasons because otherwise there would have been a lot of speculation about my future with the team in the press.

"One day, out of the blue, John Redmond of *The Irish Press* rang me up just for a chat and casually and absolutely innocently asked me if I had any plans to retire. I said that I had not made up my mind.

That same day Ned was on the phone to me and I mentioned that I had been talking on the phone earlier to John. Ned's media instinct took over and he said, with my permission of course, he had to run with the story straight away. Ned did not force me to make the decision to retire but what was forced was the timing of the announcement. In fairness to John Redmond if I had been him I would have been hurt by the deception. I wrote to John later and apologised for the manner of the announcement of my retirement – a gesture he appreciated.

"Throughout my career I had the knack of landing myself in it without meaning to do so. I would like to think it was the sensitive side of me trying not to hurt people but in the process I ended up making a mess of it when my intention was the exact opposite.

"One thing that really annoys me about certain rugby correspondents is the way they complain about the fact that certain former players have 'infiltrated', as they see it, the Press Box. They talk about this using a very wounded tone but I feel very strongly that the advantage any former player has, provided he is intelligent and articulate enough to communicate his views, is that he's seen it and done it himself and therefore he has a sensitivity that journalists who have never played the game, (certainly not at representative level at any rate) can never have and I defy any journalist to argue otherwise."

There's No Criticism Like Self-criticism

Plato wrote: "An unexamined life is not worth living." Having read millions of words about his game down through the years Ward decided the time was right for him, five years after his retirement from representative rugby, to subject himself to a rigorous examination of his own game. There would be no room for sentiment. Brutal honesty was required. He prefaced his remarks by referring to the type of out-half he now prefers as a coach with St Andrew's:

"I always pick a Paul Dean type player in my school team rather than an out-half like Ollie or me. This is not to say Deano was the finished article. He wasn't. Ollie Campbell was. However, my school sides always have a Deano type out-half who will act as a link with the rest of the backs and bring the wingers into the game. I never think about defence when I am picking my sides. I always want three-quarters who will attack at every opportunity and a full-back who comes into the line.

"As I, as dispassionately and as clinically as possible, look back on my career I have to confess that I did have a tendency to unconsciously drift sideways. Now, as a coach, I always try to ensure that my players' first step is forward but subconsciously my first step was always sideways. That was particularly so going right to left. I was always good at side-stepping but I was stronger for some reason off my left foot. On the right hand side I had a particular tendency to drift across. It was part of a subconscious strategy to give myself the option of taking the ball wide and being able to step inside the man marking me, forcing him to drift across as well. In doing that I was bunching the outside backs. For that reason the criticism often levelled against me that I did move across is valid.

"Like most people I'm a much stronger passer right to left. Accordingly, on the left hand side, my left to right passing was often a weakness.

"I wasn't the quickest man to pressurise my opposing out-half. Equally I always came up on the out-half as far as it is the out-half's role to come up on his opposite number. Even though Ollie was a great tackling fly-half his forte was sweeping across the pitch and tackling anybody who threatened the line rather than rushing up and taking his opposite man. So I don't fully accept the criticism that was sometimes made about me that I didn't come up on my out-half.

"I favoured my right foot but could kick with my left though I was not an equally two-footed player like Ralph Keyes, few are.

"My greatest strength was arguably my greatest weakness – my unpredictability. Watching Ollie, for example, you could see his computer brain at work and appreciate that he was such a methodical player. He always seemed to have the time to make things happen the way he wanted and that truly is the sign of a great player. On the other hand, while I too could always make time and space, I reacted to events instinctively as the situation demanded. Of course, many times that led me to run up blind alleys but equally it led many times to openings and try scoring opportunities. I think perhaps if you asked which aspect of my play appealed most to the sporting public it would be that one.

"However, I never went into any game with preconceived notions or try and play to the gallery, and I reject out of hand any accusations of selfishness on my part, for example the suggestion by Karl Johnston that I only passed the ball when I had finished with it myself.

"I was not a physical player but few out-halves are. I won't be remembered for my crunching tackles nor would I want to be.

"I think I had a good footballing brain. I wasn't particularly fast, but I was very fast over the short distance where it mattered most.

"I was able to stay on my feet when tackled and had the ability because of my low centre of gravity to weave in and out of tackles. In saying that I must acknowledge that sometimes after stepping inside once, I was prone to do it a second time and got swallowed up in the process. That was a big failing and one I really had to work on."

Top Of The Pops

The most surprising sight in the trophy-laden writing room, which Ward calls his study, is a platinum disc. In the sea of soccer and rugby memorabilia, where the most striking thing of all is the almost complete absence of videos from any of his big matches – he has only one recording of a match he played in himself – the platinum disc stands out like a sore thumb.

This momento was presented to him in 1990 by virtue of his role in the World Cup song "The Team That Jack Built" penned by Michael Carwood of *The Sunday Press*. Although Carwood had been responsible two years earlier for the biggest selling single in Ireland in 1988, the 'classic' hit: "We are the Boys in Green" it is highly improbable that either song will feature prominently when the history of popular music is written.

The song was funded by the Penneys' fashion chain with all the proceeds going to the Irish Society for Autistic Children. The song was recorded at Lansdowne Studios with the singers assembling in full World Cup regalia. Football's heavenly choir included such well known singers as Jimmy Magee, Ray Tracey, Jimmy Greely, Teresa Lowe, Olivia Treacey and future Eurovision winner Linda Martin. The project was coordinated by Alma Carroll whose father, Billy, was a former Shamrock Rovers player. When the song became a best seller all the singers were presented with a platinum disc.

A notable absentee from the recording was the melodic talents of Eamon Dunphy – causing one wag, who shall remain nameless, to mutter: "A good singer, not a great singer"!

Ward is a big music fan, particularly of U2. He once got the chance to see his musical heroes close-up when they shared the same plane to London. It is not an experience he will forget in a hurry:

"It was the night after the premier of their film *Rattle and Hum* in Dublin when they gave a kind of free concert in their native city. It was just after Eamon Dunphy had written his book about U2, and Bono and Dunphy had a big falling out. I was travelling over with John O'Shea, Moss Keane, Eamonn Coghlan and Eamon Dunphy for the launch of the sporting charity GOAL in London. It was a big night with anyone who was anyone in the Irish community in London there like David O'Leary, Niall Quinn, Tom MacGurk and his wife Miriam.

"When we got on the plane Dunphy sat in beside 'the Edge' because there was no rift between them. Within a short space of time a U2 minder came up to Dunphy and asked: 'Would you mind moving please?' We got off the plane and U2 were let straight through. What I remember most though is seeing the eye contact between Bono and Dunphy in the baggage area. Whoever coined the phrase 'if looks could kill', he must have had the type of look that passed between them on his mind."

However, Ward is forced to admit that his knowledge of music is not up to the same level as his knowledge of rugby as was dramatically illustrated by an incident in 1989:

"I called out to Mount Argus to meet Fr Brian D'Arcy. It was the feast of St Blaise and there were hundreds of people at Mass having their throats blessed and afterwards I went to meet Brian in the dining hall for a cuppa. There were two other men there. One I knew well – Joe Dolan. The other I genuinely didn't know from Adam. However, his star has certainly risen a lot since . . . It was Daniel O'Donnell!"

14. Go Placidly Amid The Noise And Haste

*Fame is a vapour, popularity is an accident; the only earthly certainty is
oblivion.*

Mark Twain

One of the many striking things about a visit to Ward's home is his
apparent fondness for the old song 'Desiderata':

"Luxembourg was the only station when I was growing up. I
remember doing my homework listening to it, and they had this
power play, every hour, on the hour. I remember one year there was a
Les Crane song called 'Desiderata' which was in the form of a prayer.
The other power play of the time was Joe Dolan's 'Make Me An
Island'. To this day I have the words of that prayer hung up in three
different places in my house. I'm sure everybody has heard it even if
they don't recognise the title. It is the one that begins: 'Go placidly
amid the noise and haste. . . "

Ward's life, like his career, has been a mixture of extraordinary
highs and lows. Although he is no 'Holy Joe', religion has been
something of a comfort to him in the bad times like the Australian
experience in 1979:

"I was a long way from home and I was really down and lonely and
I think it's at times like that you seek and find God. I've said this to
Brian D'Arcy a few times, because Brian has been a good friend down
through the years: 'Surely when you are down, or have a problem, or
need something, it is wrong to turn to God?' But Brian replied: 'No,
because that is why God is there'. I think as long as you can carry on
your life in the proper way, God is there as a friend and I don't think
with that philosophy you can go far wrong.

"There's a line in Desiderata that says: 'Be at peace with your God, whatever or whoever you believe him to be'. I'm at peace with my conscience, I'm at peace with my mind and I'm at peace with my maker. At the end of the day, what it's all about is that when you are called to meet your maker you can look into your soul and say you did it the right way, and more than that I don't know."

The Wannabes

Such is Ward's state of contentment that he has no plans for major changes in his life. One thing is clear coaching young players will continue to occupy a significant part of his future.

The influence of coaching in sport in general and rugby in particular is sometimes overstated. The great English prop forward, Fran Cotton, observed: "I'm a great believer in coaching. But I believe in players even more. Look back at all the great coaches and you'll find that they had some pretty useful players to work with."

With the benefit of "hands-on" experience Ward has strong opinions on the development of schools rugby in Ireland:

"Schools rugby has traditionally been the strength of Irish rugby. However, I would argue that if we don't look after it we will have serious problems. If you trace the history of the schools game in Ireland you will discover that much of its strength was derived from Religious Orders. With the fall off in vocations that situation no longer pertains and I believe the falling off in standards of back play in particular can be traced to this development.

"What you have today is a lot of enthusiastic parents who get very involved when their own child is playing. The problem is that they have, in the main, no experience of coaching kids. This is a difficulty the IRFU is addressing – how to coach people who coach kids. It's one thing to have played the game yourself or watch the matches on television but it's a totally different thing to coach children. What happens is that we get coaches taking what they see on television in

Parc de Princes or Twickenham and applying it to the schools situation with rolling mauls, double loops etc.

"The shop window teams in schools rugby are the senior and junior teams and naturally the best coaches are given to those teams. I would argue quite vehemently that the best coaches should work with the under-thirteen teams as well because that's the most important age when habits are formed and so kids should then be taught the basics: passing, running, tackling and kicking. Unless you have people to teach them those skills you have a huge problem. It's a problem of expertise. The IRFU are confronting this issue through their development officers.

"Another huge problem is the histrionics of over enthusiastic parents on the sideline. Those parents who want their children to be what they never quite were. Perhaps because of my 'Party Dress' experience I am very careful to ensure that none of the comments made by parents from the sideline are destructive or indeed in anyway negative.

"Since 1985 the buzz phrase after Fitzy's outburst has been: 'Where's your ****ing pride?' The amount of times I have heard the phrase in schools' rugby: 'Where's your pride in your jersey?' defies belief. It sickens me because it is aping the game at the highest level and applying it to kids."

Heather McKay the great Australian squash player remarked: "Part of the problem with sport today is that the parents want their kids to be what they weren't, and are trying to live through them."

Other aspects of schools rugby in Ireland perturb Ward:

"A further huge problem in schools rugby is the standard of refereeing. It's not the Union's fault but with the fall off in manpower, the people who referee schools matches are often student teachers or else staff members with little, if any, playing experience. Unfortunately, with the way the game has evolved in rugby, there so much scope for skullduggery and cheating. I see it at first hand week-in week-out. As a result, kids are being taught the wrong ethical values, i.e., it pays to cheat. I think schools should be actively encouraged to get children who love the game of rugby, but for one reason or another who haven't got what it takes to make it as players, to think about becoming referees and let them referee internal school league matches, etc.

"In fairness to the IRFU and the Leinster Branch, some improvements have taken place with the establishment of a Leinster Schools League to give more competitive games to the weaker schools.

"Two people who have had a huge impact on the game at this level are George Spotswood and John Murphy. It's a great pleasure to watch John in action at grassroots level with kids. He has a natural rapport with children and is a brilliant communicator at that level."

Ward is a great believer in greater sporting ecumenism in Ireland not just as a matter of ideology but as a practical measure to improve standards in the different sports:

"I understand the GAA has to fight its corner, particularly where soccer is concerned. I'm not so sure it has to fight its corner so hard in relation to rugby. The close season in Gaelic games is prime time in relation to rugby. I believe the GAA and the IRFU should actively encourage their members to participate in each others' sport in the close season. Surely this would help maintain the standard of fitness in both codes.

"I remember doing some coaching one Sunday morning in Monivea in Co. Galway at the request of 'Mr Rugby' in the area, Pauraic McGann, a cousin of Barry's. Pauraic had a system whereby the local boys trained every Sunday morning and then went to his pub for minerals, chocolate and biscuits. Their pitch was on the side of a hill with a telephone pole intruding on the side and farmyard manure much in evidence. What struck me most though was the number of travellers' children who were involved. It was the opposite side of the coin to my experiences in the children's hospital in South Africa in 1980. Here rugby was an integrating force. I drove back that evening humbled. To me people like Pauraic McGann are the real heroes in Irish rugby. That is the road the IRFU must go down. To be fair, they are moving in the right direction.

"The first time I can recollect having a hurley in my hand was doing a coaching course with Dave Weldrick in Thomond College. I couldn't hit the sliotar. It was alien, even though we are told it's part of what we are. Because I went to a certain type of school in Dublin I had never experienced that. Likewise the first game of Gaelic football I ever played was in Thomond.

"I can appreciate the skill level in hurling but I can really relate to Gaelic football because of my rugby and soccer involvement. When I was growing up, before the Dubs made the breakthrough in 1974, Gaelic games were 'bog' games because civilisation ended at the Naas Road. Now, as a teacher, in September every year I do a teaching block in Gaelic games because it ties in with the good weather and also the All-Ireland finals. I want my pupils to appreciate what is a major part of their heritage and provide them with an opportunity I never had."

Although Ward has never been one for thumping fists on tables he makes his point forcibly:

"I think there is so much pressure now to win that the enjoyment may be going out of rugby and that shouldn't happen because rugby is still an amateur sport and a leisure activity. As a PE teacher my job is to offer as many sporting opportunities as possible and schools are increasingly providing more sports for children. I believe that if they leave school and choose to play any one sport afterwards, no matter what sport it is, then I have succeeded as a teacher.

"One philosophy I have is that I never ever transmit negative comments to kids on the field. The day that I do that is the day that I hang up my coaching gown so to speak. Certainly on the training field a few days later I will point out the mistakes that were made. No player goes on the field deliberately trying to make a mistake and I get very annoyed when I hear teammates chastising a player on the field or worse still a coach shouting abuse at a child from the sideline."

He is tailormade for the role of coach and likes to believe that you can survive with the elite on sound principles and good habits. Naturally he has the respect of all his players, he talks a good game and has a definite strategy that takes no account of injuries, bad luck or referees - the traditional quicksand of winning rugby. He is organiser, cajoler and ever willing to offer words of affirmation and advice.

Regrets. I've Had a Few

Looking back over his life, Ward is the first to admit that he made a number of mistakes. One of his biggest has to do with his involvement in business:

"The context of my business involvement was that when I went to college I had one sole thought in mind – to become a PE teacher. I never even thought there might be other options available to me until one day in 1978, during my final year in college, I remember driving down to Cork for one of Garryowen's matches with one of our second rows, Eddie Molloy, a smashing player who should have played for Ireland. Eddie just remarked in passing that I might consider a career other than teaching. It was the first time it even crossed my mind that I might have other possible employment alternatives.

"I put it out of my mind because the exams were looming on the horizon. I am not a crammer but a worrier. My chief concern at the time was that if I failed my final exams I would have to resit them the following summer which meant I would have missed out on the Australian trip. Perhaps in the light of what happened I might have been better off failing my exams and missing out on that tour down under!

"Coming up to the exams, one of the lecturers in college, Dave Weldrick, asked me if I had thought about my career plans and mentioned the possibility of me getting involved in a sports shop. I explained that I had more or less a teaching job in St Mary's arranged with Fr David D'Arcy.

"I got my exams but I was very unsettled when I went back to Dublin. I was really missing Garryowen and Limerick once the rugby season started. I used to play the Wolfe Tones record 'Sean South from Garryowen' just to feel closer to my home from home. During October I met Frank Hogan in the Aisling Hotel and discussed his plan of going into business with him and opening a sports shop. I spoke to Dave Mahedy about it. He was living in Dublin but he had not yet secured a teaching post. We decided that because we had our degree, if it didn't work out, we could always return to teaching but if we didn't try it then we would always wonder if we had missed the boat. Frank Hogan, Pa Whelan and I were to be partners and Dave Mahedy was to be the manager.

"From day one in Limerick the business was great. In 1982 I moved back to Dublin and Dave and I opened a new shop in Cathedral Street, the two of us having bought out Frank and Pa. That shop did a great trade also. Dave remained on to look after the business in Limerick, Gerry Smith came in to manage the Dublin one and I commuted between the two. This constant coming and going was getting too much for me and we decided to sell the Limerick shop and set up a new one in Dun Laoghaire. That decision killed the business. Whereas the Limerick shop was generating a very healthy turnover, because of the recession that situation was not replicated in Dun Laoghaire. Our problem then was that we couldn't get out of our lease no matter how hard we tried. It was a dreadful business decision.

"From a personal point of view the situation was not helped by the fact that I am anything but a salesman. I was brought in for my name not for my ability to sell. The downside of that was that naturally everybody seemed to be looking for and at me, like an animal in a cage in the zoo. I became so self-conscious about this I just wanted to hide away from it all. Moreover, I have no flair for negotiating over money, or bargaining. The whole thing in business of course is to make money but I was trying to do everybody a favour and giving discounts left right and centre. The less I was behind the till the better the business did. Even though I was totally unsuited to the retail trade that was not the reason why the business failed. It was the lease in Dun Laoghaire which broke the camel's back. The proof of the pudding is that Gerry has made a great business out of our first Dublin shop and has now opened two other shops throughout the city.

"It was a year and a half after I was offered the teaching job in Andrew's that the business bit the dust. Inevitably people will put two and two together and conclude that because I was not actively involved in the shops we had to close down. Perhaps there is something in that. I'm not so sure.

"More positively I consider myself lucky because I have gone the reverse road from most teachers. After six or seven years teaching some get disenchanted and leave the profession to try something else. I did it the opposite way round and am happy to have tried something else and now to be teaching."

In the early 1980's Ward went with Colin Patterson to play an exhibition match in Parma in Italy. He was shocked by the blatant way he was approached to join one of the leading club sides in Italy with an attractive financial package which would in effect have made him a rugby professional. He never had any interest in turning "pro".

However, after he retired from international rugby in 1988 he was very tempted by an offer from Italy to go and play for one of the leading club sides, Rugby Amatori Milano, David Campese's club, for a year. Ward actually flew to Milan and back in the one day to discuss terms with the club's chief executive. A tempting offer was put to him comprising of: living accommodation for himself and his family, the use of a small car, four or five family trips home to Ireland during the course of the year, and two thousand dollars per month. With so much free time after training he could have made quite an additional income teaching English. The problem was that the offer came just at the beginning of the academic year and he was forced reluctantly to turn it down because he would have been unable to get the year's leave of absence from school at such short notice.

Fools Rush In . . . .

The single biggest surprise which a study of Ward's life throws up, is the discovery that he was a founding patron of Family Solidarity. The episode gives a real insight as to what is meant by that much used cliché "the price of fame". Even now Ward is bemused by it all:

"The problem you have when you are in the public eye is that you get requests to help a million different charities. A lot of the time it's just a request to let your name be associated with something or other and you try and help as many worthy causes as possible – sometimes foolishly so because you don't really know what you are letting yourself in to. While it's not true to say that people always have ulterior motives, you are used a lot of the time.

"I was talking to Colin Patterson's wife, Gail, recently and she said: 'Your biggest problem Tony was that you could never say no.' She was so right. Ollie Campbell was the same. I remember once we both went down to open the Drimoleague festival together in West Cork and we went on to another charity function in Bandon the following day. I went home to Dublin after that but that same day Ollie drove up to some charity event in Carrick-on-Shannon no less!!

"I was always snowed under with requests so when I was asked to be a patron of Family Solidarity I agreed without giving it much thought. Moss Keane was one of the founding members also. Sometime after, when they published their list of patrons, all the newspapers were on to me like a flash asking me if it was true to that both myself and Mossy had agreed to be patrons and inquired if I knew the beliefs and methods of the organisation.

"Immediately I moved to have myself removed from the list of patrons. A prominent personality in Family Solidarity came to meet me in our shop in Dun Laoghaire and I explained how my first marriage was breaking up and for that reason alone I didn't think it appropriate that I should be involved in any such movement. He argued the very opposite to be the case. I would be the perfect role model because I would be advocating family values even though my own marriage was over. I just had to say no because I could not go along with some of their views or methods.

"On a related matter I also got roped into appearing at a vigil to atone for abortion in Whitefriar Street Church along with Ciaran Fitzgerald, Mossy, Ollie and Brendan Mullin. Brendan had been asked to introduce a decade of the rosary when he hit a blind spot and forgot the words of the Hail Mary. There was a deadly silence. It was a really frightening experience for him.

"Some time later, Ascension Thursday, in 1985, I was one of a number of personalities brought down to Knock by Monsignor Horan to participate in a special first national Youth Prayer Rally For Peace to mark international youth year. Fr Michael Cleary was the Master of Ceremonies and as usual he did a really brilliant job. Before the ceremony I was telling him and the others the story of what had happened to Brendan. The Basilicia was overflowing and there were hundreds of people standing outside listening on the speakers. I got up to say the 'Glory Be to the Father', I got through the first line when I went totally blank. Thankfully Fr Cleary saw what had happened and he moved in immediately and told the congregation how I had been telling him the story of what happened to Brendan and now the same thing had happened to me. He made a joke of it, everybody laughed and I lived to fight another day.

"I remember coming home after that feeling very uplifted. There were people there from every corner of Ireland, including over 5,000 teenagers. There was an amazing atmosphere of love and devotion."

Power To All Our Friends

One offer Ward did not pursue came from the political arena. He turned his back on a "safe seat" in 1989 when there was a lot of press speculation that soon it would be Tony Ward T.D.:

"I have little interest in politics though my family have traditionally leaned towards Fianna Fáil. A few times I had been approached to join the local Cuman in Dun Laoghaire but I had never bothered. Eventually, to get them off my back I said I would join provided I didn't have to attend any meetings."

In the spring of 1989, the minority Fianna Fáil government were riding high in the opinion polls, suggesting that they would have no difficulty getting the few extra seats they needed to snatch the elusive overall majority which they coveted so much and which had been denied them since the landslide of '77. One of the key constituencies where they stood an excellent chance of winning a second seat was Dun Laoghaire, particularly as long serving Labour T.D., Barry Desmond was not contesting the election but concentrating his energies on becoming an MEP.

Fianna Fáil only held one seat out of five in the constituency - that of David Andrews. There had been almost a media consensus that the party would run high profile Kieran Mulvey of the ASTI in the election to win them the second seat but just before the election that situation changed and Fianna Fáil were left to find a candidate who could win them the second seat. A high profile Irish sporting hero with the right professional qualifications seemed just what the party doctor ordered and Ward was approached to run in the election:

"The night before I was approached I received a telephone call from my former colleague and great mate on the Irish team, Jim

Glennon, who is actively involved in the party in Dublin North, and he told me that the word was that I would be asked to run for the party and that the offer would come from the top. I said: 'Yeah, sure Jim' not believing a word of it.

"The next evening I was attending an important meeting in the school about funding our new sports hall when a number of times we were interrupted by the secretary saying that Seamus Brennan was on the phone looking for me. The school board were impressed that I had a Government Minister on the line for me but I wanted to concentrate on the business at hand and declined to take any of the calls. Eventually I got a different message that Charlie Haughey was on the line. The principal told me that I had better take the call. The man chairing our meeting was Lyle Collen, head of Collen's building firm with his brother, Standish, who is a close friend of CJH and they go hunting together.

"When I went out it was actually Seamus Brennan who was on the phone but he said: 'I have the Taoiseach on the line and he wants to have a few words with you.' CJH came on and said he wanted to meet me straight away in his office. I explained that it was not possible because I was attending an important meeting about funding our new school sports' hall. He said quick as a flash: 'If you don't get down here immediately you can forget about your sports hall.' The remark was made in jest but there was an undercurrent of 'do this or else' in his tone. He didn't know our sports hall was being funded totally without recourse to state assistance.

"It was about 7.15 p.m. when I drove down to Mount Street to meet him. The election campaign was well underway at that stage and it was like what I imagined the CIA or KGB headquarters to be. In fact, what it most reminded me of was the opening of the television series, *Get Smart*, when Maxwell Smart walks in and there are all those doors he has to go through. There seemed to be minders everywhere. It was a real eye-opener for me.

"Eventually I made it up to Charlie's office. The first thing that struck me was a giant portrait of CJH up on the wall behind his desk. It seemed to be of him performing in the Dáil. The next thing I saw was Charlie and Seamus Brennan sitting behind a huge director's desk. The whole thing was very impressive.

"It was the first time I had met him and my immediate impression was of a very charming man and as the discussion progressed I could sense that he had great charisma. He had obviously been very well briefed and knew everything about my career down to the minutest detail. Not surprisingly I suppose, he was very flattering in his comments about me.

"He explained that the party's polls confirmed that they would get a second seat in Dun Laoghaire and that if I agreed to stand in the constituency that he could all but guarantee me a seat in the next Dáil. If by some chance that didn't happen he would make me one of his nominees for the senate. I knew so little about politics that I didn't even know the Taoiseach nominates people to the Seanad.

"The meeting lasted for a half an hour and I knew straight away that I was not interested. I supposed I felt a bit intimidated and did not want to say so immediately. I asked for 24 hours to consider my position and then I said no. I could see that somebody who was a bit more impressionable could easily have been charmed into saying yes to him. In the end Brian Hillery ran and won a second seat for Fianna Fáil.

"I met Mr Haughey a few times afterwards and he was always a very affable and pleasant man. However, my clearest memory of him after that was of a meeting with him in RTE. It was just after Seán Doherty's revelations about the phonetapping and just before Charlie resigned. He went in to RTE to defend himself and I happened to be on business in the Sports department. I saw all these minders coming and cameras and lights filming him as he walked into the studio. I stood back and tried to make myself as invisible as possible. Then he noticed me and said: 'Tony, how are you?' and chatted with me for a few minutes. I was so dumbfounded that I was unable to address him properly. The fact that he bothered to speak to me at such a traumatic time for him left a very deep impression on me."

Don't Forget To Remember Me

Ward uncharacteristically ponders at length when asked about his hopes for the future. His answer is slow and deliberate:

"When I was a kid I had one goal – to play for the Irish schoolboys soccer team. I thought it would never happen but it did. My second goal was to sign for Shamrock Rovers. When I started playing rugby my third goal was to play for Ireland. The only unfulfilled goal in my life is that since I was a child I wanted to live looking out over the sea, ideally on the Vico Road on Killiney hill looking out towards Bray Head. That to me would be Utopia. Sadly that will never happen unless of course, I win the Lotto –which I never enter!

"I hate confrontation and a big wish would be to go through life without making too many enemies along the way.

"My life revolves around our family and all my hopes are that my children will develop their talents and abilities in whatever areas they see fit. If I can maintain the stage of contentment that I have now I will be happy for the rest of my life. I am very lucky that my broadcasting and journalistic work allows me to keep very much in touch with my main hobby – rugby."

Ward laughs when asked about how he would like to be remembered. Although the legs can't do all they used to there is still plenty of life in him yet:

"What I do like now is that people are both very familiar and friendly with me. They feel they know me and want to have a chat with me. Whether you have 99 caps or 19 you can't put a value on that. It's lovely to be remembered with affection when you are alive. To this day people come up to me and say: 'I just want to shake your hand and say thanks for the memories.' I'm very self-conscious in public and I'm mortified when this happens but it is very nice to be remembered with such fondness.

"I would like to be remembered for one quality – dignity. In my career I didn't go out and kick up a fuss or fly off the handle. At the end of my life I'd like to be remembered with having the same dignity as I am presently remembered for in my rugby career."

What's It All About?

Up to '79 Ward had led a sheltered life wallowing in the delight of a successful career which had brought all his childhood fantasies to reality. The greatest tragedy of that time was that he lost his inherent faith in his own ability.

He feels he can better cope with any adversity or cruelty life can throw at him. He is a much stronger character for the traumas he endured before finding blissful happiness through his marriage to Louise and the love of his three children. He has less interest in raising a glass to the past than toasting the present and the future. Now rugby has been placed in its proper perspective:

"I got a great insight into the transience of fame one day in school earlier this year. It was the Monday after one of Ireland's international matches. I am normally on RTE's programme *Rugby After Dark* which shows the highlights of the previous day's international match and Doyler and myself analyse the game. It is usually on very late on Sunday night and I suppose for that reason some of my younger students never get to see it for whatever reason. It was on early the Sunday evening after Ireland defeated England and I was astonished to discover so many of my pupils talking about it. The next morning we were coming from the sports hall after a PE class and I heard two of them talking. One of them asked the other: 'Did you know Mr Ward played for Ireland?' 'Oh I do. My dad told me. He said there was always a major fuss about himself and some other guy – Ossie something or other'!"